Polish Literature as World Literature

LITERATURES AS WORLD LITERATURE

Can the literature of a specific country, author, or genre be used to approach the elusive concept of "world literature"? **Literatures as World Literature** takes a novel approach to world literature by analyzing specific constellations—according to language, nation, form, or theme—of literary texts and authors in their own world-literary dimensions.

World literature is obviously so vast that any view of it cannot help but be partial; the question then becomes how to reduce the complex task of understanding and describing world literature. Most treatments of world literature so far either have been theoretical and thus abstract, or else have made broad use of exemplary texts from a variety of languages and epochs. The majority of critical work, the filling in of what has been traced, lies ahead of us. **Literatures as World Literature** fills in the devilish details by allowing scholars to move outward from their own areas of specialization, fostering scholarly writing that approaches more closely the polyphonic, multiperspectival nature of world literature.

Series Editor
Thomas O. Beebee

Editorial Board
Eduardo Coutinho, Federal University of Rio de Janeiro, Brazil
Hsinya Huang, National Sun-yat Sen University, Taiwan
Meg Samuelson, University of Adelaide, Australia
Ken Seigneurie, Simon Fraser University, Canada
Galin Tihanov, Queen Mary University of London, UK
Mads Rosendahl Thomsen, Aarhus University, Denmark

Volumes in the Series
German Literature as World Literature, edited by Thomas O. Beebee
Roberto Bolaño as World Literature, edited by Nicholas Birns and
Juan E. De Castro

Polish Literature as World Literature

Edited by
Piotr Florczyk and K. A. Wisniewski

BLOOMSBURY ACADEMIC
NEW YORK • LONDON • OXFORD • NEW DELHI • SYDNEY

BLOOMSBURY ACADEMIC
Bloomsbury Publishing Inc
1385 Broadway, New York, NY 10018, USA
50 Bedford Square, London, WC1B 3DP, UK
29 Earlsfort Terrace, Dublin 2, Ireland

BLOOMSBURY, BLOOMSBURY ACADEMIC and the Diana logo are trademarks of
Bloomsbury Publishing Plc

First published in the United States of America 2023

Cover design by Simon Levy

Library of Congress Cataloging-in-Publication Data
Names: Florczyk, Piotr, editor. | Wisniewski, K. A., 1981– editor.
Title: Polish literature as world literature / edited by Piotr Florczyk and K.A. Wisniewski.
Description: New York : Bloomsbury Academic, 2023. |
Series: Literatures as world literature | Includes bibliographical references and index. |
Summary: "Provides an overview of Polish authors and works from the 16th century
to today, highlighting their contributions to and interactions with world literature and
cultures"– Provided by publisher.
Identifiers: LCCN 2022025131 (print) | LCCN 2022025132 (ebook) |
ISBN 9781501387104 (hardback) | ISBN 9781501387142 (paperback) |
ISBN 9781501387111 (epub) | ISBN 9781501387128 (pdf) | ISBN 9781501387135
Subjects: LCSH: Polish literature–History and criticism. |
Polish literature–Appreciation. | LCGFT: Literary criticism. | Essays.Classification:
LCC PG7015 .P549 2023 (print) | LCC PG7015 (ebook) | DDC 891.8/509–dc23/eng/20220722
LC record available at https://lccn.loc.gov/2022025131
LC ebook record available at https://lccn.loc.gov/2022025132

ISBN: HB: 978-1-5013-8710-4
ePDF: 978-1-5013-8712-8
eBook: 978-1-5013-8711-1

Series: Literatures as World Literature

Typeset by Newgen KnowledgeWorks Pvt. Ltd., Chennai, India

To find out more about our authors and books visit www.bloomsbury.com
and sign up for our newsletters.

CONTENTS

ACKNOWLEDGMENTS

The editors would like to thank the University of Washington in Seattle, the University of Southern California, and the American Antiquarian Society for their support. In addition, they are deeply grateful to the contributors to this volume; to the series editor, Thomas Oliver Beebee; and to the readers, the editors, and the staff at Bloomsbury.

Introduction

Piotr Florczyk and K. A. Wisniewski

While the concept of world literature remains both elusive and controversial, especially in the eyes of the critics of globalization's reach into spheres of literary production and dissemination, Polish authors' engagement with worldly themes and styles is undisputed. Counting no fewer than five Nobel Prize in Literature laureates,[1] the Polish literary canon has played a vital role in shaping literary conversations around the world, reaching new heights in popularity, ironically, during the Cold War.[2] This is particularly true of Polish poets, whose works have long been revered in Germany, France, and the United States. Engaging themes with global purchase—themes as timeless as history, memory, and civil and personal liberties—Polish poets became models for their foreign counterparts, thus enabling a transfer of art and ideas that now flow both ways to this day. Indeed, as is the case with most countries where one of the so-called minor languages is spoken, translation, as core mechanism of world literature, plays a vital role in initiating and sustaining intercultural dialogue that traverses physical and imaginary frontiers.

Goethe's words, which gave rise to the concept of world literature— "National literature no longer means much these days, we are entering *Weltliteratur*—world literature—and it is up to each of us to hasten this development"[3]—continue to influence literary scholars, translators, and authors around the world. No matter what approaches they take, however, their positions are fraught with ethical and political considerations that go beyond questions around what to study, translate, and write. In their introduction to a volume of interviews with some of America's most noted translators, Esther Allen and Susan Bernofsky remind us,

Weltliteratur is no longer (and may never have been) politically, culturally, or ethically neutral. At the same time, the failure to translate into English, the absence of translation, is clearly the most effective way of all to consolidate the global monoculture and exclude those who write and read in other languages from the far-reaching global conversation for which English is increasingly the vehicle.[4]

In other words, focusing on translators as key players in the grand scheme of literary production and dissemination illuminates the concept of world literature as understood by Goethe or, more recently, by David Damrosch, who reminds us that "world literature is writing that gains in translation."[5]

Translation makes reading literature beyond its local contexts and national borders, a foundational aspect of world literature, possible, but how translators approach and perceive their activity is of paramount importance to understanding its effects, especially since translation "is not simply an act of faithful reproduction but, rather, a deliberate and conscious act of selection, assemblage, structuration," that, according to Maria Tymoczko and Edwin Gentzler, editors of *Translation and Power*, puts translators on par with politicians and other agents whose opinions and behaviors dictate what's culturally fashionable or even acceptable.[6] In that sense, it is helpful to use Jerzy Jarniewicz's classification, whereby all literary translators can be divided into "ambassadors" or "legislators,"[7] where the former aim to introduce foreign classics into a new cultural realm, while the latter set their sights on upending the target literature by exposing it to hitherto unknown formal and linguistic trends. Regardless of which category they are comfortable, most English-language translators would reject the charge that they work in the service of monolingualism, believing instead, given the ascendancy of English as today's international language, that they are helping make the literature of the globe available to the masses everywhere, seemingly fulfilling yet another of David Damrosch's definitions of world literature, which foregrounds us, the readers: "World literature is fully in play once several foreign works begin to resonate together in our mind."[8] This perceived contribution to what Allen and Bernofsky call "pluralism of world languages and cultures" fits the romantic paradigm according to which writers and publishers and audiences are natural allies. It does not, however, take the larger structural, especially market-driven, forces into consideration. While all authors, including Polish authors, would no doubt appreciate appearing in English, they often have little input in how their work is presented and, consequently, received in the target language. Ironically, this state suggests a global readership, since, as Darwish argues, "a work only has an effective life as world literature whenever, and wherever, it is actively present within a literary system beyond that of its original culture."[9]

Among Polish authors, there is no better case study illustrating this conundrum than that of Czesław Miłosz and his disagreement with the British poet and critic, Al Alvarez. In *Under Pressure: The Writer in Society: Eastern Europe and the U.S.A.*, Alvarez toes a fine line between a naïve observer, a tourist, and a critic who senses that things are not as they seem. His observations pertaining to Eastern European countries, gleaned during travels in the region, were meant to provide a counterpoint to the propaganda emitted from both sides of the Iron Curtain at the time:

> In Poland it is impossible to write even about the birds and the bees without someone reading into it a political metaphor or allusion. Polish art runs instinctively to allegory. It is all, whatever its appearance, written in what they call "Aesopian language," in which each detail can always be translated into terms of something else—something relevant to the immediate Polish situation.[10]

When Alvarez fell back on the same worn-out clichés while reviewing Miłosz's *The Collected Poems, 1931–1987* in *The New York Review of Books* twenty years later, characterizing the poet and his peers as Eastern or, at times, Central European moralists who wrote "poetry that occupies the moral high ground yet is proof against ridicule and impervious to pretension,"[11] Miłosz responded publicly.

Alvarez's otherwise overwhelmingly positive review, full of insights acquired over decades of reading and study, would have made many a writer, especially an émigré like Miłosz, happy. Yet the Polish poet replied to Alvarez in a letter of protest for having been depicted as exotic and traumatized. The war events that Alvarez dwelled on so much instead of discussing the poems, Miłosz argued, have added "an aura of nightmare to the vagueness that has always characterized the presence of Central and Eastern European countries in the Western imagination." Miłosz hit the nail on the head when he wrote that Western critics, by way of attempting to provide a context for the writer's work, invariably bring up events that "distort the image of their author in the minds of readers and of literary critics, by presenting him as more obsessed with historical events than he is." Yet in calling for a more individualized literary criticism that focuses on the poet and his artistic journey as much as on historicizing his or her aesthetics, Miłosz argued that poetry "should not freeze, magnetized by the sight of evil perpetrated in our lifetime," then explained that he took offense because Alvarez "seems to be impervious to the dynamics at the very core of any art: after all, a poet repeatedly says farewell to his old selves and makes himself ready for renewals."[12] This appeal to individuality—as fitting the American ethos as it gets—shows that many authors are split when it comes to embracing and defying the world literature bona fides.

Indeed, Alvarez's reading seems to counter rather than support Darwish's definition of what constitutes world literature, for if the Polish poems that Alvarez had in mind were inaccessible to readers unfamiliar with their regional or local characteristics, then what made it possible for them to enter and shape the Anglophone poetic conversating for several decades?

Clearly, it might not have been what the Polish poets might have valued about their own work, for as Justin Quinn reminds us, "Cultures ... take what they want and need from other cultures, without much regard for the proprieties. Wordsworth has never been considered a great poet in France or Germany, but Byron changed the course of European culture."[13] Indeed, the irony isn't lost on critic Magdalena Kay, either: "Major Eastern European poets make it clear that the discourse of poetry must be separate from the discourse of politics, yet their Western readers keep viewing them in political terms, and they serve as (unwillingly) touchstones in the ongoing debate regarding politics and literature."[14]

If nothing else, the Miłosz–Alvarez exchange disqualifies the idea that knowledge or meaning can be fully transparent. Believing that he had written an enthusiastic review, Alvarez likened Miłosz's rebuke to a case of literary chest pounding, even though he clearly employed ready-made schema in his review. The past, as experienced by Poles and documented in their cultural output, was, in Alvarez's eyes, the portal into Miłosz's work. Still, as Tejaswini Niranjana claims, "The drive to challenge hegemonic representations of the non-Western world need not be seen as a wish to oppose the 'true' other to the 'false' one presented in colonial discourse." In an ideal situation, world literature would embrace difference without erasing it. "It is here," Niranjana argues, "that translators can intervene to inscribe heterogeneity, to warn against myths of purity, to show origins as always already fissured."[15]

A decision to translate and publish a particular book is largely based on its local representativeness; however, the standards used to evaluate such title's alleged representativeness are often foreign. Consequently, a majority of titles whose quality has been recognized by the middlemen fit "a particular category of literature that might be recognized as properly 'global,' a literature whose fields of production and of reception could be mapped—and whose individual works could be valued—only on a world scale."[16] It is obvious why this kind of cultural globalization has been met with skepticism; some view it as profit-motivated push to homogenize literature by turning it into a product that can be sold to the largest possible number of customers. Those critics believe that a book branded as "world literature" is "an essentially false and touristic product, specially, if not always consciously, made for Euro-American consumption, masquerading as a representative form of indigenous cultural expression."[17] From a more artistic standpoint, this critique also extends to the work's alleged literary value, or rather lack thereof; since much of a book's linguistic excellence is lost in translation, books with a subject matter deemed universal have a larger chance of becoming products of mass consumption.[18]

In her essay "Comparison Literature," Rebecca Walkowitz offers a broader view of world definition. Although she, too, is interested in the ways in which writers, translators, and editors shape the literary landscape, her approach also brings in concepts related to historical cultural identity and the global book trade into the fold. She explains, "It is no longer simply a matter of determining, once and for all, the literary culture to which a work belongs. Comparison literature ... implies the intersection of three major methodologies: book history, theories of globalization, and translation studies."[19] While the latter two fields have received much attention in recent decades, book history—especially in relation to Polish literature and authors—remains underdeveloped at the present. The foundations for building such studies have been planted, however, by the anthology *The Book: A Global History* (2013), edited by Michael F. Suarez, S. J. and H. R. Woudhuysen. For example, in her chapter dedicated to "Poland," Janet Zmroczek presents a concise history of the rich and complicated structures of book trade in Poland from the tenth century to the present. This story highlights the ways in which Polish literature and Polish authors have been active agents of cultural and artistic exchange beyond their local borders since the rise of print culture and the ways in which "Polish writers, thinkers, and theologians were integrated into mainstream European culture."[20] This vigorous network, however, was interrupted when Poland ceased to be a sovereign state and was partitioned between Russia, Prussia, and Austria in 1795. While the Polish publishing industry faced tremendous obstacles in the nineteenth century, émigré communities abroad were politically active, and Polish authors maintained their relationships with their European counterparts. Beyond Europe, Thomas P. Gladsky notes American authors' interests in the Polish people and literary landscape are visible in their writerly output.[21] As Gladsky and others note, cultural exchanges were limited under German occupation during the Second World War and throughout the Cold War, despite some breakthroughs. While scholars and theorists often examine asymmetrical power relationships and marketability in their definitions of world literature and the global book trade, it is also helpful to seek alternatives, such as Pheng Cheah's explanation of literature as a world-shaping factor.[22]

As we have seen, the need for meaning, especially of the kind that satisfies the West's craving for knowledge of a particular people or culture, must be redefined, especially—how ironic!—when a country sees its political and economic fortunes rise. Poland along with the rest of Eastern Europe is a case in point. In the introduction to his study of the post-Communist writer, *Remaining Relevant after Communism: The Role of the Writer in Eastern Europe*, Andrew Baruch Wachtel recounts being asked, quiet frequently, "Why has no new Milan Kundera appeared in Eastern Europe since the collapse of communist regimes?" His answer is predictable: of course there have emerged writers just as talented, successful, and significant, but the issue, given the domestic and international forces involved, is as much sociocultural as it is literary. "Publishers must wish to make [a new] Kundera available," he writes, "critics must decide to review him, states and privately funded groups must award him prizes, and readers (both in his own country and abroad) must chose to buy and, at least in some cases, to read his work."[23] The forces and entities that had performed the invaluable service of promoting literature, making it important to audience both domestic and international, collapsed right after the 1989 transitions. Some have been rebuilt, but still it is highly unlikely that Eastern European writers will again commend the kind of respect they once did. The blame, according to Wachtel, should be placed squarely at the (largely) positive change in their countries' geopolitical situation:

> In the post-cold-war world there is no longer a political reason to pay attention to East European literary developments. What is more, as these societies have become more Westernized, they are less exotic, less "other," and hence less interesting to Western readers. In a word, just as the material base for their individual and corporate prosperity eroded at home, writers of serious literature began to seem less relevant abroad.[24]

Not surprisingly, some writers deliberately strip their work of any so-called local flavor in hopes of getting translated. This "new internationalism," as Wachtel calls it, is about getting translated as well as obtaining legitimacy, because for authors hailing from minor countries and writing in minor languages, "it is increasingly impossible to consider oneself a 'real' writer unless one has been published in major European languages (particularly English) and because such a perspective provides a way to overcome the lack of interest in Eastern Europe on the part of Western publishers now that the 'automatic' political reasons for publishing East European literature have disappeared."[25]

The risk with this kind of writing, however, includes dumbing things down for the foreign audience, thus insulting its own sense of self, as well as generalizing. Nonetheless, writing for a foreign audience (again, English-language audience seems to matter more than any other) has taken hold of homegrown authors. The English novelist and critic, Tim Parks, who's lived in Italy for over thirty years, claims—citing research by his Milanese colleagues—that "contemporary Italian prose increasingly places adjectives before nouns, uses possessives rather than reflexives to indicate body parts, and expresses subject pronouns, all as a result of contact, through translation, with English."[26] For his part, David Williams uses the term *trümmerleute* and *trümmerliteratur*[27] ("rubble literature" or "literature of the ruins") to designate writers who feed the West an expected cocktail of political strife and historical misfortune.[28] However, the case of Polish poets of the *bruLion* generation that burst on the scene after 1989 illustrates another side of the same discussion. While Marcin Świetlicki and others have in fact increased the amount of local flavor in their poems—seemingly all of a sudden, the loneliness, the humor, the whimsy, and, above all else, the individuality of the American artist became a trademark of the young Polish poet[29]—some might argue that, given the influence of Frank O'Hara and John Ashbery on him and his peers, there is no point of translating "a Polish O'Hara" back into English. This would be, of course, nothing short of disingenuous. Still, poets stripping their work to meet demands of "world poetry," according to Stephen Owen, often produce work that's strikingly "a version of Anglo-American modernism or French modernism, depending on which wave of colonial culture fist washed over the intellectuals of the country in question."[30]

In the words of Czech-French author Milan Kundera, "large nations resist the Goethean idea of 'world literature' because their own literature seems to them sufficiently rich that they need take no interest in what people write elsewhere."[31] The pitiful size of the market of translated books in the United States compared to its overall size seems to support this idea.[32] Be that as it may, *Polish Literature as World Literature* introduces key figures of Polish literature from the sixteenth century to the present and their impact on and relationships with world literature. Covering a wide range of texts and approaches, the essays in this collection not only contribute to the debates surrounding the very concept of world literature but also engage aspects of print culture and literary history, translation studies, cultural studies, LGBTQ studies, and the production and dissemination of literary works.

While our volume should not be considered a history of Polish literature, it is nonetheless in conversation with its predecessors that aimed to situate Polish literature and culture in the global narrative, especially the two most recent volumes *Being Poland*[33] and *Światowa historia literatury polskiej*.[34] Both of these works are much larger in scope—the first volume features some sixty contributors, while the second volume consists of over thirty chapters—than the present volume, whose scope is dictated by Bloomsbury's excellent series *Literatures as World Literature*. Likewise, our volume acknowledges its debt to even earlier milestones in the field of Polish literary studies, especially Manfred Kridl's *A Survey of Polish Literature and Culture* (1956), Czesław Miłosz's *The History of Polish Literature* (1969), and Julian Krzyżanowski's *A History of Polish Literature* (1978), but again eschews the panoramic and comprehensive approach in favor of a more focused approach dictated by the interests and scholarly expertise of its editors and contributors. As David Damrosch reminds us, "different readers will be obsessed by very different constellations of texts,"[35] and truly enough a completely alternative selection of authors, works, and even time periods than what is presented here would be entirely possible.

As the editors of *Being Poland* state in the introduction to their volume, Poland has always been "a culture roiled with radical changes, a history of greatness and of misery, a society of rifts and restorations."[36] However, these characteristics alone do not make the country and its literary works unique in any sense of the word; in fact, many other nations, in East Central Europe or elsewhere, would fit the bill. Nevertheless, we felt that organizing the volume chronologically would help the readers make sense of the times and conditions, from the sixteenth century onward, in which Polish authors wrote and published. Furthermore, given the prearranged, as it were, theoretical focus of the series, we felt it germane to invite contributions that focused on a specific author or authors, especially lesser-known figures. Ironically, for the reasons outlined above, we likewise feel that readers who wish to sample the chapters at will would not be at a loss, as our volume is not meant to present a continuum of Polish literary output but rather its most interesting examples of Polish authors embracing and/or resisting the pull of world literature.

Our anthology embraces what's inherently Polish in the authors and works under discussion and what makes them worldly, too. Hence, as readers might have inferred by now, we posit the role of the translator and the processes that make translation and international dissemination of literature possible at the forefront of our approach. While we do not disagree with Rebecca L. Walkowitz's notion that many books "appear simultaneously or nearly simultaneously in multiple languages. They start as world literature,"[37] in fact we are fully cognizant of the homogenizing aspect of today's global publishing and the authors' wish to partake in it; we do, however, believe that most Polish titles are selected for translation due to their domestic rather than global pedigree, which makes their global success less than certain. In that sense we find ourselves closer to Emily Apter's arguments,[38] one of whose aims is to bring more attention to how, why, and when translation takes place, which in turn leads us away from literature rooted in a particular nation or literary tradition, and toward embracing of authors for whom transgressing national norms or ideas was or has been of paramount importance.

Arguably, studying Polish literature itself fits the efforts to decentralize the reading of literature. But there is an interesting paradox at work here: Polish literature, just like the country and its people, wants to be seen as firmly European, perhaps even worldly, yet to fully appreciate it, we must read it as belonging to the periphery. Would doing so bring it into the center and thus strip it off the qualities that make it most interesting to foreign readers?[39]

The present volume, which consists of thirteen articles by leading Polish and world literature scholars from the United States, Canada, Italy, and, of course, Poland, aims to answer that and other pertinent questions. Applying a historical approach—essays are organized chronologically—and focusing on both authors and concepts, we hope to illustrate how Polish authors, from Jan Potocki in the late eighteenth century to the 2018 Nobel laureate Olga Tokarczuk, have engaged with their foreign counterparts and other traditions into the global literary network and have taken an active part in the conversations of their day. While it might be read by some as a survey of Polish literature, *Polish Literature as World Literature* acts itself as an intermediary to other aforementioned works; it seeks to investigate the ways in which a national literature and its authors have interacted with the world and how these engagements can resituate the histories and current state of Polish literature and its studies. Readers with some background in Polish literature will be greeted with familiar names from the canon—Adam Mickiewicz, Czesław Miłosz, Bruno Schulz, and Witold Gombrowicz—but, hopefully, this work will introduce them to new authors and works, as well. Henryk Sienkiewicz, Joseph Conrad, Wisława Szymborska, and Stanisław Lem are among the writers notably missing from this work. This is not to say that these individuals' respective works could not add additional insights to the larger questions underway in this volume; like some of the other globally recognizable authors noted above, there is a great deal of excellent scholarship on their work for readers to investigate. Their absence reflects the editors' decision to offer balance to this volume by including Polish authors perhaps less familiar to the novice reader and to ultimately reflect on how various definitions offered here might extend and reshape the literary canon of Polish authors to a global readership.

Building upon this introduction's interest in translation, Michał Paweł Markowski's opening chapter delineates two dominant cultural Western paradigms of understanding "world literature." Markowski argues that those two models are rooted not only in divergent models of translation but also in two different theologies. Drawing on works by Czesław Miłosz and Witold Gombrowicz, it questions the very paradox of Polishness. In Chapter 2, "Jan Potocki, the Greatest Author of the Polish Enlightenment as a French Writer," Emiliano Ranocchi extends this theoretical inquiry into a reassessment of the life and work of Polish Enlightenment writer Jan Potocki. It reexamines the writer's Polish aristocratic status and the impact of writing originally in French on his travel writings and novel *Manuscript Found in Saragossa*.

In Chapter 3, Grzegorz Marzec focuses on the Polish romantic poet Adam Mickiewicz. Upon reviewing recent criticism surrounding the ways in which Polish identity and memory is tied to the romantic paradigm, Marzec complicates traditional "Polish" readings of Mickiewicz's *Konrad Wallenrod* by uncovering parallels between it and Shakespeare's *Hamlet*. Whereas Marzec deconstructs Poland's complicated literary history with romantic archetypes, in Chapter 4, "The Global Rise of the Novel: Poland and World Literature," Katarzyna Bartoszyńska argues for more nuanced formalist readings of Polish novels. Building on critiques that challenge the notion of a stable category of realism, she argues that new readings of the complexities of early Polish fictions offer not only a new account of the Polish novel but also an opportunity to rewrite the paradigmatic theories of the form, to produce a more robust account of the global novel. Chapter 5 continues this thread of investigating nineteenth-century literature; Lena Magnone demonstrates how Polish women's writing parallels texts by women in the West. She examines the ways in which the dominant model of British female novel was transformed for American and Polish contexts using Eliza Orzeszkowa and Edith Wharton as her prime examples.

Chapter 6 transitions into the twentieth century. Here, Agnieszka Jeżyk examines the cannibalistic tropes in the texts of Polish futurists, Jerzy Jankowski, Anatol Stern, and Bruno Jasieński. The author views these themes as a lens through which the poets address some of the crucial problems of modernity: imperialism, social injustice, changes in gender roles, and the problem of originality of art. Whereas this chapter focuses on writers working on the periphery of the literary arts, Chapter 7 explores Bruno Schulz and the ways in which translation and reviews marketed and reframed the work for commercial success. Zofia Ziemann surveys how Schulz's work was alternately categorized as Polish, Jewish, Central and Eastern European literature, and, ultimately, as world writing and argues that his global recognition is largely owed to Celina Wieniewska's widely marketed translation. Finally, in Chapter 8, Jacek Gutorow continues these close readings of world literature and Polish identity with his evaluation of Witold Gombrowicz. Popular readings highlight the writer's flair for the absurd and antinationalist flavor; however, Gutorow explains how Gombrowicz can be viewed as an advocate rather than a parodist of inherited conservative traditions of writing. Examining his novel *Trans-Atlantyk* and *Diary*, Gutorow inspects the ways in which Gombrowicz's use of parody tackles questions of national and individual identity and the ways in which those writings are tied to Polishness even as they work to break from them and embrace the ideals of world literature.

With the fall of the Eastern Bloc in 1989, Poland experienced a production boom with thousands of new publishers and the privatization of state publishers and a surge in the accessibility of books previously banned from readers. In Chapter 9, "Beyond Identity: John Ashbery's and Frank O'Hara's Impact on Polish Poetry" Kacper Bartczak probes the ways in which Polish poetic culture was transformed in the 1980s and 1990s. The New York School was an informal collective of American poets and artists active during the 1950s and 1960s in New York City. Concentrating on Frank O'Hara and John Ashbery, Bartczak shows how this group's interests in surrealism and the avant-garde inspired new thought and practice in poetry in the Polish literary scene as seen by the exchanges with and the works of Bohdan Zadura and Andrzej Sosnowski. With the transition to liberal democracy and the geopolitical reorientation to the West, Poles also began to travel abroad on an unprecedented scale.

The next set of chapters returns to questions of Polish identity within this new global context. In Chapter 10, Andrzej Brylak attempts to trace the processes of cultural cross-pollination among Polish-language literature in Israel, Israeli literature, and Polish theater, focusing on the circulation of the figure of a melancholic, constipated post-Holocaust subject. The author interprets Leo Lipski's largely unknown 1960 novella "Piotruś" as a forgotten *urtext* and outlines the historical context responsible for its silencing, particularly the complicated position of Holocaust survivors within the Zionist project. Chapter 11 argues for the importance of rethinking both world literature and Polish literature from the perspective of queer Polish literature. Author Ela Przybyło focuses on Tomasz Jedrowski's novel, *Swimming in the Dark* (2020), and the use of water in the novel to uncover themes of border imperialism, sexuality and national identity, and transnational circulation of queer texts. The chapter contends that by reading "against the tide" and being attentive to queer movements in writing through an analytics of water, Polish and world literatures can continue to be reimagined and reinvigorated.

In Chapter 12, "Between the Mythical and the Modern: Polishness in the Work of Olga Tokarczuk and Dorota Masłowska," Marta Koronkiewicz and Paweł Kaczmarski compare various depictions of Polishness in the work of two contemporary Polish novelists. By drawing on the concept of *proza środka* (*the middlebrow prose*), they show how Tokarczuk's understanding of Polish history and identity is rooted in a desire to project a certain aura of mystery and mysticism, which in turn stems from a particular approach to the legacy of the modernist novel: namely, Tokarczuk's attempt to make modernism more accessible to a new type of middle-class Polish audience. Meanwhile, Dorota Masłowska reinvents certain modernist gestures under the guise of postmodernism, ultimately subverting the expectations of her readers and demystifying Polish identity by pointing out the impossibility of Polishness as a coherent construct. The final chapter serves as a bookend—a counterpoint to the introductory essay by Markowski. In Chapter 13, Katarzyna Bazarnik deconstructs the multimodal literary genre of liberature, first proposed by Zenon Fajfer. Representing the future of literary practice in the digital age and critical questions surrounding the sociology of texts and role of materiality, Bazarnik illustrates the ways in which liberature was formulated as a result of such an approach to world literature. While it has emerged from a local movement, it has positioned itself as a global reference point and as a genre that can enable us to reread and reexamine the literary past with the view to uncover a specific strand in the history of world literature.

While many of the articles collected herein highlight a key literary figure— or several figures, in case of a particular school or movement—we have also aimed, as evidenced by the opening and closing chapters, to feature the views of scholars working in Polish literature and culture that pertain to theories of world literature or literary systems, with a particular attention paid to the resurgence of the idea of the physical book as a cultural artifact.

This seemed especially important to us in light of the fact that so much of today's global literary output stems from Anglophone perceptions of what constitutes literary quality and even tastes. As seen from this overview, the collection sheds light on not only specific issues pertaining to Poland, such as the idea of Polishness, but also other global phenomena, including social and economic advancement as well as ecological degradation. Some of these authors, like the romantic poet Adam Mickiewicz or the 1980 Nobel laureate Czesław Miłosz, were renowned far beyond the borders of their country, while others, like the contemporary travel writer and novelist Andrzej Stasiuk, embrace regionalism, seeing as they do in their immediate surroundings a synecdoche of the world at large. Nevertheless, it is our sincere hope that the picture of Polish literature and Polish authors that emerges from these articles is that of a diverse, cosmopolitan cohort engaged in a reciprocal and mutually rewarding relationship with what the late French critic Pascale Casanova has called "the world republic of letters."[40]

Notes

1   Or six, if we include the Polish American writer Isaac Bashevis Singer (1902–91).

2   See, for example, Clare Cavanagh, *Lyric Poetry and Modern Politics: Russia, Poland, and the West* (New Haven, CT: Yale University Press, 2010).

3   Milan Kundera, *The Curtain: An Essay in Seven Parts*. Translated by Linda Asher (New York: Harper Perennial, 2008), 35–6.

4   Esther Allen and Susan Bernofsky (eds.), *In Translation: Translators on Their Work and What It Means* (New York: Columbia University Press, 2013), xvii.

5   David Damrosch, *What Is World Literature?* (Princeton, NJ: Princeton University Press, 2003), 281.

6   See Maria Tymoczko and Edwin Gentzler (eds.), *Translation and Power* (Amherst: University of Massachusetts Press, 2002), xxi.

7   See Jerzy Jarniewicz, *Gościnność słowa: Szkice o przekładzie literackim* (Kraków: Znak, 2014). Unless noted otherwise, all translations are our own.

8   Damrosch, *What Is World Literature?*, 298.

9   Ibid., 4.

10   Al Alvarez, *Under Pressure: The Writer in Society: Eastern Europe and the U.S.A.* (New York: Penguin Press, 1965), 22.

11   Al Alvarez, "Witness," *New York Review of Books*, vol. 35, no. 9 (July 2, 1988): 21.

12   Czesław Miłosz, "A Poet's Reply," *New York Review of Books*, vol. 35, no. 12 (July 12, 1988): n.p.

13   Justin Quinn, *Between Two Fires: Transnationalism and Cold War Poetry* (Oxford: Oxford University Press, 2015), 11.

14 Quoted in ibid., 189.

15 Tejaswini Niranjana, *Siting Translation: History, Post-Structuralism, and the Colonial Context* (Berkeley: University of California Press, 1992), 186.

16 James F. English, *The Economy of Prestige: Prizes, Awards, and the Circulation of Cultural Value* (Cambridge, MA: Harvard University Press, 2005), 304.

17 Ibid., 307.

18 English singles out books whose appeal stems from their alleged social value. This echoes some of the criticism leveled against the Nobel Prize Committee, which some see as overtly favorable to books and authors with leftist political leanings. However, Alexander Beecroft, the author of *An Ecology of World Literature: From Antiquity to the Present Day* (London: Verso, 2015), introduces a key caveat into the discussion of the Nobel Committee's preference for European writers, when he writes, "There is, however, nothing wrong per se with the idea that the Nobel exists primarily to recognize literature in European languages (and particularly from the European periphery), so long as we do not continue to make the historic error of making universal whatever happens in European languages" (qtd. in English, *The Economy of Prestige*, 297).

19 Rebecca L. Walkowitz, "Comparison Literature," *New Literary History*, vol. 40, no. 3 (2009): 580–1.

20 Zmroczek demonstrates that Polish travelers engaged with intellectual communities as far as Ireland, France, and Italy. In the sixteenth century 724 titles by Polish authors were printed abroad and over five hundred in the seventeenth century. See Janet Zmroczek, "The History of the Book in Poland," in *The Book: A Global History*, edited by F. Michael S. J. Suarez, and H. R. Woudhuysen (Oxford: Oxford University Press, 2013), 470–9, esp. 470, 473.

21 See Thomas S. Gladsky, *Princes, Peasants, and Other Polish Selves: Ethnicity in American Literature* (Amherst: University of Massachusetts Press, 2009).

22 See Emily Apter, *Against World Literature: On the Politics of Untranslatability* (London: Verso, 2013) and Pheng Cheah, *What Is a World? On Postcolonial Literature as World Literature* (Durham, NC: Duke University Press, 2016).

23 Andrew Baruch Wachtel, *Remaining Relevant after Communism: The Role of the Writer in Eastern Europe* (Chicago: University of Chicago Press, 2006), 1.

24 Ibid., 47.

25 Ibid., 122.

26 Tim Parks qtd. in Alexander Beecroft, *An Ecology of World Literature: From Antiquity to the Present Day* (London: Verso, 2015), 279–80.

27 David William, *Writing Postcommunism: Towards a Literature of the East European Ruins* (Basingstoke: Palgrave Macmillan, 2013), 4.

28 The charge of exploiting her country's bloody past is commonly brought up by her Croatian countrymen against émigré writer Dubravka Ugrešić. According to Williams,

Ugrešić … has (implicitly and explicitly) been accused of performing a kind of *Auftragskunst*—of willingly meeting the demands of the western literary marketplace for "the fairy tale about good and evil, which a good child likes to hear again and again." The accusation is doubly chauvinistic, implying both that Ugrešić's talent has played no part in her success, and that western readers are too stupid to see that they have had the wool pulled over their eyes. It would, however, be disingenuous to suggest that extraliterary factors have played no part in the attention Ugrešić has received—when Anna Akhmatova learned of Brodsky's exile even she is alleged to have responded to the effect of "oh what a biography they have written for our little redhead" (92). See David Williams, *Writing Postcommunism: Towards a Literature of the East European Ruins* (New York: Palgrave, 2013).

29 Here is how critic Joanna Niżyńska of Indiana University explains the context in which their new poems came to operate:

Prior to 1989, Poles regarded the dominant metanarrative in their literature and culture as the paradygmat romantyczny (Romantic paradigm) or, as it was sometimes called, the paradygmat romantyczno-symboliczny (the Romantic-symbolic paradigm). The question of whether the influence of the Romantic heritage was on the wane in the new reality became a focal point of cultural discussions in the 1990s. In these discussions, the term Romantic was clearly associated with beliefs originating in the nineteenth-century period of high Romanticism in Poland. Literature at this time was tied to the fate of the community that produced it and was invested with the power to create an alternative ("spiritual") community in the face of external political oppression. Literature was also charged with the ethical responsibility of witnessing the community's misfortunes and working toward its survival.

See Joanna Niżyńska, "The Impossibility of Shrugging One's Shoulders: O'Harists, O'Hara, and Post-1989 Polish Poetry," *Slavic Review*, vol. 66, no. 3 (2007): 465.

30 Qtd. in Quinn, *Between Two Fires*, 121.

31 Kundera, *The Curtain*, 37.

32 For a detailed discussion of how many and what kinds of translations are published each year in the United States, see *Three Percent*: A Resource for International Literature at the University of Rochester or the "Translation Database" at *Publishers Weekly*.

33 Tamara Trojanowska, Joanna Niżyńska, Przemysław Czapliński, and Agnieszka Polakowska (eds.), *Being Poland: A New History of Polish Literature and Culture since 1918* (Toronto: University of Toronto Press, 2019).

34 Magdalena Popiel, Tomasz Bilczewski, and Stanley Bill (eds.), *Światowa Historia Literatury Polskiej: Interpretacje* (Kraków: Wydawnictwo Uniwersytetu Jagiellońskiego, 2020).

35 Damrosch, *What Is World Literature?*, 281.

36 Trojanowska, Niżyńska, Czapliński, and Polakowska *Being Poland*, xv.

37 Rebecca L. Walkowitz, *Born Translated: The Contemporary Novel in an Age of World Literature* (New York: Columbia University Press, 2015), 4.

38 See Apter, *Against World Literature*.

39 For a discussion of Orientalizing of Eastern Europe, see Larry Wolff, *Inventing Eastern Europe: The Map of Civilization on the Mind of the Enlightenment* (Stanford, CA: Stanford University Press, 1994).

40 See Pascale Casanova, *The World Republic of Letters* (Cambridge, MA: Harvard University Press, 2004).

1

Polish Neurosis and the World Literature

Michał Paweł Markowski

Polish Neurosis

"There are many arguments against defining Polish literature by comparing it with world literature," wrote Andrzej Kijowski, an influential intellectual, critic, and writer, in the late 1950s.[1] History and geography, being radically different in each case, leave specific environments without a common ground. Culture, though, suggested Kijowski, is something distinct: "In the realm of culture, there is no strict determination," because creation "is a process of liberation, a process of transcending limitations, a process of getting rid of frailty." In culture, in contrast to the material condition of life, everything can be done. "Striving for completeness, maturity, and universality puts culture in motion; without it, it becomes a particular myth."[2]

Having established this Hegelian perspective in which cultural development happens only by a gradual elimination of the particular on the way to the absolute knowledge transcending all empirical limitations, Kijowski immediately turned it against the Polish mentality and argued that from its emergence in the sixteenth century, Polish literature seemed to have performed "a drama of its existence." This drama had consisted of a constant clash of two contrasting tendencies: a centripetal move of "searching for a reflection of local issues that will never find their way to the world literature," and a centrifugal movement of crossing the limits of "national form,"[3] and reaching a more cosmopolitan level. By not adjusting these moves peacefully, Polish literature subjected itself to an irresolvable conflict between the local and the universal. "Polish literature is like a young lad during his puberty: he lives only by defining himself and spends hours before the mirror, making faces and asking himself whether a person with such a face can be useful at all."[4]

Two decades later, Kijowski maintained but refined his position. While reading a draft of Kazimierz Brandys's novel *Nierzeczywistość*,[5] he first acknowledged the book's seriousness and then immediately launched a polemical discussion with the author, which is worth quoting at length:

> It [the part of the book Kijowski calls "a questionnaire"] puts too much stress on Polishness, and therefore on the narrator's personality. You imply that what makes the Polish experience distinct from a universal one can be understood only by Poles—here lies their tragic fate—and you invite the addressee of the "questionnaire" to the secret only because he is a descendant of a Polish family. You say on page 1: ... "Poles suffer from the locality complex, they know that they speak in riddles and that deciphering those riddles is of no interest to foreigners" ... How do you know that it is "of no interest" to them? In order to strip a mysterious thing of its mystery, to turn something local into something universal, you have to use the universal mode of narration to attract a reader, you have to make use of categories of history, psychology, morality, anthropology, and you have to use metaphors. Has the Irish code diminished the popularity of Joyce's books, has the complex of the South—how Polish, how cavalry-like!—shut the door to universality on Faulkner's face? ... A fear of looking too weird against the background of the world is stifling your voice, represses your energy.[6]

You cannot formulate the paradox nourishing modern Polish literature more clearly. If it is too particular (too Polish), it will become a curio inaccessible to anybody outside the Polish ken and unavoidably obscure forever. However, if it is going to be purely universal, detached from the Polish ground and Polish network of references, it will lose all its substance and cease to be Polish.[7] Kijowski saw a solution to this uncomfortable paradox in the repertoire of literary (narrative and stylistic) devices that would help Polish authors "turn something local into something universal" and preserve the Polish substance by carrying it over to the level of worldwide understanding.

However, this universal appeal can come from an altogether different tradition than a more worldly, cosmopolitan one. In an essay on *Sienkiewicz and Polish Neurosis*, Kijowski made a double move. First, he attacked an ultraconservative late nineteenth-century writer who won the Nobel Prize for a historical novel about the martyrdom of early Christianity (*Quo Vadis?* 1896). In doing that, Kijowski joined a large group of Polish critics for whom Sienkiewicz, turning popular literature into a national monument, petrified Polish sensibility in all-too-easy propaganda of mediocrity.

There is in Polish culture a phenomenon, which I would like to name a Sienkiewiczian structure of the idea. It shapes the literary characters' fate by cleansing themselves from the contemporary world to return to the mythical, foggy origin, source, and primeval Arcadia. ... Why do you need, he said, the world, history, movement, progress, transformation, a plethora of ideas, and adventures? Come back, be a child, a husband, a father. Be something you were born as a Pole, a Catholic. It will heal you.[8]

Having pointed to the infantilization of Polish readership,[9] Kijowski hit an altogether different note, when he wrote that "Sienkiewicz brought to the light a hidden theme of Polish culture and gave it an art form. He conducted psychoanalysis of the Polish cultural soul: a joy one feels in the presence of his oeuvre is a relief of a patient healed from neurosis."[10] Suppose the source of this national neurosis (which now, in Kijowski's vocabulary, replaces "the tragic fate" of Polish culture) is a discrepancy between history and myth, between what makes you particular and what allows you to go beyond your idiosyncrasy. In that case, the remedy comes "in the form of classic order," which in Sienkiewicz takes the shape of a fairy tale or comedy (in a sense, Northrop Frye defined this category in 1965[11]). Kijowski, however, also opens here the door for "the Christian doctrine," the lesson of which consists not in returning to a mythical source but in projecting into the future "a discipline" that infuses everything contingent with "absolute values."

For an attentive reader of Kijowski's texts in the 1960s, his complete turn into Catholicism a decade later was hardly a surprise. In 1977, not long after the liberal opposition in Poland was established with prominent help from the Catholic Church, he confessed in his diary: "What I miss is a full religious act, a complete identification with a religious community."[12] Later, in 1981, he cowrote a script for Krzysztof Zanussi's movie *From a Far Country*, a biopic about the newly elected pope, John Paul II (the confessor of his mother in Kraków). It seems to have been a typical trajectory for postwar Polish cultural critics other than national believers to counterbalance the powerful universality of the communist ideology[13] with their anti-particular agenda. They had to choose either classicism (I will return to that in a moment) or Catholicism, sweeping a painful tension between the particular and the universal under the rug of newly adopted transnational tradition.

The Horror, the Horror!

In a classic account of neurosis,[14] Sigmund Freud suggested that it results from a conflict within the psychic apparatus and not—as in the case of psychosis—from the direct conflict between the psyche and external reality:

The ego defends itself against the instinctual impulse by the mechanism of repression. The repressed material struggles against this fate. It creates for itself, along paths over which the ego has no power, a substitutive representation (which forces itself upon the ego, by way of a compromise)—the symptom. The ego finds its unity threatened and impaired by this intruder, and it continues to struggle against the symptom, just as it fended off the original instinctual impulse. All this produces the picture of neurosis. It is no contradiction to this that, in undertaking the repression, the ego is at the bottom following the commands of its super-ego-commands which, in their turn, originate from influences in the external world that have found representation in the superego. The fact remains that the ego has taken sides with those powers, that in it their demands have more strength than the instinctual demands of the id, and that the ego is the power which sets the repression in motion against the portion of the id concerned and which fortifies the repression. ... The ego has come into conflict with the id in the service of the superego and of reality; and this is the state of affairs in every transference neurosis.[15]

Although it is clear that the Id launches the major blow at the ego (*das Ich*), the central conflict develops between the Id and the superego (*Über-Ich*), which takes over the ego. The latter must subject itself to the superego to defend its supposed identity against what it perceives as an eruption of irrational and chaotic forces. The subjectivity results from this defensive mechanism and combines the ego with the superego. It comes into being only at the price of repression of the spontaneous forces of the psyche. If, then, the subjectivity is what the ego shares, through others, with the superego, the Id seems to be a drive that others cannot accept for its tendency of undermining the institution of the ego. In splitting the psyche into the subjective part and the individual part (even if the latter works through the biological drives of sexual determination to procreate: individuality for Freud is closely related to the somatic), Freud made it clear that neurosis results from the irreconcilable tension between what strives for identity (the ego subjected to the superego) and what this identity struggle deconstructs.

If we were to translate this conceptualization into a discourse of cultural studies, we would say that cultural neurosis emerges at any time dialectics of the particular and the universal become troubled and off-balance. By looking briefly at Czesław Miłosz's take on the conflict between the repressed individual drives and the subjective imperative to gain identity,[16] we will understand how to graft the Freudian idea onto our argument about Polish neurosis.

In *Road-Side Dog*, awarded in 1999 with the Nike Award, the most prestigious literary prize in Poland, Miłosz had a paragraph titled *Tropics*:

A parrot screeches. Ventilators turn. An iguana walks vertically up a palm trunk, a shining ocean wave puts foam on a beach. When I was young,

I was driven to despair during vacations by the boredom of obvious things. In my old age, finding myself in tropics, I already knew that I had always searched for medicine against this horror, which lasts because it means nothing. To give a meaning, any, only to get out of this bovine, perfectly indifferent, inert reality, without aims, strivings, affirmation, negation, like an incarnated nothingness. Religions! Ideologies! Desires! Hatreds! Come to cover with your multicolored fabric this blind thing, deprived even of a name.[17]

Miłosz struggled with this "incarnated nothingness" within himself for decades, and the only good rescue from its "horror" was literature, understood as "need for order, for rhythm, for form, which three words are opposed to chaos and nothingness."[18] In my reading, Miłosz was a persistent classicist for whom literature was an efficient weapon to "cover this blind thing," which he liked to equal with the demonic, chaotic side of reality.[19] According to Paweł Hertz, a friend of Miłosz and the intellectual who effortlessly combined his Mediterranean ideals with Roman Catholicism, classicism should be defined by two major factors: (1) by neglecting personal perception of the world and entering any human community, either religious or philosophical, either cultural or national, and (2) by penetrating the obscure reality with one's imagination.[20] In both cases, the ego has to find its identity beyond a shapeless and nameless mass of phenomena and subject itself to "the forms of classic order."

In an essay explaining his "private duties" as a professor of Polish literature in America, Miłosz wrote, "I would prefer if Polish literature had a more developed sense for the classical form and it did not consist of blind chances, surprises, gargoyles, and monsters with angelic wings." He incessantly called for this "classical form" as an antidote to any individual excess and a chaotic assault of the bare existence. In *Rodzinna Europa*, a historical account of his Lithuanian genealogy, "instead of thrusting the individual into the foreground," he chose to "looking upon [himself] as a sociological phenomenon." He did it out of respect for "those undergrounds that exist in all of us and that are better left in peace." In the same vein, he tried to explain the essence of Polishness, which I am also taking as an excellent approximation to what Kijowski called the Polish neurosis:

It was not contemplation he [= Miłosz's teacher of religion in the elementary school] was encouraging, but the ritual purification of our own person. I see this, too, as a trait of Polish Catholicism, which, in putting the accent on responsibility to collective organisms (i.e., to Church and Fatherland, which are largely identified with each other), thereby lightens the responsibility to concrete, living people. ... Perhaps this is the source of the Pole's capacity of heroic élan and of his casual or careless way of relating to another person, his indifference even to another's suffering. He wears a corset—a Roman corset. After a certain amount of alcohol, it bursts open, revealing a chaos that is not often met with in Western Europe countries. ... His literature is filled with the problem of duty towards the collective (the Church, the Nation, the Society, the Class) and the conflicts it engenders.[21]

The uncomfortable paradox of Polishness Miłosz emphasizes is that if a Pole fully dedicates his life to the subjective, that is, transindividual community of any sort, this dedication is nothing but repression of his monadic individuality on the surface of his consciousness.

In order to cover this shapeless horror, he has to apply a rigid form, which, in its turn, will deprive him of a suspicious particularity. Polishness, a formless, chaotic force closing up the channels leading to the world, does not let build any relationship with other communities, other ethnic groups, and other nations. The only way out of this stifling position is to strip oneself of individuality[22] and subject oneself to the universal community of shareable forms and rituals. This dichotomy of form and chaos repeats faithfully the Freudian description of the source of neurosis, from which, as Kijowski intelligently remarked, the most common way out, mastered by Sienkiewicz, was a withdrawal from history through history.[23] The individual chaos (always associated with what is contingent in the self) undermines the urge to form-giving, taking place both personally and collectively. It follows that the Polish side of these dialectics identified with the inability of moving into a transindividual dimension of being-in-the-world must be abandoned if the personal/collective psyche of a Pole strives for recognition in and of the world at the price of his or her individuality.

Myth and Translation

Not being able to communicate with the world through common language leads to depression,[24] from which only a transfer beyond the bounds of personal or cultural periphery seems to pull one out. Consider, for example, the case of Bruno Schulz, an assimilated Jew from a small provincial town in the borderlands of Poland who chose a literary career in Polish and, during his lifetime, published two slim volumes of prose. In 1938, his friend Rachel Auerbach gave him the following advice: "I firmly believe that your stuff can become a world-class revelation and since you are not writing in Yiddish and do not belong to the culture you grew up in, be a part at least of ... the world."[25]

Auerbach was confident that there was a strong incompatibility between a Jewish culture growing at the outskirts of pre-Holocaust Europe and the world. The world was defined here in contrast to the local and peripheral cultural environment, to which you pay allegiance when looking for the most useful—and most limiting—markers of identity. Either one writes in one of those minor languages of Central and Eastern Europe, or one belongs to the world, *tertium non datur*.[26]

In order to achieve a world-class level, writers should write in the language of one of the literary elites. Unfortunately, neither Yiddish nor Polish belonged to that family and were like "poor relatives," with a limited impact on the world. Schulz attempted to become a world-class author not once but twice. The first time he wrote a short story in German and sent it to Thomas Mann, whom he adored,[27] and in whom he saw a paradigmatic mythologizing writer.[28] The second attempt was to submit a proposal to an Italian editor to publish his first collection of prose. Both these efforts came to naught.

Schulz, as a man struggling with depression in most of the days he spent as a teacher in a local vocation school,[29] tried to extricate himself from a mundane routine by creating literature accessible on a deeper level of universal symbolism. When he was not depressed enough to not writing at all, he embarked on a mission to widen the thematic scope of his literature to hook it up on the level transcending both Polish and Jewish backgrounds.[30] In an authorial commentary to his first collection of prose, *The Cinnamon Shops*, sent to a potential Italian publisher, Schulz made it clear that in the book, he ventured to "create a history of a family, of a certain home in the provinces, not out of real events, or real fates, but seeking above them a mythical content, an ultimate sense of their story."[31] The local stories die if they do not descend (or, as Schulz suggested, ascend) into a myth (a lesson learned from Thomas Mann), the definition of which is a narrative easily understandable across the multiethnic board. One does not belong to the world if one writes in a language incomprehensible beyond its original milieu, but also one does not belong to the world if this language does not carry in its translation "an ultimate sense," ready to be appropriated by foreign readers. An apt allegory of this depressive lack of passage between the individual and the collective is Schulz's quasi-autobiographical short story *Loneliness*,[32] a grim confession made by a vanishing character irrevocably locked in a room without exit. As myth seemed to Schulz to secure comprehensibility of his dense prose on the level of content, translation into foreign languages was for Schulz the only accessible pass to the world. Nevertheless, even then, due to its hyper-stylistic inventiveness, a second translation was needed.

When Michael Hofmann, a great translator of German literature and a skilled poet himself, embarked on a mission to elucidate Schulz's style to the American readers, he went on an endless comparative spree:

The usual way of encompassing something strange and original is to offer a few points of reference. So, for gorgeous sensuousness of language, Schulz is like Keats or Dylan Thomas; in his febrile, hallucinating quality he is like Robert Louis Stevenson (the Stevenson of counterpanes and armies and dreamy lamp lighting); in his uncanny closeness to childhood, he recalls the first pages of Joyce's *Portrait of the Artist*. Further, there is

Rilke (whom he loved) in his appetite for metaphor, perhaps something of Virginia Woolf's *Orlando* in his ability to gather up and jump through time. There is also something 18th century in his baroque loftiness and his predilection for the mock-heroic.[33]

Neither of these references, maybe except for Rilke, would ever come to the mind of Polish readers, who—by the way—do also experience in reading Schulz "something strange and original."[34] If a piece of literature resists easy appropriation in a foreign cultural context, it must be ignored or adjusted to the new readers' agenda. The subjection to the rules of world literature amounts to having a cake eaten and not kept if by cake we understand the eccentric individuality that goes beyond a repertoire of the widely received forms.

Poland or Yourself?

As I am suggesting, Polish cultural neurosis results from the incompatibility between a desire to be authentically Polish and the impossibility of fulfilling this desire. A good formula for these contradictory imperatives that blows up any idea of peaceful integration of both the personal and the collective psyche came from Witold Gombrowicz, who in 1957 wrote, "I cannot be myself, yet I want to be myself, and I must be myself—this is an antinomy, one of those that do not let themselves be resolved ... and do not expect me to provide you with medicine for incurable diseases."[35] If this antinomy is an "incurable disease," then the Polish neurosis cannot be cured unless the whole premise of the disease—the antinomy itself—is put into question, especially since the solution provided by Kijowski, Miłosz, Hertz, and other Polish writers—remove yourself as far as possible from any touch of individual disruptive forces—seems more to strengthen the grip of the repressive ego than releasing the psyche.

When Gombrowicz started to publish excerpts from his diary in the Paris-based émigré monthly *Kultura* in 1953, he began almost immediately with criticizing an article "Polish Literature and Literature in Poland" by another Polish émigré writer Jan Lechoń.[36] Especially one passage from that article attracted his attention:

> Because our men of letters were preoccupied chiefly with things Polish, they could not fulfill the mission of designating the right place for our literature in the ranks of other literatures, or of establishing the world standing of our masterpieces. ... Only a great poet, a master of his own language ... could give his countrymen an idea of the level of our poets, equal to the greatest in the world, and could convince them that this poetry is of the same mettle, of the same fineness as the poetry of Dante, Racine, and Shakespeare.[37]

Of the same mettle, really? Gombrowicz begged to disagree: "To compare Mickiewicz to Dante or to Shakespeare is to compare fruit to preserves, a natural product to a processed one; a meadow, field, or village to a cathedral or city; an idyllic soul to an urban one which is rooted in people, not in nature, which is loaded with knowledge about the world of the human race."[38] With this quintessentially modern dualistic worldview (nature–culture, rural–urban, particular–universal, local–global), supported by the geopolitical division between the (supposedly free) West and the (supposedly restricted) East, Gombrowicz in 1953 set the tone for the discussion we have been following from the beginning of this article. Are we, Polish writers, unacknowledged representatives of still another minor literature produced in an incomprehensible language, or are we just writers without a national pedigree, confronted daily with issues of universal significance? In 1957, after solidifying his position among the postwar Polish readership (both in Poland and in exile), Gombrowicz, still living in Buenos Aires, returned to this question, translating it into an imaginary dialogue about the dominating allegiance to the nation:

> I walk up to a Pole and say to him: —You have spent your whole life falling to your knees before It. Now try something just the opposite. Rise up. Think not just that you must serve It—but that it is also supposed to serve you, your development. Therefore get rid of the excessive love and honor that shackle you, try to liberate yourself from the nation. To which that Pole would answer furiously: —You've gone crazy! What would I be worth if I did that? To which I say: —You must (because today it is unavoidable) decide what is the highest value to you: Poland or yourself. We must finally know what your ultimate reason for being is. Choose what is more basic to you: being a man in the world or a Pole?[39]

You cannot say it more openly: either you are a Pole or you belong to the world. Of course, if trapped in this kind of binary opposition, a Pole cannot be a "citizen of the world," and that was the reason so many writers and intellectuals in the postwar period, when the Soviets kept Poland behind the Iron Curtain, tried to locate their "true" motherland in different traditions and different communities. However, this neurotic grip was difficult (if not impossible) to avoid, as it was established precisely at the moment Polish literature replaced the erased political body (after the third, and definitive partition of 1795) in the mission of preserving national sovereignty.

Polish Literature or Literature in Poland?

After the defeat of the November Uprising and the consequent Russian-Polish war in 1831, which put an end to the relative freedom of the Warsaw

Duchy and gave way to the administrative annexation of Poland by the Russian Empire, one of the brightest Polish Romantic minds, Zygmunt Krasiński wrote bitterly to his father, a former general in the Napoleon army and now an official in the service of the Czar:

> Nothing organic, complete, comprehensive has ever been with us: there was no aristocracy, no bourgeoisie, and people. We have been shapeless political organisms and not individuals, which is why the end came so quickly. ... And in sciences and arts—what have we created? Is there Polish poetry, architecture, painting, or music? Have we had anything Polish in the world except coarseness? The clothes were borrowed from the West first, then from the Orient. Polish language left behind in favor of the dead one, Latin, then left behind in favor of the living one, French. Our small literature is a patchwork of Italian concepts, Cicero's maxims, French verses, and German ballads.[40]

Complaining at the imitative nature of Polish culture (which Gombrowicz called "being a pale moon shining with borrowed life"[41]) and at yielding originality to repetitiveness has been a constant motive in modern Polish thought.[42] Karol Irzykowski, an eminent cultural critic of the interwar period, an heir to German *Geisteswissenschaften* himself, made a powerful claim about the plagiaristic character of Polish literary turns,[43] and all critics eager to undermine any Polish originality enthusiastically accepted his thesis.

Krasiński ends his complaint with Polish cultural mimicry, which another Romantic poet, Juliusz Słowacki, had also in mind accusing Poland of being "a peacock and a parrot of other nations"[44] but begins with reproaching Poles for having, again, no sense for form. The only form they could have come up with was a recycled, second-hand form borrowed from the foreigners.

This Romantic blow at the Polish literature had a surprising follow-up 150 years later. Not long after the Oval Table conference in 1989, which forced communists to share power with the liberal opposition, one of the newly established critics suggested that we abandon the term "Polish literature" in favor of another term, "literature in Poland." Kinga Dunin intended to strip Polish literature of any social responsibility it had been burdened since Romanticism and acknowledge (against the call for authenticity) that foreign literature was as crucial in building a modern or postmodern sensitivity as the Polish one.[45] To say that John Le Carré, Stephen King, or Ursula Le Guin were much more important for the contemporary Polish sensibility than outdated classics from the Polish canon amounted to a total revaluation of established aesthetic hierarchies the liberal Polish society had lived with for decades. However, the attack was not only aimed at the "pathos, boredom, and obligations" of Polish literature at the threshold of political transformation and was not only made to say that "the true Polish culture" equals popular culture created abroad, in "the global village." "Busy with contemplating its aching tail," wrote the critic, "contemporary Polish literature is unable to cope with reality," the latter being the world of values shared by average Polish contemporary reader fed up with "costumes pulled out of an old drawer."

For the Polish audience, the change of 1989 was as significant as the one experienced after 1945 (the political annexation of Poland by the Soviet regime), or 1957 (a short-term revival of freedom known as "thaw"). It is not then by chance that the article by Kinga Dunin (a feminist reader undermining a patriarchal Polish canon) was a hidden rebuke of the problem expressed in an article Gombrowicz attacked in 1953.[46] Although the title of those two pieces was almost identical, the idea could not be more different. Lechoń was a poet who, just a year before Poland gained independence in 1918, wanted to see "spring and not Poland."[47]

Nevertheless, several decades after, only Polish literature, well aware of its belonging to the greatest although universally neglected Romantic tradition, could serve as a model for "literature in Poland," totally subjected to ideological manipulation. For Dunin, "literature in Poland" included everything Polish readers, liberated from their national prejudices, really wanted to read. For Lechoń, "literature in Poland" was a poor simulacrum of the genuine Polish literature in exile whose moral superiority over the collaborators in the native country was proven by its firm allegiance to the glorious past.

Despite unbridgeable differences between Lechoń and Dunin, their primary diagnosis seems to have been the same: Polish literature and world literature have nothing to do with each other. The cure, however, was altogether different: for a post-Romantic poet, Polish literature should be fully acknowledged by the world if the latter does not want to suffer from its incompleteness; for a postmodern critic, Polish literature has nothing to say to the world, because Polish readers do not even appreciate it. When a literary guru of the progressive left in interwar Poland, Stefan Żeromski, announced during the Great War almost the same—"We are not bringing to the world any artistic news about a complicated human soul. We are still talking about a complex Polish soul"[48]—what he had in mind was that the time for that delivery had not come yet. For Kinga Dunin, this moment was never to materialize.

Redefining the World

In a provocative essay against Sienkiewicz (a usual culprit, as we have seen), Gombrowicz pointed to the fact that the greatest weakness of Polish writers consisted in being incapable of seeing "the nation from the outside, as something 'existing in the world'." For Gombrowicz, it was a matter of choice. One could choose a unique way of defining oneself and emphasize what disconnects them from social networks (Gombrowicz himself), or, inversely, one could stress one's place in a more extensive system of links (Miłosz et al.). If individuality reveals the stubborn concreteness of a human being, subjectivity aims at sharing individual properties with selected others. Under this banner, Gombrowicz ran his anti-Polish campaign in the 1950s, when Polish writers (both in the country and in exile) needed to redefine their artistic status against the fatal political circumstances. Gradually, however, as patriotic calls began to fade and Polish literature moved beyond the realm of national obligations, Gombrowicz switched gears, realizing that his criticism of Polish subjectivity is a dead end as long as the main category of this relation—the world—remains untouched.

When we look at Gombrowicz's anti-Polish campaign in the early 1950s, we see that he understood "the world" as a synonym of the anti-parochial perspective, a distance that one should adopt in talking about local issues rather than a total rejection of it. In contrast to Kijowski and Miłosz, he did not want Polish idiom translated smoothly into a universal language understood by foreign readers but wanted the world to make an effort to acknowledge the idiom. The world, Gombrowicz suggested, was not there, beyond the Iron Curtain, but here, in every act of "confronting with reality," which, in Poland, violently subjected to the extraordinary historical circumstances, could have been more interesting than in other countries, routinely immersed in the well-being. However, within years, Gombrowicz moved from this "humanistic" perspective on the world to include a more uncanny and demonic view.[49]

> There exist two orders: the human and the inhuman. The world is an absurdity and a monstrosity to our indestructible need for meaning, justice, love. A simple thought. A sure one … Don't make a cheap demon out of me. I will be on the side of human order (and even on God's side even though I am not a believer) to the end of my days and in dying as well.[50]

Identified only with this "indestructible need for meaning, justice, love," the world seems to be "an oversimplified concept."[51] Gombrowicz would agree with Miłosz that the chaotic powers of the accidental ceaselessly attack the human world, putting the ego into a constant crisis. However, he would also disagree with Miłosz or Kijowski and their view of literature as a therapeutic imposition of form on the formless.[52] Already in the 1930s, Gombrowicz made his name by insisting on "confronting with each other all areas [of life], especially not forgetting about those most private and secret." Moreover, he added, anticipating Miłosz's resistance to what boils under the surface of consciousness, "they do not stand the light, so let us drag them out into the daylight."[53] For Gombrowicz (in stark contrast to

Miłosz), literature is set to report the human wrestling with the unofficial, underground, immature, ungovernable forces and not ignore them.[54]

Into the Unknown

Diagnosing himself with "a crisis of 'universalism'" and gravitating toward what is "concrete and private," Gombrowicz assigned literature a task of coping with the existential and not national concrete. "I want to topple the accursed 'universality' that shackles me more than the most confining prison and escape into the freedom of the limited!"[55] This "freedom of the limited" is now *not* the Polish particularity infused with a dollop of universality but a radical descending into the gaping abyss of the accidental deprived of any safeguarding coordinates.

To choose a nation (Polish or Argentine), religion, or any other institutionalized belief as an identity marker saving from the assault of "the unknown, inconceivable" was to lie to the monstrous contingency of human existence devoid of any transcendence.[56] The terrifying lack of transcendence, however, was also dispossessing the self from its personal properties. When Gombrowicz encouraged Polish writers to abandon their national safety net, he was not pushing to adopt a more cosmopolitan approach; that would be just a variation of a self-assuring and self-gratifying take on life.[57] Instead, he wanted them to throw themselves headfirst into a dark cosmos deprived of any form of identity and stabilized meaning, chaos in which neither individuality nor subjectivity would have a chance to emerge. This radical move aimed at breaking a dead-end dialectics between Poland and the world. In the turbulent undercurrent of existence, any alleviating principle of human identity dissolves, and the dichotomies between the ego and the Id, Poland and the world, individuality and subjectivity, dichotomies of which the Polish neurosis had been born, cease to be an obsessive factor to be included in the writers' fight for independence.[58] As long as the world is a place that does not protect you from the devil and where no form can ever gloss over the chaos boiling under the steps of any human being, the only way out of the neurotic trap set by Polish collective psyche leads toward piling up scenes of confrontation with the formless, the material, and the contingent. The healing of Polish neurosis cannot be complete unless the total deconstruction of geography is on the way, and you realize that "the world" is not there, but here, in the "bottomless abyss" of yourself.

Notes

1   Unfortunately no major work by Andrzej Kijowski (1928–85) has been translated into English so far. In Polish the best monograph is still Dariusz

Skórczewski, *Aby rozpoznać siebie: Rzecz o Andrzeju Kijowskim–krytyku literackim i publicyście* [To recognize oneself. On Andrzej Kijowski, a literary critic and opinion writer] (Towarzystwo Naukowe Katolickiego Uniwersytetu Lubelskiego: Lublin, 1996).

2   Andrzej Kijowski, "Czy istnieje polska literatura?" [Does Polish Literature Exist?] in Szósta dekada [The Sixties] (Warszawa: PIW, 1972), 26–30. First published as "Czy istnieję?" [Do I exist?], *Przegląd Kulturalny*, no. 44 (1958): 8]. If not indicated otherwise, all translations from the Polish are mine.

3   Andrzej Kijowski, "Krajowa czy z importu?," [Polish, or imported?] in *Szósta dekada*, 25.

4   Kijowski, "Czy istnieje polska literatura?," 29.

5   *Nierzeczywistość* (in English *A Question of Reality: A Novel of Poland*) was the first Polish novel to be published for underground circulation in 1977.

6   Andrzej Kijowski, *Dziennik 1970–1977* [Diary 1970–1977], edited by J. Błoński, K. Kijowska (Kraków: Wydawnictwo Literackie, 1998), 301–2.

7   The same issue, although expressed in different historic and cultural circumstances, was crucial for Dostoevsky who hated Russian émigré culture for having been detached from the Russian soil and therefore betraying the Russian soul. We are not facing the problem of "minor literature" then but the problem of repressed cultural backwardness.

8   Andrzej Kijowski, "Sienkiewicz i polska nerwica," *Tygodnik Powszechny*, no. 46 (1966): 1–2. Reprinted in *Granice literatury. Wybór szkiców krytycznych i historycznych* [The Limits of Literature: Selected Critical and Historical Essays], edited by Tomasz Burek (Warszawa: Biblioteka "Więzi," 1991), 238–40.

9   First diagnosed by S. Brzozowski, *Legenda Młodej Polski. Studia o strukturze duszy kulturalnej* [The Legend of Young Poland: Studies on the Structure of Cultural Soul] (Połoniecki: Lwów 1910), in chapter 3: "Polska zdziecinniała" [The infantile Poland].

10 Kijowski, "Sienkiewicz i polska nerwica," 241.

11 As a narrative pattern "moving from death to rebirth, decadence to renewal, winter to spring, darkness to a new dawn." See Northrop Frye, *A Natural Perspective: The Development of Shakespearean Comedy and Romance* (New York: Columbia 1965), 121.

12 Kijowski, *Dziennik 1970–1977*, 413.

13 Czesław Miłosz made this point several times in prose, conversations, and poems, that the acceptance of communism among Polish intellectuals and writers came not from personal cynicism but from subjecting to the "objective" laws of history (see especially *The Captive Mind*, trans. Jane Zielonko, New York: Knopf, 1953).

14 In a broader sense, as applied to European modernity, I am using the category of neurosis in "Między nerwicą i psychozą. Rzeczywistości Rolanda Barthesa [Between neurosis and psychosis: Roland Barthes's realities]," *Teksty Drugie*, no. 3 (2012). Translation of this analytical category into a cultural discourse

was possible thanks to Karen Horney and her book *The Neurotic Personality of Our Age* (1937), which, by the way, was "the Bible" of Polish psychotherapists in the last decade of the communist regime (see *Polska ucieczka od wolności* [Polish Escape from Freedom]: *Z Wojciechem Eichelbergerem rozmawia Adam Puchejda*, "Kultura Liberalna," nr 432, 18 kwietnia 2017 (https://kulturalibera lna.pl/2017/04/18/eichelberger-puchejda-zdrowie-psychiczne-polska/). The Polish translation of Horney's book came out in 1976.

15 Sigmund Freud, *Neurosis and Psychosis*, translated by Joan Riviere, *Standard Edition of the Complete Psychological Works of Sigmund Freud*, Volume XIX (1923–1925): *The Ego and the Id and Other Works* (London: Hoghart Press, 1971), 149–50.

16 In separating the individual from the subjective, the former being a marker of idiomatic tendencies in the self, the latter aiming at belonging to community of any sort, I am following the conceptual frame of my most recent books: *Wojny nowoczesnych plemion. Spór o rzeczywistość w epoce populizmu* [Wars of Modern Tribes: Arguing about Reality in the Age of Populism] (Karakter: Kraków, 2019) and *Polska, rozkosz, uniwersytet. Opowieść edukacyjna* [Poland, *bliss*, university: an educational story] (Kraków: WUJ, 2021).

17 Czesław Miłosz, "Tropics," in *Road-Side Dog*, translated by the author and Robert Hass (New York: Farrar, Strauss, and Giroux, 1998), 41.

18 Czesław Miłosz, *New and Collected Poems 1931–2001* (New York: Ecco, 2003), 452.

19 "What reasonable man would like to be a city of demons, / who behave as if they were at home, speak in many tongues, / and who, not satisfied with stealing his lips or hand, / work at changing his destiny for their convenience?" ("Ars Poetica?" [1968], in *New and Collected Poems*, 240.)

20 Paweł Hertz, "O klasycyzmie [On classicism]" in *Świat i dom. Szkice i uwagi wybrane* [World and Home: Selected Essays and Remarks] (Warsaw: PIW, 1977), 47–8.

21 Czesław Miłosz, *Native Realm: A Search for Self-definition*, translated by Catherine S. Leach (Berkeley: University of California Press 1981), 84–5.

22 Kijowski: "Accept Christ's way, ... annihilate myself and consider myself secondary, and bring to the fore the good of God and other people" (*Dziennik 1978–1985*, 54).

23 That was also a key problem for Miłosz at the time he struggled with the "Hegelian bite": "Do you agree then / To abolish what is, and take from movement / The eternal moment as a gleam/On the current of a black river? Yes." [*A Notebook: Bon by Lake Leman* (1953)].

24 See Julia Kristeva, *The Black Sun: Depression and Melancolia*, translated by L. Roudiez (New York: Columbia University Press, 1989).

25 Letter from July 25, 1938. In Bruno Schulz, *Księga listów*, edited by Jerzy Ficowski, Stanisław Danecki, and Dzieła zebrane [Collected Works], (słowo/ obraz terytoria: Gdańsk, 2012), 5, 453 [sprawdzić paginację].

26 Here is the most significant difference between Kafka and Schulz (who translated Der Prozess into Polish). Kafka, an assimilated Jew like Schulz, although living in Czech Prague, chose as his literary medium German, the language of a cultural minority immersed in the Czech linguistic landscape. For Schulz Polish was the language of the cultural majority in the multiethnic community of Western Ukraine. From this point of view, Schulz's literature did not belong to the "minor literature" defined by Deleuze and Guattari with three factors: "the deterritorialization of language, the connection of the individual to a political immediacy, and the collective assemblage of enunciation." (Gilles Deleuze and Felix Guattari, "What Is Minor Literature," in *Kafka: Toward Minor Literature*, translated by Dana Pollan (Minneapolis: University of Minnesota Press 1986), 18.)

27 *Die Heimkehr* (Homecoming), written in 1937, did not survive the war.

28 In an open letter to S. I. Witkiewicz published in 1935, Schulz wrote,

> Mann shows that at the bottom of all human events, if only to shell them from the husk of time and multitude, certain Ur-patterns, "histories" emerge, serving as bases for those events, which forms in big repetitions. In Mann, these are biblical stories, eternal myths of Babylon and Egypt. As for myself, I tried to find my private mythology, my own "histories," my mythical genealogy on a much smaller scale. (B. Schulz, *Szkice krytyczne*, *Dzieła zebrane*, 7, 18)

29 "I am in a deep mental collapse, and I believe that I will not be able to write anything more! I am persuading myself that it's neurasthenia, but this repulsion to writing has lasted more than six months, and it makes me think a bit" (letter to Z Waśniewski, June 5, 1934 [*Księga listów*, 112]). "I so much detest returning to school. I am in despair when I start thinking on working with metal, of which I don't have the slightest idea. And in general, I despise all this business and am bored with it to the highest degree" (to the same, August 27, 1934 [*Księga listów*, 115]).

30 Today we witness a countermove made by various scholars in Polish-Jewish academia to retrieve this rich local background of Schulz. See especially sixteen volumes of Schulz/Forum edited by scholars associated with słowo/obraz terytoria, the publisher of Bruno Schulz's *Complete Works*, and a book by K. Underhill, *Bruno Schulz and Galician Jewish Modernity*, forthcoming.

31 [Bruno Schulz], "Exposé o książce Brunona Schulza Sklepy cynamonowe" [A summary of Bruno Schulz's book The Cinnamon Shops], in *Szkice krytyczne*, *Collected Works*, edited by Włodzimierz Bolecki, Mirosław Wójcik, Piotr Sitkiewicz, 7, 203.

32 B. Schulz, "Loneliness," in *Collected Stories*, translated by Madeleine G. Levine (Evanston, IL: Northwestern University Press, 2018), 231–2. First printed in "Studio" in 1936 under the title "O sobie [About myself]."

33 M. Hofmann, "Young Man from Drohobycz," *New York Times*, March 9, 2003. https://www.nytimes.com/2003/03/09/books/young-man-from-drohobycz.html.

34 After the second collection of Schulz came out in 1936 (dated 1937), he was immediately accused by critics of "hideous ornamentality" and "artistic immorality." See K. Wyka and S. Napierski, "Dwugłos o Schulzu" [Two Voices about Schulz], *Ateneum*, no. 1 (1939): 156–63.

35 Witold Gombrowicz, *Diary*, translated by Lillian Vallee (New Haven, CT: Yale University Press), 289.

36 J. Lechoń, "Literatura polska i literatura w Polsce," *Wiadomości*, nos. 36–7 (September 14, 1952): 1.

37 I am using here a translation provided by L. Vallee.

38 Gombrowicz, *Diary*, 5.

39 Ibid., 298.

40 Z. Krasiński, *Listy do ojca*, edited by S. Pigoń (Warszawa: PIW, 1963), 311–12.

41 Gombrowicz, *Diary*, 294.

42 An instructive anthology and summary of Polish self-hatred gives A. Leszczyński, *No dno po prostu jest Polska. Dlaczego Polacy tak bardzo nie lubią swojego kraju i innych Polaków* [Poland Is Simply At The Bottom: Why Poles Don't Like So Much Themselves and Other Poles] (Warszawa: WAB, 2017).

43 Karol Irzykowski, "Plagiatowy charakter przełomów literackich w Polsce," [The Plagiaristic Character of Literary Turns in Poland], in *Słoń wśród porcelany: Studia nad nowszą myślą literacką w Polsce* [Elephant in a China Shop. Studies on the Most Recent Literary Thoughts in Poland] (Warszawa: Rój, 1935).

44 Juliusz Słowacki, "Agamemnon's Tomb," in *Juliusz Slowacki's Agamemnon's Tomb: A Polish Oresteia*, edited by Catherine O'Neil, Z. Janowski (South Bend: St. Augustin's Press 2019).

45 Kinga Dunin, "Literatura polska czy literatura w Polsce," *Ex Libris*, no. 48 (1994).

46 Lechoń, "Literatura polska i literatura w Polsce."

47 In a poem "Herostrates [Herostratus]" written in 1917 and published in a volume *Karmazynowy poemat* [A crimson poem] in 1920.

48 Stefan Żeromski, *Literatura a życie* polskie (1915) [Literature and Polish Life], in *Snobizm i postęp oraz inne utwory publicystyczne*, edited by Antonina Lubaszewska (Kraków: Universitas 2003), 228–9.

49 "I felt that something was happening endlessly, something demonic" (*Diary*, 141)—this sentence could serve as a motto for Gombrowicz's adventures in Argentina and Europe as well.

50 Gombrowicz, *Diary*, 294.

51 Ibid., 21.

52 On this category in the context of the twentieth-century art see Yves-Alain Bois and Rosalind E. Krauss, *Formless: A User's Guide* (New York: Zone Books, 1997).

53 Witold Gombrowicz, "Grzechy naszego wieku przejściowego" [Sins of Our Transitional Age], *Kurier Poranny*, no. 10 (1936). Reprinted in: W. Gombrowicz, *Varia*, t. 1: *Czytelnicy i krytycy* (Kraków: Wydawnictwo Literackie 2004), 203.

54 M. P. Markowski, *Czarny nurt: Gombrowicz, świat, literatura* [Black Current: Gombrowicz, World, and Literature] (Wydawnictwo Literackie: Kraków, 2004).

55 Gombrowicz, *Diary*, 349–50.

56 See Ł. Tischner, *Gombrowicza milczenie o Bogu* [Gombrowicz's Silence about God] (Kraków: Wydawnictwo Uniwersytetu Jagiellońskiego, 2013).

57 "I am not admirer of cosmopolitanism—neither the scientific, dry, theoretical, and abstract cosmopolitanism with its cerebral schema of ideally universal systems—nor that which is born, in murky heads, od a sentimental anarchy, of a mawkish dream of 'freedom' " (Gombrowicz, *Diary*, 299).

58 M. P. Markowski, "Du vomi ou au-déla de l'économie: Gombrowicz contre Sartre," in *Witold Gombrowicz entre l'Europe et l'Amérique*, edited by M. Tomaszewski (Lille: Presses Universitaires de Septentrion, 2007), 171–80.

2

Jan Potocki, the Greatest Author of the Polish Enlightenment as a French Writer

Emiliano Ranocchi

Jan Potocki was a man of paradoxes. The first of them, without any doubt, is that this major Polish author of the Enlightenment was a French writer— by French meaning not nationality but language, as Jan Potocki's native language was not Polish but French. This situation was a consequence of the role played by the French language as a sociolect and status symbol within the Polish-Lithuanian aristocracy in the eighteenth century, as was the case in many other European countries, and due to the unrivaled prestige of French literature and culture in Europe at the time. However, this is still insufficient to explain how it transpired that Jan Potocki was not bilingual, as most of the representatives of his class (if they were), but a French native speaker like anyone else in France, Wallonia, or Romandy. Hence, his situation differed from that of the second most famous Polish author to write in a language that was not that of the country of his birth: Józef Konrad Korzeniowski, alias Joseph Conrad, who was not a native speaker of English but chose to write in this language, nonetheless. As a matter of fact, Potocki's linguistic identity is at the border between a social habit and an individual feature. Furthermore, one should not forget that in early modern Europe, language was not yet connected with national identity. In other words, Potocki's linguistic identity played no role in defining his national identity. Born into one of the most prominent and influential Polish families, he left Poland for the first time around 1770, at the age of nine, along with his younger brother

Seweryn, following the upheaval caused by the Bar Confederation. In 1774, the brothers were sent to Switzerland to be educated by a Protestant pastor, Louis Constançon, and Jan Potocki's Swiss education may account for the dominance of his French over his Polish.[1]

Therefore, the question of language, as a *pars pro toto*, showcases the inadequacy of mere historical and sociological parameters to explain the emergence of such an uncommon mind as that of Jan Potocki. Up to a point, he was a typical representative of his class at his time, but he very soon transcended what was considered typical for his milieu. For instance, in the case of Jan Potocki, it would be inappropriate to speak of a Grand Tour in the sense that this practice had for the education of young aristocrats from northern and eastern Europe. To appreciate Jan Potocki's originality, the best touchstone would be a distant cousin of his, Stanisław Kostka Potocki, his future brother-in-law, as both young men would marry two sisters of the Lubomirski family. Stanisław had taken a fairly similar educational path as Jan and Seweryn: he had also been educated under the direction of a Swiss governor abroad, in Turin's Royal Academy and longer stays in Switzerland, and from then on he undertook several trips to Italy, which would make him the first Polish art historian and the translator of Winckelmann's *History of the Art of Antiquity* into Polish.

Without taking anything away from Kostka Potocki's unusual competence and merits, his journeys fully accord with the standard version of the aristocratic educational practice of the time, which aimed at furnishing him with the requisite skills of a future statesman, even if the stress on art and architecture is specific for Stanisław Kosta's personality. In this context, the case of Jan Potocki is quite singular: without considering the four years spent in Switzerland and a brief episode as an officer in the Austrian army, he had begun to travel at the age of seventeen, but his first destination was not Italy or Paris or London but Africa, which he reached from Malta.[2] After this first encounter with Africa, Potocki also visited Italy in 1779 and, seven years before Goethe, Sicily, which was not yet on the must-see-places list, then Spain, Morocco, and Tunis. In subsequent decades would come Turkey, Egypt, Morocco again, the Caucasus, Crimea, and the Asian part of the Russian Empire. Beginning with the journey to Turkey and Egypt in 1784, some of his travel experiences have come down to us in print or manuscript form: *The Voyage to Turkey and Egypt* (1788), *The Voyage to the Empire of Morocco* (1792), *The Voyage to Astrakhan and to Caucasus* (several manuscript versions and a posthumous editions from 1829), *The Memoir on the Embassy to China* (manuscript dated to 1806).

In the list above, I have deliberately omitted the European countries between which he continued to shuttle in the same period. This is because Europe (which he knew like a few others) in this paradigm was not merely the final destination, like in the educational travels of young European aristocrats, but a term of comparison and a starting point. He sought the discovery of an extra-European space that in turn would influence and change the comprehension of Europe itself in a relentless play of mirrors. Indeed, at least two of his literary journeys took place in Europe:[3] the *Journey to Holland during the revolution of 1787* (1788) and the *Journey to some parts of Lower Saxony in search of Slavic and Wend remains, made in 1794* (1795). Even when he traveled within Europe and set himself radically different goals (the attempt at understanding the dynamics of the Small Revolution of 1787, the exploration of archeological evidence of the Slavic presence in Saxony), the gaze is the same.

Compared with the Eurocentric, relatively fixed itinerary of the Grand Tour, Potocki's way of traveling shatters all points of reference and can be regarded as a precursor of twentieth-century anthropological and ethnological journeys, for traveling is an instrument of thinking in the same way that walking was for the Peripatetics. For some of his travels, we do not even know the real task or reason: this is especially true for the trips to Turkey, Egypt, and Morocco. Scholars are quite unanimous in supposing some secret diplomatic missions for them.[4] Be that as it may, reading his travel reports, we do not feel that ignoring these missions, if there were any, really affects our understanding of the text. This may lead to the conclusion that, no matter how important these purported missions were, the real and deep reason of Potocki's travels never changed from the first to the last, despite their sheer scale. Formally, they either consist of letters (*Journey to Turkey and Egypt, Journey to Holland, Memoir on the Embassy to China*) or are composed as a journal (*Journey to the Empire of Morocco, Journey to some parts of Lower Saxony, Journey to Astrakhan and to Caucasus*). The two forms blend into each other, as the letters are also structured as journals. Moreover, there are letters written during other voyages (to the Polish king, Stanisław August, from the Caucasus, to Prince Adam Kazimierz Czartoryski during Potocki's participation in the diplomatic mission to China) that the writer did never collect or edit as separate works.

At the very beginning of his *Journey to the Empire of Morocco* Potocki claims to be the "first stranger who came to this country as a simple traveler,"[5] which is untrue, moreover—he was aware of that, as in his text he quotes the works of other travelers to this country. However, this utterance is ultimately true, as he was the first in Europe, or at least one of the first, to adopt traveling as an epistemological and methodological instrument to question the fixed scale of the values of European culture. In this sense, while being a chapter in the complex history of European Orientalism, Potocki's journeys contain tremendous potential to overcome the Orientalist paradigm itself, as only a very few works in contemporary Europe did. He was the first of a long list of European travelers to go to extra-European countries in search of the requisite tools to question the abstract paradigm of European universalism and supply a critical definition of human culture. Potocki's travel ethic is perhaps best expressed in a well-known passage at the beginning of his *Journey to the Empire of Morocco*: "Alas! Travelers usually do not have other glasses to observe, but those they have brought with them from their countries and do not take care of letting the lenses cut in the countries they are visiting. Hence, there are so many bad observations."[6] Moreover, at the beginning of another journey, the one to Astrakhan and Caucasus, he makes a promise: "I promise to the reader but one thing, never to close my eyes. Everything I will see I will tell you. Sometimes, I will add some observations that I like to believe will not be poorly received, even by educated men."[7] To a certain extent, this justifies the use of the journal form, which ensures a basic standard of reliability and exactitude: the traveler reports his travel in chronological order and leaves the reader to his own conclusions, limiting himself to marginal notes. The same approach "can be found again in his historical works, in which ancient writers take the place of travellers' 'notions'."[8]

In addition to this objective approach (even if applied to subjective impressions), another unexpected element in Potocki's journeys opens the way to a different dimension, namely that of fiction. Already in the *Journey to Turkey and Egypt*, Potocki weaves five tales into the relation (in the second edition of 1789 they increase to six). The first of them is said to have been gathered in a café of Constantinople. The rest are presented as written in an "Oriental" style and explicitly adapted for the European reader. However, since the oldest manuscript of the *Journey* (1784) does not contain any tales, it is rather unlikely that they could have been written in Constantinople. Another "tartar apologue" was published in May 1790 in the *Weekly Magazine of the Diet*. This fictional narrative element returns in the *Journey to the Empire of Morocco*. Told by a Moroccan acquaintance of the writer, Bin-Otman, the narrative appendix to *the Journey to the Empire of Morocco* is, as Potocki himself informs the reader, "a work of pure imagination." This makes in total nine Oriental tales, the only narrative texts written by Potocki before his novel. Their fictive reliability provides a foretaste of Potocki's mastery of pastiche and penchant for fake references which abound in his future novel. The various metalinguistic considerations accompanying the composition of these apologues, supposedly borrowed from the oral tradition, or invented by the author and stylized as Oriental tales, keeping things in proportion, create a kind of narrative parallel to Goethe's poetic cycle *West-östlicher Divan*, with the consistent difference that Potocki's Orient is not a matter of books but of experience.

In fact, the voyages, in all their variety, already contain the whole range of Potocki's creativity: on the one side the exactitude and objectivity of the gaze and the methodology of providing the gathered material/observations in the order of their occurrence—methods he employs alongside in his historical works; on the other side, there is the fascination with traditional oral narrative both in a proto-ethnological way and in a creative, fictional one, which would lead to the novel form. This tension is not accidental—it reflects the slow but relentless emergence of a critical approach to the purported transparency of speech whose expression would have a place in Potocki's major work, *The Manuscript Found in Saragossa*.

Potocki's historical works, today almost totally forgotten and neglected by all but a handful of scholars, were that part of his work (here another of his paradoxes) for which he expected to go down in history. Written at the dawn of modern history and science, at a time when breakthroughs in science and geology shattered the limits set down by the Holy Scriptures and ancient historiography, Potocki's historical works today have lost their scientific value, from the point of view of both their methodology and content. Nevertheless, they continue to reflect the clash between his erudite approach with the multiplicity, incommensurability, and randomness of historical evidence and help us understand some deep premises of his literary world. The historian gets around written testimonies and archeological relics with the same caution with which the traveler encounters different civilizations, striving not to draw hasty conclusions from his observations. For fear of falling prey to what he calls, with an expression of his times, "ésprit de système,"[9] he prefers to put together fragments and quotes from ancient authors, relying on an unquestioned traditional principle of authority, without adding anything of his own and leaving the task of making sense of them to the reader, in a manner that has been compared to an epistolary novel.[10] This is, of course, what makes them so difficult to read today. His interest in the past of the Slavs began already at the time of his service in the Austrian army and led to his first major publication in the years around the Great Sejm. It was then that the young Potocki, dressed eccentrically as a Sarmatian with shaved head and sable, agitated for the safety of the Republic from its aggressors and founded a printing press in Warsaw (called "Free Press").

The *Essay about Universal History and Investigations about That of Sarmatia*, printed in six volumes by the Free Press in Warsaw between 1789 and 1792, is the erudite expression of his political patriotism. In this work the traditional narrative of the Polish *szlachta*, identifying the Polish nation (synonymous with the nobility) with the ancient tribe of the Sarmatians, thanks to the broadest possible meaning of Sarmatia, ends up embracing all Slavic peoples and turns into an anticipation of nineteenth-century pan-Slavic ideology. After the failure of the revolution and the end of the Republic, this would help Potocki put an end to his political engagement and readdress his political loyalty to Russia, turning his juvenile commitment to the national cause into a purely scientific interest. A testimony of this turn is the already mentioned *Voyage to Lower Saxony* of 1794, written in parallel with *the Historical & Geographical Fragments about Scythia, Sarmatia & the Slavs* (III volume Berlin, 1795, I-II Brunswick, 1796). His interest in the archeology of the Slavs would last at least for another decade and culminate in a book Potocki was very proud of: *The Early History of the Peoples of Russia with a Thorough Exposition of All Local, National and Traditional Notions That Are necessary for Understanding the Fourth Book of Herodotus* (Saint-Petersburg, 1802).

In this work, the radical approach of the previous ones is mitigated by an extensive commentary and the two main topics of Potocki's historical research—the exploration of the past of the Slavic peoples and the history of early Antiquity—which are so strictly connected as never before or since. The search for the origins of human history would become his next focus and lead first to the essays on Ancient Egyptian chronology: *The Dynasties of the Second Book of Manetho* (Florence, 1803), The *Chronology of the First Two Books of Manetho* (Florence, 1803), then extend to cover biblical chronology: *Hebrew Chronology to Continue Manetho* (manuscript, 1803) and later to the *Principles of Chronology for the Times Anterior to the Olympics* (Saint-Petersburg, 1810) and to the *Principles of Chronology for the Twelve Centuries Preceding the Olympics* (I vol. 1813, II vol. 1814, III vol. 1815, Krzemieniec). Again, destiny played him a trick for the hieroglyphs were deciphered only a few years after the writer's tragic death, with the subsequent access to a countless number of sources disqualifying all his labors and consigning them to the past. Moreover, Potocki writes for a reader who is potentially his partner, someone perfectly acquainted with all the sources, effectively freeing Potocki from quoting them, which makes his work very hard to grasp even for initiated readers, since they have to reconstruct his unexpressed thoughts and connections. The chronological inquiries during the last years of his life took the appearance of a real mania Potocki himself was aware of, since he drew his own caricatures in two characters of his novel: Hervas and Velasquez. However, though it may seem so, the laboratory of history is not detached from his literary creation, as it provided some of the questions Potocki was unable to answer without questioning the medium itself, the discourse, and this was only possible by quitting the field of history for that of literature. Since the travel journal, whose possible variants he had extensively and successfully experimented with, was still on the border between objectivity of the gaze and literary invention, the next step could only be the most audacious one, that of fiction.

However, before we proceed to an examination of his masterpiece, we must say a few more words on another field of Potocki's literary oeuvre that was a hotbed of invention: theater. In terms of dimensions, compared to the rest of his work Potocki's theatrical output occupies a somewhat negligible place. All of his pieces belong to *théatre de société*, represent minor literary genres, and were written for fun in three different periods of his life and each time for a specific audience: the first six *Parades* were composed for the theater of Łańcut Castle, the residence of his first mother-in-law, Izabella Lubomirska, where they were staged in 1792, and published anonymously in Warsaw the following year;[11] the comedy *The Gypsies of Andalusia*, the only more extensive play, was written in 1794, when the writer was a frequent guest at the court of Henry of Prussia (brother of Friedrich II) in Rheinsberg; finally, the last pieces come from the period between 1798 and 1802, when Potocki entered into his second marriage, with Konstancja Potocka, daughter of Stanisław Felix Potocki, another distant cousin of his and one of the former leaders of the Bar Confederation. At this time, the writer often stayed at his cousin's magnificent residence in Tulczyn, in Ukraine. Two little plays also date from this period. The first of them, *The Blind*, belongs to the genre of the so-called proverb, a play built on a proverb that the spectators are expected to guess, which was found and published in the early 1990s. The second, *Gile Married*, is again a parade whose subtitle explicitly claims to be the continuation of one of the *Parades* written for Łańcut, *Gile in Love*, and has recently been discovered in the Central National Historical Archives of Ukraine in Kiev.

The genre parade was originally a form of very short folk scene played outside theaters to draw the attention of the passersby and entice them to buy a ticket and enter the real playhouse. It became very popular in the eighteenth century, and from the oral environment of street theaters it became a literary genre. Parades began to be written and played in the courts to amuse the nobility with the stylization of a peasant milieu. Like in the Commedia dell'Arte, the characters of the parades are always fixed and stereotyped, and, like masks, they are always the same: Cassandre (father or husband of Izabelle), Léandre (lover of Izabelle), Izabelle (in Potocki's work, Zerzabelle), Gile or Arlequin (Cassandre's or Léandre's servant). Due to their origin in a form of advertising, as a rule the parades are single short scenes that are complete in themselves. Already this shows that Potocki's idea of making *Gile Married* the continuation of *Gile in Love* is a break in the tradition of the genre (let alone that of making Gile, the servant, Zerzabelle's lover, instead of Léandre, with consequent metaliterary jokes and allusions).

Potocki's characters are aware of the roles assigned to them in the genre's tradition and often make open references to it at the same time they break it. In fact, even if *Parades* were born from leisure and conceived to amuse an exclusive society, nothing is ever simple with Potocki, and yet in these apparently innocuous divertissements we find numerous allusions to contemporary literature and society, to what was going on in France,[12] stylistic pastiches making fun of contemporary French literature, but also allusions to contemporary Polish culture and society. This is the case, for example, of *The Calendar of Old People*, which is an adaptation of an original of La Fontaine (who in turn drew on Boccaccio) and, as the subheading openly states, a parody of Madame de Genlis's plays (more precisely of a one-act play called *La cloison*). However, the reference to this play is a pretext. The real target is Madame de Genlis herself with her prudish Catholic theater. At the same time, the calendar of the seniors is a quite perspicuous allusion to a famous Polish comedy of Franciszek Bohomolec, *Marriage*

According to the Calendar, in which the calendar (often the only reading of Sarmatian nobility), with its information about moon phases and saints employed in both Potocki and Bohomolec to gauge the auspiciousness of a marriage, was a sort of synecdoche of the backwardness and superstition of the Polish *szlachta*.[13] *The Bourgeois Comedian* in turn plays humorously with Rousseau's *Pigmalion*.[14] However, the most modern aspect of Potocki's *Parades* is undoubtedly the specific verbal absurd, the frequent nonsense and verbal jokes reminding us of Ionesco and Jarry.[15] Like in his novel, in these theatral miniatures Potocki transcends the nineteenth century to appear directly in the twentieth.

The Gypsies of Andalusia represent another form of playing with literary tradition. Here the main plot, a quite tearful history of two couples and a father written in alexandrines, is interspersed with eleven ironical airs sung by the gypsies, which turn the apparently serious story into a comedy. The sophisticated, uncommon gimmick has prevented most of the critics from recognizing its humoristic intention, described by Dominique Triaire as a "delayed" parody.[16] In fact, the skill for pastiche and the play with the frame reversing or calling into question the content of the frame itself would be one of the many narrative strategies of *The Manuscript Found in Saragossa*. Curiously enough, *The Gypsies of Andalusia* already contain some of the characters, including the gypsies, who would return in the novel.

The Manuscript Found in Saragossa is one of the most astonishing novels in the history of world literature, a novel written by a Polish nobleman in French, whose action occurs mainly in Spain and in other countries of the Mediterranean basin and in which neither Poland nor Eastern Europe make even the slightest appearance. To introduce the reader to this extremely complex work, we cannot gloss over questions concerning its composition, reception, and editorial history. In recent decades, thanks to the investigations and discoveries of Dominique Triaire and François Rosset, our understanding of the composition process has substantially improved. The work on the novel has occupied the writer for more than twenty years. Three major steps of composition are documented: the first one dates to around 1794, the second one between 1804 and 1808, and the third and final one, the only completed version, around 1810. In fact, *The Manuscript Found in Saragossa* is not a single novel but rather a cluster of texts linked with each other by the characters, the general compositional idea (even if a substantial change of structure takes place between the second and the third version, as we will see), and number of stories and plots. We do not know precisely when Potocki started working on his masterpiece, but we know that in 1791 he traveled through the region where the novel's plot would take place. The history of the editions of the *Manuscript* is also no less romantic. Until Rosset and Triaire's critical edition (2006), we could either read Potocki's novel in the fragmentary version of Roger Caillois (1958) or in René Raddrizzani's edition (1989), which was partly a retranslation of the Polish translation of Edmund Chojecki of 1847. In fact, until Rosset and Triaire's discoveries, we did not have at our disposal a complete French text of the novel. The only complete version known was the Polish translation. For a long time, Chojecki was considered to have had access to a lost French original of the work, believed to be the last definitive version.

Today, after the discovery of many manuscripts (both signed and unsigned) has allowed the reconstruction of three versions of the novel, we know that Chojecki did not have any source unknown to us today and that he simply added the missing connections himself between the French original parts he knew, according to his understanding of the novel and what he knew were the first four decamerons of the 1804 version and the last three of the 1810 version. However, since the two versions of 1804 and 1810 differ substantially in the distribution of the narrative material, their conflation could not be achieved mechanically. The translator had to cut some plots occurring in both versions and to complete the broken ones. Thus, the text Polish readers have read for more than one and a half centuries (and European readers after 1989) is a fake made up of original fragments of the two main versions of the novel joined together by sutures written by the translator. Chojecki's version counts up to sixty-six days, while the last and complete version of 1810 has only sixty-one. The editions by which the first readers could read the novel have of course influenced its comprehension and interpretation. So, the highly incomplete version of Roger Caillois (approximately one-third of the novel) happened to mainly contain texts in which Potocki plays with the genre of the fantastic tale, with the consequence that, stripped of the wider context of the novel, this edition has contributed to making Potocki a precursor of the nineteenth-century fantastic literature. This misunderstanding has proved an enduring one since Roger Caillois's partial edition is still in print in many countries and both editions of Caillois and Radrizzani are the only available ones on the market, as up to now the French critical edition has only been translated into Polish, Spanish, and Japanese. Similarly, once the critical edition had proved that Potocki had originally envisaged sixty-one days, all other interpretations that followed the number of days of Chojecki's version (sixty-six) lost legitimacy.

Already in the first fragmentary version of 1794, the narrative of *The Manuscript Found in Saragossa* was subdivided into days according to a tradition deeply entrenched in Western culture, with Boccaccio's *Decameron* as the exemplary model of the genre, but also with a paradigmatic achievement from outside the European space, well known to Potocki, as that of *A Thousand and One Nights*. However, what already differentiates Potocki's novel at the structural level from the traditional models of Boccaccio or Mary of Navarra is that the frame in Potocki is neither static nor exterior to the tales told by the single characters of the story, but it is a story itself, namely that of the protagonist of the novel, the Walloon guard Alfonse van Worden. On the way to Madrid, he becomes lost in the mountains of Sierra Morena and meets a number of characters who, in turn, tell him their stories. Some stories in turn become frames for other stories, and these stories for other stories in the form of a potentially endless *mise en abîme*. Precedents of nested stories were practiced already in Antiquity and were well known to Potocki,[17] yet the writer contaminates this technique with another one, the Romance technique of *entrelacement*, originally employed in the medieval French versions of the Arthurian cycle and then borrowed by Italian Renaissance poets like Boiardo and Ariosto, but revises it as a three-dimensional form, where the narrative structure is not only horizontal, like in the traditional *entrelacement*, but also vertical, as some tales are contained in other tales and so on. In fact, some major frame stories are partitioned and intertwined with other stories with the consequence that not only the reader but even the characters feel lost.[18]

This is especially true for the second version of the novel, that of 1804, in which this narrative strategy is carried to an extreme. If we add that all these tales are representative of different narrative traditions—like that of travel writing, the picaresque novel, the gothic novel, the fantastic tale and so on, together with sectorial texts of scientific, philosophical, technical, or legal character, akin to textual *objets trouvés* naturally embedded in the story by means of their narrative motivation, but at the same time deconstructed and made unfamiliar as the result of their new context (a technique also employed in *Goethe's Wilhelm Meister's Journeyman Years*)—we get the image of an extremely sophisticated narrative machine. Since no one genre dominates over the others (which makes any interpretation based on one genre paradigm senseless) the theme of the novel is not a single narrative tradition but narrative itself. What Marie de Gournay wrote about Montaigne's *Essays*, mainly that "others speak about things, he speaks both about his own discourse and about things," could be applied to *Manuscript* as well.[19] Thus, the stories do not mean anything by themselves (or not only by themselves) but only within the context of the "intertextual protocol,"[20] which put them in relation with each other and with the whole of the literature of the present and of the past (and we, as readers, could add the literature of the future). In fact, each text is not only related to other texts by choice of genre but also by means of allusions, open, and hidden references. Open references, whose aim is to substantiate the fictional world of the novel, sometimes turn to be false, inaugurating the taste for fake bibliographies, which would lead in a direct line to Borges. The most macroscopic example of such a strategy is Hervas's encyclopedia, at once a mockery of the Enlightenment's obsession with categorizing and cataloging and the self-ironic portrait of an erudite striving to encompass the whole of human knowledge but who ends up defeated twice by rats and a narrow-minded bookseller.

The complexity of the 1804 version was such that the writer left it unfinished and began to write a new novel following the advice of one of its characters, Velasquez (another figure endowed with quite strong autobiographical features), to write "novels and other such works ... arranging them in several columns like chronology treatises."[21] The 1810 version is therefore characterized by a complete structural rearrangement of the narrative stuff: the division into days is maintained, but it has lost its mimetic character; it has now only a functional reason (not very far from that of chapters), the stories are no longer intertwined but are told in cycles (Velasquez's columns): the story of Alfonso, that of the Gomelez family, that of the Gypsy Chief, and that of Velasquez. The major narrative loss of this version is the total disappearance from the novel of the story of the Wandering Jew, which was already problematic in the previous two versions, as it was made of a different narrative stuff, not always successfully amalgamated with the rest of the stories (however fascinating it seemed with regard to its content). In return, the story of Velasquez is much more developed. The character has lost some of his comic features, which he possessed in the previous version, and gained both gravitas and philosophical depth. In particular, his "system," an extensive secular interpretation of the book of Genesis in the context of the most up-to-date geological theories of that time, is the major asset of this version. As mentioned above, the 1810 version is also the only completed one and this has huge consequences for its interpretation. At the end of this version, Alfonso learns that all the characters he met on his way were emissaries of Gomelez Sheik sent his way to test his loyalty. Thus, two more genres are added to the others: that of the pedagogic novel (with strong Masonic suggestions) and that of the *Bildungsroman*.[22]

In the absence of any metatextual commentary from the author, one could be easily misled by the logic of linear sequence and take the 1810 version as the definitive one erasing the previous ones. However, the reader who takes the time to read both versions, even though due to its fragmentary state the 1794 version cannot be yet read on its own, will have to admit that this is not the case of a complete and an incomplete version of one and the same novel but two different books, organized differently and even reflecting two different visions of the world: one more avant-gardist and centrifugal in form and libertine in the *Weltanschauung* (1804), the other one oriented toward the moral final *anagnorisis*, more philosophical and, to a certain degree, moderate and conservative in its views (1810). In fact, one could regard the uncompletedness of the 1804 version as a structural and ideological impossibility deriving from the very premises of the work—a foreboding of the open works and impossible novels of the twentieth century. Moreover, considering *The Manuscript Found in Saragossa* as one project in three distinct phases allows one to identify in it the harbingers of many examples of experimental twentieth-century prose: from Cortazar to Calvino, from Saporta to B. S. Johnson, from shuffle literature to hypertext.

After a short journey to Vienna and Italy in 1803, Potocki settled in the Russian Empire and never again visited Western Europe. Initially he was full of hope for having his work recognized, and he remained professionally busy by taking part in a diplomatic mission to China, being named editor-in-chief of an anti-Napoleonian journal in St. Petersburg, and working at a large-scale project of expansion of the Russian Empire in Asia (called "Asian system"), but with time his disappointment with the authorities and unfulfilled ambitions pushed him to leave the capital and return to his homeland, in the Podolia governorate. There, in Uladivka, very close to the place he was born, he took his own life on September 23, 1815.

Notes

1   However, it is worth noting that his brother Seweryn, who shared the same education, was fluent in both languages as his correspondence shows.

2   This was the first, unfortunately undocumented, of many trips that he would take to Africa and Asia.

3   It seems that a *Voyage in Spain, Portugal, England, France, and Germany* has been lost.

4   Daniel Beauvois, "Entre l'analyse et l'action politiques: Jean Potocki voyageur 'éclairé,'" in *Modèles et moyens de la réflexion politique au XVIIIe siècle* (Villeneuve-d'Ascq: Publications de l'université de Lille III, 1973), 39–63; Daniel Beauvois, "Un proche encombrant de Stanislas Auguste: Jean Potocki et ses papillonnements politico-diplomatiques entre la Grande Diète et le voyage au Maroc (avec une lettre inédite)," *Wiek Oświecenia*, vol. 15 (1999): 229–46; Rosset François and Dominique Triaire, *Jean Potocki: Biographie* (Paris: Flammarion, 2004), 91, 207–9.

5   Jean Potocki, *Œuvres I* (Louvain: Peeters, 2004), 91.

6   Ibid., 99.

7   Jean Potocki, *Œuvres II* (Louvain: Peeters, 2004), 141.

8   Rosset François and Dominique Triaire, *De Varsovie à Saragosse: Jean Potocki et son œuvre* (Louvain: Peeters, 2000), 119.

9   A set of improper conclusions in which systematics prevail over adherence to reality or truth.

10   Jean Potocki, *Œuvres III* (Louvain: Peeters, 2004), 99.

11   The copy was found only in the 1950s, until then they were unknown.

12   The first *Parades* were written soon after Potocki's return from revolutionary France.

13   Marek Dębowski, "Parades: le début de l'idée subversive dans l'œuvre de Potocki," in *Jean Potocki à nouveau*, edited by Emilie Klene (Amsterdam: Rodopi, 2010), 67–9.

14   Ibid., 70–4.

15 Tadeusz Kowzan, "La parodie, le grotesque et l'absurde dans les *Parades* de Jean Potocki," *Les Cahiers de Varsovie, Centre de civilisation française de l'Université de Varsovie*, vol. 3 (1974): 236–8.

16 Dominique Triaire, "Le théâtre de Jean Potocki," *Cahiers de l'Association Internationale des Études Françaises*, vol. 51 (1999): 163.

17 See Apuleius' *Golden Ass* or Ovid's *Metamorphoses*.

18 Jean Potocki, *Œuvres*, IV/2 (Louvain: Peeters, 2006), 290.

19 Marie de Gournay, "Préface sur Les Essais de Michel seigneur de Montaigne par sa fille d'alliance," in *Les Essais de Michel seigneur de Montaigne* (Paris: 1652), ciii.

20 François Rosset, "Manuscrit trouvé à Saragosse et protocole intertextuel," in *Le Manuscrit trouvé à Saragosse et ses intertextes* (Louvain: Peeters, 2001), 24.

21 Potocki, *Œuvres*, IV/2, 291. It is no coincidence that the work on the last version of the novel coincides with Potocki's commitment to chronology.

22 The structural resemblance to Goethe's *Wilhelm Meister's Apprenticeship* is striking, but the two works were composed independently of each other.

3

Adam Mickiewicz: A Very Short Manual for Non-Polish Users

Grzegorz Marzec

1

Throughout history, Central and Eastern Europe, with the sole exception of Russia, has rarely enjoyed the interest of the English-speaking world, and certainly almost the same might be said of Adam Mickiewicz (1798–1855), one of the greatest bards of the Slavic peoples and cultures. Most importantly, it is somehow difficult to imagine that the foreign reception of Polish Romanticism and Mickiewicz could match the rank that Mickiewicz and Romanticism have for Polish consciousness and culture, where, invariably for two centuries, they have occupied a key position, and where the dominant "Romantic paradigm"—as Maria Janion put it—does not seem to lose any of its luster despite the new political, economic, and social situation emerging after 1989.

It needs to be remembered that the Romantic paradigm was traditionally associated with Poland's struggle for independence: Mickiewicz himself was the bard of a country that, throughout his life and until the end of the First World War, was absent from the map of Europe. However, the post-1989 change of the political and economic system in Poland—and many other Central European countries as well—did not necessarily need to result in the breakdown of the Romantic paradigm, because Polish Romanticism was so deeply involved in the social and political fabric of the country that it offered ideas and notions that could be implemented in brand-new societal circumstances.[1] It even seems that it is difficult to talk about the Romantic paradigm without the political context, and the only question to be discussed is whether this paradigm is more of a leftist or rightist, that is, of a liberal or conservative concept.

Although it is true that Polish Romantics showed some anti-urbanist and anti-modernization tendencies, the assessment of their attitudes is not entirely unambiguous: contrary to what some commentators have previously pointed out, Romanticism is not inevitably in conflict with liberal social and political thought, and for instance from Mickiewicz one could extract both conservative and liberal aspects. Anyway, the constant significance of the Romantic paradigm, not only in Polish but also in a wider European context, is proved by the very recent words of Sviatlana Tsikhanouskaya, the former counter-candidate of Alexander Lukashenko in the 2020 Belarusian presidential. Having fled the country following the unfair elections and the regime's crackdown on opposition, she wrote for *Gazeta Wyborcza*, the largest Polish daily magazine, the following in connection with the arrest of the Polish-Belarusian journalist Andrzej Poczobut:

> Last week, together with Polish and Lithuanian diplomats in Paris, we honored the memory of our common genius, Adam Mickiewicz. At this point, I clearly realized that for me, personally, Mickiewicz was not only a talented writer. The history of his life, emigration, and struggle for freedom is a living example of heroism, courage and sacrifice in the fight *for our freedom and yours*. I appeal to all Poles to be as brave as Andrzej Poczobut and Adam Mickiewicz.[2]

Mickiewicz himself is widely recognized as the greatest Polish poet and at the same time one of the greatest bards of the Slavic world. His legend was influenced not only by his poetry and writings but also by his activity in exile, mainly in Paris. In the full sense of the word, Mickiewicz was a citizen of the world. In Russian Empire he knew the Decembrists and Pushkin; he visited Goethe in Weimar, and in Berlin he attended Hegel's lectures; he was friends with American authors such as James Fenimore Cooper and Margaret Fuller, and in Italy his 1832 "Księgi narodu polskiego i pielgrzymstwa polskiego" ["Books of the Polish Nation and the Polish Pilgrimage"] had a significant impact on the independence leaders such as Giuseppe Mazzini and Niccolò Tommaseo; during the revolutions of 1848 he also formed the so-called Polish Legion to participate in the liberation of Italy. Above all, however, he was considered one of the most important figures of Polish diaspora in Paris, and his lectures on Slavic history and literature at the Collège de France strengthened his position as a national bard. When the poet applied, unsuccessfully, for French citizenship, in police reports he was labeled "the most dangerous of all Polish refugees, because the strength of his mind and imagination allows him to proclaim, with great success, anarchic and subversive doctrines."[3] These doctrines were mostly spread through the leftist *La Tribune des Peuples* of which Mickiewicz was the founder, editor-in-chief, and main writer. In 1855, during the Crimean War, his belief in the expected liberation of nations compelled him to arrive in Constantinople, where he expected to organize Polish and Jewish legions to fight against Russia, but he died the same year, probably after contracting cholera, though it was also suggested that he might have been poisoned by his political enemies.

Of the many, at times very obvious reasons for why Mickiewicz has not become an important point of reference for English-speaking researchers, at least four need to be mentioned. First of all, East-Central European languages, literatures, and cultures have traditionally remained outside the main area of interest of Western academia. Secondly, even at a time when Slavic faculties and studies were developing in the United States, especially during the Cold War, it was the Russian language and culture that were usually the main focus, with the space for researchers dealing with Polish, Balkan, Bohemian, Ukrainian studies, and so on being much smaller. Thirdly, it is certainly not very attractive for Western researchers to deal with a kind of literature—and that is, for sure, the case of Polish Romantic literature, and probably other Slavic literatures as well—that is so inherently involved in the complex history of the nation and its various symbols, often too vague and obscure, even though some of them, like the idea of Polish or Slavic messianism, are not of course essentially Polish or Slavic, but they often tend to be interpreted in a very simple and reductionist way. Fourthly, it is hard to expect that any increase in this interest could take place without new translations of Mickiewicz into English, and without the extensive exegesis of his work accompanying these translations, especially in the contexts that might be regarded as interesting for English-speaking audiences.

However, it must be noted that the two most recent and most important attempts to promote Mickiewicz in the United States, and the whole English-speaking world, came from non-Polish authors. Bill Johnston, a distinguished translator of Polish literature into English, and a professor of comparative literature at Indiana University, Bloomington, is responsible for a new and much needed translation of "Pan Tadeusz," widely regarded as the national poem in Poland. Moreover, in 2008, we have witnessed the monumental work by Roman Koropeckyj entitled *Adam Mickiewicz: The Life of a Romantic*, which has already been translated into Polish (2013). Koropeckyj, for whom it was the second large-scale meeting with the poet,[4] and whom various Polish researchers consider to be perhaps the greatest non-Polish expert on Mickiewicz, joined the great predecessors such as Manfred Kridl, Wiktor Weintraub, Wacław Lednicki (editor of the 1956 anniversary volume "Adam Mickiewicz in World Literature"), and, finally, Czesław Miłosz, all of whom could be described as ambassadors of Polish literature in the United States. Regarding Miłosz, we still must not forget that this longtime lecturer at UC Berkeley did not necessarily contribute to the promotion of Polish Romantic literature, since he is considered one of the most anti-Romantic poets in Polish culture. Indeed, while his relations with Romanticism and Mickiewicz are much more complicated than it is usually assumed,[5] his 1969 *History of Polish Literature* does contain many simplifications and even prejudices concerning Polish Romanticism. On the other hand, it would be difficult to deprive Miłosz of his right to perceive literary facts and processes in his own way; furthermore, this makes his book all the more interesting.

A few words need to be said of Koropeckyj's biography of Mickiewicz, which is not only a historical account but also resembles an adventurous novel, full of episodes, incidents, and plots. Koropeckyj's Mickiewicz is a pan-European phenomenon, going far beyond the parochial and narrow issues of Polish Romanticism, because, as the subtitle suggests, not the life of a Polish Romantic is presented here but simply the "life of a Romantic." In a broader sense, however, it is a story about crossing borders and about a nomadic life that Koropeckyj, a descendant of Ukrainian emigrants in America, shares with the Polish poet. To Koropeckyj, Mickiewicz is, of course, important as a writer, but perhaps above all, same as for Tsikhanouskaya, he is important as a political and social activist and leader, a factor stimulating social and political unrest, in the all-European dimension: wherever he puts his foot, something is happening there or it will happen in a moment. This order of biography certainly makes it more attractive to an English-speaking reader who, through Mickiewicz's biography, can simultaneously follow the history of Europe in the first half of the nineteenth century along with a long list of poets, philosophers, political activists, and revolutionists. This was not, however, a mere coincidence, because Poland, although not present on the map of Europe, shared the same currents, trends, and tendencies—national, societal, political, artistic, and religious—with the rest of Europe at the time. Mickiewicz's great merit was the fact that, as a poet and social activist, he was the best Polish exponent of these tendencies, and he both presented and represented Polish and Slavic affairs on the European forum. This image of Mickiewicz that we supposedly knew well, but thanks to Koropeckyj's book we got to know much better, is also an interesting proposition from the point of view of current social movements in Europe and in the world of the last two decades, for example, anti-austerity demonstrations and protests.

Koropeckyj very carefully unearths hundreds or even thousands pieces of textual evidence, but at the same time his scholarship is deliberately balanced by the overt literary or novelistic elements of his book. Therefore, it is not an old-fashioned biography with straightforward and suspicious ambitions to simply say "the truth, the whole truth, and nothing but the truth," because the reader is constantly made aware of the fact that Mickiewicz is presented from a certain perspective, established by the author, and that the story is dedicated equally to Mickiewicz or his contemporaries, and to Koropeckyj or his contemporaries. This makes this biography even more interesting for those raised on recent critique of historical methodologies and totalizing historical narratives. Certainly, one of the takeaways from this book is that it would be difficult to speak about overall identity of the Slavic nations without knowledge of how the bards of these nations perceived their place and role in Europe.

Indeed, a careful study of authors such as Mickiewicz in Poland or Shevchenko in Ukraine might lead to "a revision of the self-image that these various cultures [East-Central European] have constructed of themselves in the course of the nineteenth and twentieth centuries."[6] Romantic poets have played a special role in this process because they were largely involved in the questions of national identities and in the "institutionalization of literature."[7] In Poland this process could have been different, compared to some other East-Central European nations that were just awakening to independence, because Poland, at least since the Renaissance and Jan Kochanowski, had already constructed its identity and institutionalized literature, but upon losing its independence in the partitions at the end of the eighteenth century it needed to absolutely redefine itself. From the Polish perspective, Mickiewicz was a key figure in this work of "national redefinition," and he more than carried out what was often attributed to the bards of East-Central Europe, including "reviving the vernacular poetry," "writing new national epics and historical fiction," and "(re)constructing the national literary past."[8]

Reading Mickiewicz, especially his lectures on Slavic literatures and cultures at the Collège de France, is undoubtedly the key to understanding not only what Poland is and where it is located on the geographical and spiritual map of Europe but also how the Slavs understood and comprehended categories such as East, West, North, and South. In other words, that is the key to understanding what "East-Central Europe" actually is, and what role Polish Romanticism did play in the process of shaping all these concepts. Nowadays these processes are also subject to critical scrutiny, in which attention is paid to the shaping of national and supranational ideas based on deliberately created utopias, for instance, the proto-Slavic utopia,[9] as well as in research applying the methods of geography and "critical cartography" by Brian Harley.[10] And just like Jarosław Marek Rymkiewicz—a contemporary poet, literary historian, and a great expert on Mickiewicz—who believed that Poles who want to learn about their country's history and its present meaning must reread "Pan Tadeusz."[11] It would be correct then to suggest that to understand the history and situation of East-Central Europe it is necessary to read Mickiewicz's lectures at the Collège de France; journalism and booklets from the 1830s, 1840, and 1850s; and at least some literary works. This, however, would require brand-new or, in some cases, the first ever translations of Mickiewicz into English.

2

In any case, it must be noted that currently in Poland neither Romanticism nor Mickiewicz are the subject of uncritical admiration, although it also happens that they are narrowly "nationalized" and understood as a sum of such notions as Polishness, messianism, and Catholicism (if one deliberately overlooks the poet's accession to the religious and political sect led by Andrzej Towiański, which was strongly attacked by the Catholic Church). This is the opposite of what we have dealt with in the times of communist Poland, when Mickiewicz was very often interpreted through the lenses of Marxist methodologies.

Therefore, today Mickiewicz and Romanticism are being examined and reassessed not to disavow Romanticism as such but to recognize secret and hidden premises of the Romantic paradigm, its ideological foundations, and sometimes also its limitations and dead-ends: because if Polish identity is indeed largely based on this paradigm, those foundations need to be recognized and disclosed. As a result, in the last two or three decades, Mickiewicz and Romanticism have been subjected to numerous empirical tests, including—and the following list is far from being exhaustive—such theoretical tools and perspectives as:

(A)   Postcolonial studies (e.g., Michał Kuziak 2013, Dariusz Skórczewski 2013, Ewa Thompson 2014). It should be added here that the usefulness of the postcolonial theory to Polish Romanticism was sometimes questioned, as Poland was never strictly a colonial or colonized country, even after the third partition of Poland, or during and after the Second World War. It seems, however, that these reservations are not particularly strong at this very moment, and that postcolonial studies are particularly suitable for the analysis of Polish writers who dealt with Ukrainian and Lithuanian topics, and in this view, Poles are very often presented as colonial rulers. Nevertheless, it is worth paying attention to the very accurate remarks of Michał Kuziak, that during the lectures at the Collège de France Mickiewicz not only presented the Slavs to the Western world but also and more importantly tried to reconstruct the image of the Slavs that the Western world had created and imposed upon them, an image that was both symbolic and oppressive. In this sense Mickiewicz, obviously *toutes proportions gardées*, made diagnoses similar to those made over 100 years later by Edward Said. Another thing is that the postcolonial discourse in Poland is beginning to have a right-wing and conservative character, contrary to its left-wing sources, which has also already been pointed out.[12]

(B) Feminist literary criticism, gender studies, queer studies. Certainly, Maria Janion played the most significant role in promoting these research topics and methods in relation to Romanticism, both through her seminar on transgressions, resulting in several volumes dedicated to the subject, as well as the 1996 book *Kobiety i duch inności* ["Women and the Spirit of Otherness"]. Since "Polska" and "ojczyzna" [Poland, homeland] are both feminine nouns in Polish, even though "ojczyzna" should be more accurately translated as "the home of the fathers" [fatherland], it is somehow difficult to imagine that these theoretical tools are not applied to Romanticism.

(C) Animal studies, ecocriticism, and environmental humanities (e.g., Anna Barcz 2016, Justyna Schollenberger 2010, Agnieszka Trześniewska 2017, Beata Mytych-Forajter 2017). It would be a truism to repeat that Romanticism broke with sentimental decorativeness in presenting nature, that it made nature a dynamic and significant persona in literary texts, and that it largely defined the key issues for these research areas, such as the relationship between man and nature, the criticism of anthropocentrism, or the problem of responsibility for nonhuman beings. Some commentators, for instance, Anna Barcz, also suggest that in Polish Romanticism nature is marked by a national stigma, that is, it is the embodiment of Polish identity. Whether the latter is true or not, it is obvious that in Mickiewicz's poetry one will find a great deal of environmental issues.

(D) Microhistories in the manner of Carlo Ginzburg (e.g., Aleksander Nawarecki 2003), alternative histories, and fictionalization of history (e.g., Jarosław Marek Rymkiewicz, Krzysztof Rutkowski). It is extremely interesting that it was the researchers dealing with Romanticism, and especially with Mickiewicz, who largely led to a reevaluation of Polish historical writing, to its shift toward somewhat postmodern forms of writing. Perhaps the most influential in this respect were historical accounts by Jarosław Marek Rymkiewicz, dedicated to Mickiewicz, Słowacki, and Fredro. Rymkiewicz is also the creator of the concept of "żmut" (i.e., knot), and this word, taken from the Polish language spoken in the area of Grand Duchy of Lithuania, describes Rymkiewicz's historical writings as a bundle of various threads that cannot be unraveled, unless at the cost of an ideological interpretation "on behalf of the only truth."

(E) The so-called turn toward things, and toward everyday life, such as in the series of volumes of *Nowa Biblioteka Romantyczna* ["New Romantic Library"], published by the Institute of Literary

Research of the Polish Academy of Sciences and edited by Marta Zielińska. This approach results, inter alia, out of the necessity to test to what extent the great Romantic themes and ideas, which are usually associated with the Romantic paradigm, had actually influenced ordinary people's lives and social reality. Remaining only within the boundaries of great social, political, and artistic ideas and literature, in which these ideas were expressed, may lead to a significant distortion of perspective, which does not stand up to the empirical test of life.

3

However, in my own opinion, there are particularly great opportunities in the exploration of Mickiewicz and Romanticism from the point of view of memory studies. This observation is perhaps not particularly surprising, and may even seem trivial, as memory has always functioned as a Romantic leitmotif and an important interpretative clue. The already mentioned Maria Janion directly declared that "Romanticism in Poland is a certain gesture, ritual, and form of memory."[13] Nevertheless, in the tradition of Polish literary history, the Romantic memory and forms of remembrance have usually been somewhat one-sidedly depicted from the point of view of nostalgia, above all for a lost lover, that is, the homeland. This is how "Pan Tadeusz" was usually comprehended: as a nostalgic remembrance of the former noble Poland, its villages and settlements, its people, culture and customs, and as an "epic dream" dreamt by a Polish refugee in Paris. However, already a few decades ago, we had very interesting ideas that made it possible to look at the problems of Romantic memory a little bit differently.

Here, I am thinking mainly of the essay by Ireneusz Opacki, "Pomnik i wiersz" ["Monument and poem"], which was included in his 1972 book *Poezja romantycznych przełomów* ["The Poetry of Romantic Breakthroughs"]. Opacki puts forward the thesis that with regard to memory, and in contrast to the Enlightenment predecessors who gladly collected various material souvenirs, the Romantic breakthrough simply consisted in departing from material mementos, from gathering and collecting, and in the fact that during Romanticism memory and commemoration were relegated almost solely to the realm of poetry or literature. Thus, according to Opacki, commemorations in Romanticism were primarily textual and symbolic. When read retrospectively, Opacki's essay may therefore be regarded as the first project of memory studies in Poland and also one of the first in Europe, because both Opacki and cultural memory are mostly focused on the specific transformation of material memory traces into cultural signs and symbols. Similarly to German and Anglo-Saxon researchers in the field of memory studies, including Aleida Assmann, Opacki dates this change of how memory is perceived to the first half of the nineteenth century. It is only a step away from Opacki to concepts such as Pierre Nora's "lieux de mémoire," because "lieux de mémoire" only from time to time are real objects or places, and to a much greater extent they are immaterial objects, such as "La Marseillaise," the nation, the colors of the national flag, or a seven-volume novel by Marcel Proust.[14]

Romantic literature, including not only the writings of Mickiewicz but also the philosophy and journalism of that period, contains countless references, usually fragmentary, to the concepts of memory and remembrance. Anyway, they have always been one of the great Romantic themes, especially in Slavic Romanticism, and this is confirmed in Mickiewicz's first course of lectures at the Collège de France, where he said that

> Slavic peoples seem to have a special gift of memory, a love for the past. However, they do not make up the past, they do not create an image of it, but—one could rightly say—their imagination, inhabiting the past, has a constant and immediate sense of it, not only in relation to poetic traditions, but even to more common and indifferent things.[15]

It was obvious to Polish Romantics that memory cannot be understood, as it has been done for centuries starting from antiquity, as simply a useful storehouse in which news, facts, and events are collected, and a mental ability that can be exercised and kept in good shape through appropriate mnemonic exercises.[16] On the contrary, memory and remembrance are of the greatest importance, that is, as a form of identity, a language that can be shared and communicated, and, according to Jean Paul's (Johann Paul Richter's) formula quoted by Polish Romantics, as "the only paradise from which there is no exile."[17] This sentence also testifies to the quasi-religious nature of memory and commemorations, for which we could easily find dozens or even hundreds of other examples of textual evidence.

The possible perspectives in exploration of memory and commemorations are not, however, aimed at confirmation of the previous opinions and findings about the power of Romantic memory, or—what would be even less attractive—at confirmation of the very assumptions of contemporary memory studies. My point is that a closer look at how memory was perceived in the nineteenth century would above all result in the identification of "subversive" points and places, that is, those in which the Romantic view of memory stands in sharp contradiction to what we have so far thought about, or at least to reveal the very fabric of the "memory discourse" and its foundations, but mostly those that make it obscure, controversial, or perverse even. The last outcome of the proposed analysis would be to disclose those aspects of Romantic memory that defined Polish or even wider East-Central European social and political discourse, and which may be relevant to this day.[18] For example, as I tried to demonstrate in my 2016 book *Ekonomia pamięci* ["The Economy of Memory"], where, inter alia, I analyzed such works by Mickiewicz as *Konrad Wallenrod*, *Ballady i romanse* ["Ballads and Romances"], or Part 3 of *Dziady* ["Forefathers' Eve"], one might notice that in Polish Romanticism memory was associated with the ethical category of obligation or duty, which in turn led to the paradoxical effect of the almost necessary link between memory and violence, and even memory and terrorism. This is especially clear in *Konrad Wallenrod* (1828), as this poem creates a very strong bond between memory and revenge, or memory and various forms of violence.[19] But there is also another paradoxical effect, which is also very visible in this poem, that is, the fact that individuals or communities guided by obligation to remember conceal their violent intentions behind masks and appearances. It is relatively easy to show the striking resemblance between Mickiewicz's Wallenrod and Shakespeare's Hamlet, which consists of both referring to the idea of compulsive and constant remembering (Hamlet, just like Wallenrod, is obliged to not forget: "Remember thee!") but also concealing their real intentions, and pretending to be someone else. Hamlet, as he admits many times, simulates his madness. For example, before the duel with Laertes (Act V, Scene II), he explains that whatever he has done wrong to him, it was never Hamlet but only his madness. As a result, the difference between Wallenrod and Hamlet lies in the fact that the former must simulate the rationality of his actions, while the latter needs to constantly derationalize them.

It is this context that makes it worth recalling that what the protagonist of Mickiewicz's poem experiences is the constant "tension of memory" ["pamięci natężenie"], whereas an equivalent of this tension is also found in Shakespeare, because precisely in the context of this simulated insanity Hamlet uses the phrase "They fool me to the top of my bent" (Act III, Scene II). Thus, he makes reference to the degree to which a bow can be bent before it breaks. Similarly, Mickiewicz realizes that Konrad's "tension of memory" cannot grow without limits and indefinitely; thus, if someone is obliged to remember, it is also necessary to define a horizon upon the reaching of which this tension can be released, unfortunately mainly through violence. We observe this in both texts, mainly through the specific theatricalization of memory. In "Konrad Wallenrod," the intention of violence is hidden in the song about Almanzor, which foretells the coming revenge.[20] And in *Hamlet*, in the play *The Murder of Gonzago*, that is, the "Mouse-trap" in which Hamlet intends to "catch the conscience of the king."

Such an understanding of memory, somewhat preceding the later conception of memory in Nietzsche's *On the Genealogy of Morality* (1887), is rather far from everything that was traditionally associated with memory and remembrance as a Romantic heritage. In any case, Polish Romantic discourse of memory may be interesting for researchers of cultural memory, because in many respects it shows similarities to the phenomena that these researchers observe in more popular and common literatures (i.e., English,

French, German, or Spanish), and at the same time in many other respects it is also quite specific, and its inclusion could lead to the reformulation of some assumptions of memory studies. But—and here we go back to the starting point—it would be difficult to expect that Polish Romantic literature will suddenly attract many American and West European researchers. Rather, one should expect that Polish and Slavic researchers (like Roman Koropeckyj) will introduce certain texts, issues, and interpretations to a wider international circulation, just as this article is a very timid and modest attempt to introduce Adam Mickiewicz and Polish Romanticism to international readers.

Notes

1 Jerzy Kałążny, in "Kiedy właściwie skończył się romantyzm?," interestingly sketches the difference between Polish and German Romanticisms: the latter had very little interest in social affairs, as the main enemy of German Romantics was their own and inner *I*, and this attitude resulted in limiting oneself to narrow poetic or artistic activities in which various moral judgments were formulated.

2 Sviatlana Tsikhanouskaya, "Bądź jak Poczobut i Mickiewicz." Tsikhanouskaya's words contain a certain tension between the terms "genius" and "talented writer." The latter, as slightly depreciating, would be difficult for Poles to accept. However, we see that Mickiewicz is a poet of at least three countries and nations: of Poland, Lithuania, and Belarus.

3 Zofia Mitosek (ed.), *Adam Mickiewicz w oczach Francuzów*, translated by Remigiusz Forycki (Warszawa: PWN, 1999), 388.

4 See Roman Kropeckyj, *Adam Mickiewicz: The Life of a Romantic* (Ithaca, NY: Cornell University Press, 2008).

5 See, for example, Elżbieta Kiślak, *Walka Jakuba z aniołem: Czesław Miłosz wobec romantyczności* (Warszawa: IBL PAN, 2000).

6 Marcel Cornis-Pope and John Neubauer, "Towards a History of the Literary Cultures in East-Central Europe: Theoretical Reflections," *ACLS Occasional Paper*, no. 52 (2002): 7.

7 Ibid., 12.

8 Ibid., 13.

9 See Monika Rudaś-Grodzka, *Sfinks słowiański i mumia polska* (Warszawa: IBL PAN, 2013).

10 See, for example, Dorota Siwicka, *Mapy romantyków* (Warszawa: IBL PAN, 2018).

11 Dorota Siwicka and Marek Bieńczyk (ed.), *Nasze pojedynki o romantyzm* (Warszawa: IBL PAN, 1995), 276.

12 See Stanley Bill, "W poszukiwaniu autentyczności. Kultura polska i natura teorii postkolonialnej," *Praktyka Teoretyczna*, vol. 11, no. 1 (2014): 107–27. https://pressto.amu.edu.pl/index.php/prt/article/view/436/349.

13 Maria Janion, *Do Europy tak, ale razem z naszymi umarłymi* (Warszawa: Sic!, 2000), 6.

14 Nowadays, we are witnessing a significant number of works that discuss Mickiewicz and other Romantic writers from the point of view of memory studies; one of the more interesting examples is the 2011 book by Krzysztof Trybuś.

15 Adam Mickiewicz, *Dzieła: wydanie rocznicowe 1798–1998*, edited by Julian Maślanka (Warszawa: Czytelnik, 1997), 276.

16 Which is not contradicted by the fact that the nineteenth century was also the time of the heyday of various mnemonic systems, for example, in the United States, the Aimé Paris system, imported there by Francis Fauvel-Gouraud, was at least temporarily recognized. Poles also had their share in the development of mnemonics, including Major Beniowski in England and especially Antoni Jaźwiński in France and other European countries.

17 In the German original, the full aphorism is: "Die Erinnerung ist das einzige Paradies, aus welchem wir nicht getrieben werden können. Sogar die ersten Eltern waren nicht daraus zu bringen" (Richter 1842, 80). It can be translated as follows: "Memory is the only paradise from which we cannot be driven out. Even the first parents could not be banished from there."

18 For example, it seems that many features of Slavic memory can be compared with what the Jewish philosopher Avishai Margalit writes about memory in his 2004 book "The Ethics of Memory."

19 The plot of the poem could be shortly summarized as follows: Konrad Wallenrod is actually a Lithuanian revolutionist hiding under this name, who joins the Teutonic Order, in the Middle Ages an enemy of Lithuania and Poland, to become a great master of the order and destroy it from the inside (historically one of the greatest masters of the Teutonic Knights was Konrad von Wallenrode). In this work, he is supported by the Lithuanian bard Halban, who constantly reminds him of his mission.

20 In the ballad sung by Konrad about the Spaniards and the Moors, the Moorish chief Almanzor entrusts himself to the Spanish king, but only to infect the Spaniards with the raging plague in Granada.

4

The Global Rise of the Novel: Poland and World Literature

Katarzyna Bartoszyńska

The study of world literature is, more often than not, the study of the novel.[1] And the history of the novel and its rise, as it is told today, is still, more often than not, a story about British fiction. Academic monographs about British literature frequently feature sweeping titles, with geographic specificity appearing only in the subtitle—*Novel Beginnings: Experiments in Eighteenth-Century English Fiction*, or *Before Novels: The Cultural Contexts of Eighteenth-Century English Fiction*. Or, indeed, present themselves as accounts of the novel without specifying any limitations but discussing only British, or British and French, fiction.[2] Michael Schmidt's seven-hundred-page *The Novel: A Biography*, for instance, occasionally clarifies that it narrates the "life of the novel in English,"[3] yet frequently slips into more universalizing language of the novel as such. The occasional discussion of non-Anglophone writers such as Cervantes, Rabelais, Flaubert, or Tolstoy curiously serves to both acknowledge and occlude a notion of a larger world of literature: it is there, yes, but there is a reassuring sense that whatever one needed to know about it has been provided.

Polish fiction rarely figures into these sweeping narratives of the novel. At best, there may be glancing reference to a handful of authors who have attained some measure of celebrity in the canon of world literature: Bruno Schulz, Witold Gombrowicz, and of course Joseph Conrad, though he is just as often considered an adopted son in the British tradition (that all of these authors were writing in the twentieth century, and can be counted, broadly speaking, as modernists, is no coincidence: modernism, as a field, has long had a more global perspective, and world literature studies tends to be focused on the twentieth and twenty-first centuries). How then, can Polish fiction be made to count in studies of the novel? What would a more global history of the novel's rise look like?

What follows is a brief polemic, which offers only the briefest of gestures toward considering the works of some authors, such as Anna Mostowska or Maria Wirtemberska, who could potentially serve as rich case studies; my focus, instead, is on sketching out a theoretical framework for a potential approach to this problem. The process of integrating works from so-called minor traditions has frequently been grounded in a historicist framing, which sketches out a supplementary historical context for underappreciated literary texts in an effort to help readers understand them better. As I will explain, however, such approaches tend to cede a normative teleology of the novel's development, and reinforce notions of center and periphery. In this essay, I argue that appreciating Poland's offerings to a global novelistic tradition requires, instead, more nuanced formalist readings of Polish fiction. It is through careful and attentive interpretations of the intricacies of Polish prose—interpretation unhampered by the normative expectations underpinning dominant paradigms of the novel's rise—that we should read Polish literature as world literature, not only so that we can better appreciate the work of Polish authors but, more ambitiously, in order to rewrite the theory of the novel, and produce a more robust account of the novel in the world.

It is important to acknowledge that critiques of the Eurocentrism of the dominant model of the novel's emergence have been gathering force, and the need to de-provincialize novel studies is felt with increasing intensity.[4] One of the more radical upendings of the conventional pairing of the Anglo-French novel and modernity, Ning Ma's *Age of Silver*, has argued that European modernity was in fact a belated response to a global system produced in Asia by the silver trade, and that we can trace a development of the novel in the East that proceeds along similar lines to the one posited in the West, a coevolution of the realist form. But more often, efforts to globalize novel studies do not so much seek to challenge the dominant paradigms of thinking about the novel and world history as to supplement them.[5] Providing more detailed accounts of the history of marginalized parts of the world, they aim to recuperate various works of fiction from these places by reading them symptomatically, as manifestations of historical pressures.[6]

The contemporary incarnation of world literature studies has been deeply entangled with systems theory—the renewed effort to study literature from a global perspective began with an examination of the relationships between different parts of the world, and especially of the power hierarchies that structure it.[7] Pascale Casanova's groundbreaking *World Republic of Letters*, while carving out some measure of autonomy for the literary sphere, nonetheless showed it to be subject to similar kinds of power struggles as those obtaining in geopolitics, even if the standings were occasionally different. So, for instance, the rise of magical realism rocketed the literature from comparatively less powerful Latin American countries to the heights of cultural prestige, and Stieg Larsson's *Girl with the Dragon Tattoo* series made Nordic crime writing trendy. Much has been written about the complex interconnections between literary capital and political power, and the functioning of the global cultural market, in relation to contemporary fiction.[8] But when we theorize these power relationships diachronically, there is an unexpected result—our descriptions become normative, and our presentist frameworks shape how we read the texts of the past. The fiction is made to seem abnormal, or strange, because it doesn't conform to the model offered by texts written in major traditions.

The most representative version—and frequently the template—for such approaches to writing global literary history was Franco Moretti's "Conjectures on World Literature," an enormously influential text that argued that the trajectory of the novel's rise in England and France was an anomaly, in the sense of being the more rare occurrence, but was nonetheless what set the standard, creating the form of the novel, which was then exported to other areas. But in all of those other locations, the form had to be adapted to local conditions, and this effort was not always successful. The struggle, he writes, was often reflected in the texts themselves: "the historical conditions reappear as a sort of 'crack' in the form; as a fault line running between story and discourse, world and worldview: the world goes in the strange direction dictated by an outside power; the worldview tries to make sense of it, and is thrown off balance all the time."[9] This approach, informed by Marxist thinking, seeks the explanation for literary form in sociohistorical and economic conditions first and foremost. But it frequently depends upon an implicit norm—the Anglo-French realist novel—against which to consider the literary form, and in some cases, may even produce a subtle pressure for the critic to explain the divergence from that norm. This produces a circular form of argument: the realist novel emerges in France and England, and when fiction from a different place, with different sociohistorical conditions, is examined, it is found to be different—as a result of the difference in sociohistorical conditions. This reasoning may also produce a sense of inferiority, or failure: the novels are flawed, because the place is undeveloped, not fully "civilized."

Examples of such thinking abound in Polish literary criticism. Zdzisław Najder, describing the beginnings of the Polish novel, explains that Poland did not have the strong middle class that is seen as crucial to the Anglo-French novel, and that the form emerged "at a time of unprecedented and ideological turmoil."[10] Czesław Miłosz, in his *History of Polish Literature*, says that the Polish novel "encountered serious obstacles."[11] Julian

Krzyżanowski does not speak of the novel specifically, but similarly notes the exceptional sociohistorical conditions that produced Polish literature, and suggests that the novel only began to blossom in the late nineteenth century.[12]

Indeed, this is arguably the dominant view of the Polish novel—that it emerged in full force during the Positivist period, with authors such as Eliza Orzeszkowa, Bolesław Prus, and Henryk Sienkiewicz. The earlier phase of Polish prose, which included notable authors such as Ignacy Krasicki, Maria Wirtemberska, Anna Mostowska, Elżbieta Naraczewska, and Narcyza Żmichowska,[13] is not uniformly categorized or periodized, including, as it does, neoclassical, Enlightenment, and Romantic tendencies. This means that there is no clear, significant early realist tradition in late-eighteenth- and early-nineteenth-century Poland that would correspond to that of the British tradition. And from the perspective of a global literary history of the novel, this can look like backwardness, or failure.

This sense of exceptionality—and occasional note of defensiveness—is not only found in the work of twentieth-century critics but also appears in works by the authors themselves, particularly in prefatory material. So, for instance, we find Malwina Wirtemberska proclaiming that her 1816 novel, *Malwina*, "przypomni, że nie ma tego rodzaju pisma, do którego język polski nie byłby zdolnym" ["may serve to remind readers ... that there is no genre of writing of which the Polish language might not be capable"].[14] Rather than confirming the thesis that sociohistorical conditions hampered the development of fiction, however, such claims suggest authors who were quite conversant in the literary traditions of Europe, and highly engaged in reflections on literary form. Anna Mostowska, for instance, prefaces her 1806 work, *Strach w Zameczku*, by noting that a new generation of readers has emerged, with different expectations of fiction: "Jeśli matki nasze rozrzewniały się z łatwością nad losem Klaryssy, Pameli, itd., wyczerpane nasze uczucia gwałtowniejszych wzruszeń potrzebują." ["If our mothers were easily moved by the fates of Clarissa, Pamela, etc, our exhausted emotions require more violent sensations."][15] There is no sense of lag or delay here, but rather, a perceived obsolescence of the kind of fiction that is now termed realist, swept away by the Gothic boom that began in the 1790s and continued throughout the nineteenth century.

I say now termed realist, because to today's readers, the notion that *Pamela*, the story of a servant who resists her employer's repeated attempts to rape her and ultimately convinces him to marry her, is a realistic fiction— and a more realistic one than *Strach w Zameczku*, which tells of two young women who play a complex prank on their male friend, temporarily convincing him that he is seeing a ghost—is potentially puzzling. By using these terms, I wish to flag the inchoate nature of the categorization, both then and now. Writing about both *Clarissa* and *Pamela*, among other texts, in ways that complicate common understandings of how such fictions operate, Stephanie Insley Hershinow stresses "the provisionality of the realist project in this moment, the sense that realist representation was being figured out in real time and with considerable urgency."[16] Hershinow's book highlights the overlap between realism's apparent interest in mimeticism and its tendency to idealize (a tension that Thomas Pavel sees as a constant in the long history of the novel form)—and thereby invites us, further, to reconsider the purchase of realism as a category.

This connects to another strand of recent efforts to upend the Anglo-French realist paradigm of the Rise of the Novel narrative: the growing body of work that calls into question the notion of a stable category of realism as a teleological endpoint in the process of the novel's development, and reconsiders our sense of how those early fictions operated. Marcie Frank's work on the relationship between the emerging form of the novel and theater, for instance, urges us to rethink ideas of disembodiment and identification underpinning the realist paradigm, and argues for a more formally heterogeneous perspective on the form: a mixed-media aesthetic. Wendy Anne Lee's work on insensibility in the early novel likewise overturns the idea of identification as crucial to the novel's functioning, and says that, rather than recounting a progressive development of the form, her book tracks a kind of "stuckness."[17] Elaine Freedgood suggests that the notion of a stable category of realism in the Victorian period is illusory, and belies the formal messiness of those fictions. And Scott Black has boldly argued that far from being a history of realism—a narrative he sees as false in its perspective on both history and literary form—the story of the novel is a history of romance, one that is nonlinear and not progressive. This last intervention is particularly meaningful to the Polish case, because, as Black notes, "in histories of the novel as a modern form, romance tends to be discussed as the residual pole against which to measure the novel's development, the epistemological or ideological mistake corrected by the modern, mature, enlightened form of the novel."[18] And one of the key ways in which early Polish fiction can appear underdeveloped is in the persistence of romance.

I will return to this aspect of Polish prose in a moment, but I want to pause here to observe that, taken together, these various critical interventions signal that the long-standing story of the Rise of the Novel as the emergence of a particular form of Anglo-French realism is already coming apart at the seams, buckling under the weight of internal pressures. It can no longer sustain its position as the figurehead against which all other novelistic traditions are measured—by now, we know (or should know) better than to think that the Anglo-French novel was any one particular thing, an inevitable endpoint in a linear path of development. Instead, we are beginning to see this tradition as it truly was: formally diverse, filled with a variety of different approaches and techniques, some of which caught on for a period of time, others of which were abandoned (and some of which resurfaced many years later).[19]

And paradoxically, perhaps, those engaged in the effort to find new ways to describe the complexities of this diverse, multifaceted form may find it useful to turn to those traditions that were previously overlooked or ignored, to consider an archive where those many crossing paths are seen in particularly vivid detail. Polish literature offers a particularly rich case study for such efforts.

Describing Polish theories of the novel from the seventeenth and eighteenth centuries, Henryk Markiewicz begins by discussing the problem of terminology. Prose fictions went by many names, including *historia* [history], *margites*, roman (*roman*), *romans* [romance], and *powieść* [novel/tales]. And, as Markiewicz explains, even once the term "romans" had taken hold, critical examination and assessment of the form was complicated by the fact that "sama nazwa oznaczała utwory bardzo w swej zawartości różnorodne—od nieprawdopodobnych przygód rycerskich i miłosnych do realistycznego przedstawienia charakterów i obyczajów współczesnych, od moralizatorstwa do libertyńskiej erotyki." ["The very name referred to works that were extremely diverse in their contents—from improbable adventures of knights and their love affairs to a realistic portrayal of characters and contemporary customs, from moralizing to libertine erotica."][20] The debates within Polish criticism as to the function and merits of these literary texts are in many ways similar to what is found in eighteenth-century British writing—fears over the moral effects of romances (and some defenses of their pedagogical value), typologies of different varieties of literature, considerations of the relationship between fiction and truth, and so on. But the differences are perhaps useful as well, providing a helpful kind of estrangement that unsettles old habits of perspective. By exploring a different archive, that of Polish prose works of the late eighteenth and early nineteenth century, we can develop different habits of reading, which are freed from the conventions learned in examinations of Anglo-French fictions.[21] Rather than measuring these works according to a standard imported from elsewhere, how can we read them on their own terms? By attending carefully to the particularities of their form, without moving too quickly to connect literary mechanics to historical context.

Formalist criticism can appear clinical or airless ("Judging a poem is like judging a pudding or a machine"[22]). I am far from advocating that we abandon all sense of history or context in considering Polish fiction, but rather that we begin with the texts, and the effects they produce, and allow those formal readings to generate new theoretical frameworks, different historical narratives.

Anna Mostowska's prose works, for instance, offer an array of different varieties, or subgenres, of fiction, as a survey of their subtitles suggests: powieść prawdziwa [a true story], powieść ruska [a Russian tale], powieść wschodnia [an Eastern tale], powieść moralna [a moral tale], powieść mitologiczna [a mythological tale]. Wirtemberska's *Malwina*, meanwhile, is a complex hybrid of different forms within one text, blending the conventions of romance plots with a keen interest in individual psychology and a vibrant sense of sarcastic humor. Similarly, Ignacy Krasicki's *Mikołaja Doświadczyńskiego przypadki* combines philosophical fiction, picaresque, and didactic moral tale, with a bit of romance tacked on at the end. Rather than reading this generic hybridity as a flaw, a symptom of authors importing foreign forms in turbulent historical conditions, we should instead consider how it functions, what it accomplishes, and where the tensions lie. How do these authors make use of the affordances of these various modes to make something new?

To integrate the history of Polish fiction into an account of the global novel does not mean creating a new history of the novel, exactly. As Scott Black argues in his work on romance, and Julie Orlemanski has compellingly shown in her work on medieval fictionality, historical narratives are beholden to models of linear progress, privileging "firsts" and casting earlier periods as unsophisticated, naïve. The interesting question is not, as Orlemanski puts it, *who* has fiction but *how* they have it. What we seek is not a history but a hermeneutics, an exploration of different kinds of literary practice in different places and times.

So the goal, I would like to suggest in conclusion, is to allow a new account of Polish fiction to lead us to a different way of conceptualizing the global novel: a "weak theory" of the novel.

I take the term "weak theory" from Paul Saint-Amour's call for a weak theory of modernism. Modernism, Saint-Amour writes, is typically conceived in terms of strength, a muscular tradition produced by a series of rugged men (and some women). As perspectives on the period have changed, he writes, we might instead embrace the idea of weakness. This notion of weakness operates on multiple levels: naming the kinds of subjects under consideration, particularly those previously considered inferior (the female, the queer, disabled, or subaltern), as well as the multiplication of this object of study into something less clearly defined, with fuzzier boundaries (Is this text a novel? What if we treat it as one?), and the notion of a different stance in our theoretical posture—away from claims of mastery and understanding, to something more speculative, experimental. Saint-Amour writes that "modernism in a global frame should be understood not just as an *object* of weak theory but as weak thought *par excellence*—as a set of disparate sites and conversations unified by the aim of weakening the monopolistic hold of transcendental truth claims upon us." So, too, I am arguing, the global novel, a loose band of motley texts, from many different places, times, languages, and which take a variety of forms, some familiar, some strange. And so too the criticism that describes it must surrender its claim to definitive knowledge, clear-cut typology, progressive history. And Polish fiction can teach us how.

Notes

1   Of course there are notable exceptions—in particular, in poetry studies, where there is much excellent work on the problem of world literature. See, for instance, Hunter, Walt. "For a Global Poetics," or a recent special issue of *Comparative Critical Studies* coedited by Fatima Burney and Sara Hakeem Grewal. Alexander Beecroft's *An Ecology of World Literature* is also a key example of a study that examines a wide variety of genres. But the novel form is the unstated default object for much of world literature studies. Efrain Kristal critiques this aspect of Franco Moretti's "Conjectures on World Literature," a text that was arguably a kind of template for the field, in Kristal, Efrain. "Considering Coldly ..."

2   See, for instance, *How Novels Think: The Limits of Individualism from 1719–1900*, *Before Fiction: The Ancien Regime of the Novel*, or the many Cambridge Companions to the novel in various periods.

3   Michael Schmidt, *The Novel: A Biography* (Cambridge, MA: Harvard University Press, 2014), 2.

4   Some particularly important works in this vein have been the two-volume anthology, *The Novel*, edited by Franco Moretti, the two volumes of Steven Moore's *The Novel: An Alternate History*, and Ning Ma's *The Age of Silver: The Rise of the Novel East and West*. Although Elaine Freedgood's *Worlds Enough: the Invention of Realism in the Victorian Novel* is primarily an examination of British fiction, it aims to overturn the centrality of the Anglo-French rise of realism paradigm, and argues forcefully for a more global perspective.

5   Indeed, Ma's book arguably also functions in this way, in that it leaves intact much of the theoretical armature of theories of the novel's emergence, but doubles it, as it were.

6   See, for instance, work by the Warwick Research Collective that reads irrealist features of fiction as registering uneven development.

7   There was a concomitant interest in earlier approaches to theorizing world literature, such as Goethe's idea of *weltliteratur*. *Debating World Literature* offers an excellent overview of some of these debates.

8   See Gloria Fisk, *Orhan Pamuk and the Good of World Literature* (New York: Columbia University Press, 2018); Sarah Brouilette, *Postcolonial Writers in the Global Literary Marketplace* (London: Palgrave Macmillan, 2007); and Rebecca Walkowitz, *Born Translated: The Contemporary Novel in the Age of World Literature* (New York: Columbia University Press, 2015).

9   Franco Moretti, "Conjectures on World Literature," *New Left Review*, vol. 1 (January–February 2000): 65.

10   Zdzisław Najder, "The Development of the Polish Novel: Functions and Structure," *Slavic Review*, vol. 29, no. 4 (December 1970): 651–2.

11   Czesław Miłosz, *The History of Polish Literature* (Berkeley: University of California Press, 1969), 254.

12 Curiously, he attributes the flaws of the earliest works of Polish fiction, the novels of Ignacy Krasicki, to Krasicki's individual problems:

In introducing this new type of writing, which was already quite a common thing outside Poland, the excellent poet had to overcome various difficulties, namely, his own inhibitions and habits, select from his own experience of life a collective subject worth writing about, and this meant taking an attitude, deliberating as to whether to give a faithful account of situations and events or whether he should add his own comments. All these difficulties made it hard for Krasicki to succeed in his aim of writing a novel. (Krzyżanowski, *History of Polish Literature*, 195)

13 As discussed by Halina Filipowicz, a tremendous amount of work has been done by scholars, particularly women scholars, to recover the work of Polish women writers, who were for a long time largely overlooked in histories of Polish literature.

14 Maria Wirtemberska, *Malwina, czyli domyślność serca* (Kraków: Universitas, 2002), 33 (*Malvina, or the Heart's Intuition*, 3).

15 Anna Mostowska, *Powieści, Listy*. Edited and with an introduction by Monika Urbańska (Łódź: Wydawnictwo Uniwersytetu Łódzkiego, 2014), 180–1. Translation my own.

16 Stephanie Insley Hershinow, *Born Yesterday: Inexperience and the Early Realist Novel* (Baltimore, MD: Johns Hopkins University Press, 2019), 8.

17 Wendy Anne Lee, *Failures of Feeling: Insensibility and the Novel* (Stanford, CA: Stanford University Press, 2018), 3. The same could be said of Hershinow's *Born Yesterday*.

18 Scott Black, *Without the Novel: Romance and the History of Prose Fiction* (Charlottesville: University of Virginia Press, 2019), 19.

19 Lorri Nandrea examines such abandoned possibilities, and their later resurgence, and Nicholas Paige's *Before Fiction* strongly refutes any straightforward notion of development.

20 Markiewicz, *Polskie teorie powieści* (Warszawa: PWN, 1998), 8–9, translation my own.

21 Even in small ways—that Wirtemberska calls *Malwina* a romance, whereas Mostowska calls her texts powieść, novels, when one could easily argue that it should be the other way around, loosen the hold of these categories on our perception.

22 Monroe Beardsley and W. K. Wimsatt, "The Intentional Fallacy," *Sewanee Review*, vol. 57, no. 1 (Winter 1949): 468.

5

Eliza Orzeszkowa and Edith Wharton, or Worldly Rhythms of Polish Women's Writing

Lena Magnone

Eliza Orzeszkowa (1841–1910) and Edith Wharton (1862–1937) belonged to different generations, lived on different continents, and wrote in different languages. They never met or read each other's works. Nevertheless, their biographies bear striking similarities: in their youth, they were both discouraged from literary work and had to go through early, unhappy marriage and a scandal-arousing divorce to dare authorship, become professional writers, gain independence, and eventually unprecedented success. There are also puzzling similitudes in their novels, of which I propose to juxtapose two pairs: *Marta* (1873) and *The House of Mirth* (1905), as well as *Dwa bieguny* (Two poles, 1893) and *The Age of Innocence* (1920).

While using comparative reading methods, this study aims to argue the Polish writers' place within women's world literature.[1] Orzeszkowa's case is particularly compelling, for her status as the only woman novelist from the partition period to enter the national canon resulted in the conviction of general untranslatability of her work. Considered a writer of specific Polish concerns, she enjoyed little if any attention abroad, and her work appears almost at the farthest end of David Damrosch's definition of world literature.[2] Twice nominated for the Nobel Prize, she notoriously lost in 1905 to her fellow countryman Henryk Sienkiewicz and in 1909 to a more internationally successful woman writer, a Swede Selma Lagerlöf. However, as a female author, not only does she bear the comparison to other great figures of national revival in the region—the Czech Eliška Krásnohorská, the Ukrainian Marko Vovchok, the Croatian Marija Jambrišak, or the Slovak Terézia Vansová—but also deserves her place in the world republic of (women's) letters.

Two Biographies

Cynthia Griffin Wolff begins her Wharton biography with a rhetorical question: "How could she have written so well? Indeed, why did she write at all?"[3] A similar query comes to mind regarding Orzeszkowa: How is it that she even started writing? Edith Jones was a late child born to a beautiful and fashionable but emotionally withdrawn and rejecting mother, in an environment ordered according to conventions, where intellectual aspirations in women were not to be encouraged. In her unpublished memoir, she bitterly admits to never having exchanged a word with a really intelligent human being until she was over twenty.[4] Father's library was the only shelter for the ambitious girl. On the way to self-education, she followed the university studies curriculum, reading in four languages history, philosophy, and poetry. Although she was not allowed to read novels, her passion for storytelling soon led her to write one herself. She refers to those early writing experiences as intimate, almost erotic. It was her "secret garden."[5]

However, those efforts were met with disapproval, and not only from the part of her mother, who despised even the most successful women writers like Harriet Beecher Stowe. When in 1882 a planned wedding was called off by her fiancé, the Newport *Daily News* reported: "The only reason assigned for the breaking of the engagement ... is an alleged preponderance of intellectuality on the part of the intended bride. Miss Jones is an ambitious authoress, and it is said that, in the eyes of Mr. Stevens, ambitious is a grievous fault."[6]

Eventually, in 1885 she married Edward Wharton, twelve years her senior. The spouses' lack of intellectual and sexual compatibility resulted in her developing many psychosomatic symptoms, and she supposedly became a patient of the famous Dr. Silas Weir Mitchell in Philadelphia.[7] She did not release a book before she was thirty-five. However, from this moment on, she published prolifically, thus gaining the financial independence and courage necessary to divorce her husband in 1913. Still, in her social circle, the subject of her literary success was always to be avoided "as though it were a kind of family disgrace, which might be condoned but could not be forgotten."[8]

Eliza Pawłowska also showed literary talent as a child, writing her first stories before she turned seven. Her mother, "generally despotic, but the most in matters of convention,"[9] was not delighted with her early attempts and forbade her to talk about writing as a future life path, convinced that a female author could only bring shame to a respectable family.[10] The girl experienced the initiation into philosophy, science, and literature in the multilingual library left by her father, who died when she was three. At eleven, Eliza was sent by her newly remarried mother to Warsaw to attend a boarding school run by nuns. Not unlike her American counterpart, she was unattractive but wealthy. At seventeen, soon after she finished her modest education, she was married off to a distant cousin, Piotr Orzeszko, twice her age:

> I did not feel the slightest anxiety. I knew that I had to get married before long because of my mother's wishes and custom requirements. To whom? I did not care. I liked Mr. Orzeszko more than the others in terms of the appearance and the way of dancing ... I wanted to be married as soon as possible to have the right to dispose of my house, carriage, service, and finally of myself.[11]

Like Wharton, who avows that she ignored all of the processes of generation till she had been married for several weeks,[12] Orzeszkowa admits "about certain facts of a married life I knew nothing and didn't think a second."[13] Her marriage was equally unhappy. When Orzeszko was arrested and sent to Siberia as part of Russian repression after the January Uprising, she did not follow him. Instead, she tried to get a divorce, which she eventually obtained in 1869. She also decided to sell the family estate in Milkowszczyzna, perfectly aware that under the current legislation it would end up in Russian hands. Only when she became independent did she return to writing, the experience described as a "strange joy, impassive, calm, but so great" that she "would not give up ... for any pleasures of the world."[14]

Wharton, the first woman to win the Pulitzer Prize, claimed to be grateful that her mother censored her reading, as it prevented her from the sentimentality of American women writers, from whom she always felt the need to distinguish herself, envisioning her creative self as masculine.[15] According to Percy Lubbock, she had a "very masculine mind," and "she liked to be talked to as a man."[16] The same can be said about Orzeszkowa, recognized by her peers as having "a male-like head."[17] Today's scholars consider her the leading example of nineteenth-century Polish writers' self-imposed self-limitation, the champion of the "strategy of self-adjustment."[18]

Indeed, both did not appreciate other women's works, and their belief in art beyond the limitations of gender influenced their aesthetic choices. They usually wrote from a male perspective and used a male or gender-neutral narrator, which allowed them to distance themselves from the world they depicted. Like Wharton, Orzeszkowa deviated from the sentimental tradition, and her 1873 *Marta* violated woman's novel patterns as radically as *The House of Mirth* in 1905.

Marta and *The House of Mirth*

Both novels achieved an enormous financial and critical success and were translated into numerous foreign languages.[19] Most importantly, for Wharton and Orzeszkowa alike, these works were critical to their literary careers. Before *The House of Mirth*,[20] her first novel dealing with New York society, Wharton published many novellas, several nonfiction books, and her first novel, *The Valley of Decision*, situated in eighteenth-century Italy. However, it was only the process of writing *The House of Mirth* as a serial for *Scribner's Magazine* that made her turn "from a drifting amateur into a professional."[21]

Orzeszkowa, publishing since 1866, writes in her memoirs about *Marta* as if her eighth novel were her actual debut.[22] It certainly marks her transition from the romance convention she had successfully used so far—telling autobiographical stories of rash marriages by immature heroines, their disappointments and defeats on the way to get a divorce, as well as unfulfilled loves that came too late—to social issues. Literary historians praise it as a symptom of the writer's maturation and her distancing herself from female literature of the era.[23]

Both titles refer to the Bible. *The House of Mirth* is a quotation from Ecclesiastes, while the name of Orzeszkowa's eponymous protagonist brings to mind one of Lazarus's sisters. The novels, set in a time contemporary with their composition, are openly polemical toward the tradition of women writing, mocking female readers' expectations for romance and offering an acute social critique instead of a happy ending. Orzeszkowa resorts to ironic authorial commentaries to show how conventional narrative structures distort female experience. Wharton achieves the same goal thanks to double perspective, the main heroine's story being constantly misread by an unreliable male observer.[24]

When we meet Lily Bart, she is twenty-nine years old. Although Marta Świcka is five years younger, as a mother and a widow, she does not resemble the heroines of the classic marriage plot. She belongs likewise to the genre "the novel of the woman of thirty."[25] Their fate illustrates limited choices for women in a patriarchal, capitalist society. Their prematurely deceased upper-class parents brought both up to become nothing more than ornamental wives. However, Marta's husband dies only five years after the wedding, leaving his wife and a four-year-old daughter penniless. Lily fails to marry altogether. They lack any formal education or professional training and are equally unprepared for independent living. They are looking for not love but economic stabilization—Lily is thus desperate to marry, while Marta, with the same despair, tries unsuccessfully to obtain a job.

Orzeszkowa presents Marta's ineffective six-month efforts to enter professional life. Each episode describes her awakened hopes, trial, and final failure. A fiasco in the employment agency, where the protagonist fails to show off by playing piano, opens a series of defeats. Her skills prove equally insufficient to give French lessons, copy drawings, or translate. In some cases, the fault lies in gender stereotypes. For example, a potential coworker at the jewelry store stutters, "if you are ... to hire this lady as a draughtsman ... well, how would you say it ... draughtswoman," before bursting into hysterical laughter.[26] Although she has a natural talent and suitable abilities, she is thus refused a job as a jewelry designer.

As her situation becomes more and more dramatic, the woman asks for a position in the establishment where, in better times, she used to purchase dresses. Still, because she cannot sew on the machine, she ends up at Madame Szwejc's sweatshop. She loses the job after the owner suspects her of immoral conduct. She has recourse to charity, beggary, and, eventually, to theft. Caught stealing in an elegant store, she runs into an omnibus and dies—in the evening rush hour on one of Warsaw's most fashionable streets—in a desperate effort to escape the pursuit.

The structure of *The House of Mirth*, whose action expands on a year and a half, is surprisingly similar. At the beginning, Lily is just like Marta, entirely confident, convinced that her efforts will shortly bring expected results. However, starting with a failed seduction of a millionaire Percy Gryce, Lily's "hunt for a rich husband" goes through a repeating cycle of elaborate plans, missed chances, and bitter failures.[27]

If Marta's position is somewhat liminal, with her social background contradicting her current life situation, Lily's is comparably ambiguous. With no income of her own, to enjoy the pleasures of the leisure class, she relies on other people's capricious generosity: "In her bitter moods, it sometimes struck her that she and her maid were in the same position, except that the latter received her wages more regularly."[28] Living in a world where just anything can cause a scandal, both women escape the actual rape but not the consequences of the imputation that it occurred. Just as Marta loses her job as a seamstress to an intrusive admirer who ruins her reputation, Lily misses a chance for a happy relationship after Lawrence Selden sees her leave Gus Trenor's apartment. Both also prove to be equally unable to explain or defend themselves. Finally, as Marta, who was laughed at by the jeweler, Lily meets with ridicule in response to as bold a step, that is, her desperate marriage proposal to Simon Rosedale.

Each lack of success means for Lily a fall one step down, from a valued member of high society to despised circles of "new money" to the working class. Destitute, after her aunt disinherits her, she is obliged to work for a living. She becomes no better than the poor Miss Silvertons, left without funds by their brother's debts and desperately looking for a job, though all they have to offer is that one "reads aloud very nicely," and the other "paints a little."[29] The scene almost at the end of the novel, Lily's meeting them going down the stairs as she goes up on her way to Gerty Farish, resembles the one at the very beginning of *Marta* when she heads for the recruitment agency and passes on the stairs two women incarnating two prospects that lie before her. Lily has no more chance at succeeding than Marta does. She gets accepted as an apprentice at Mme Regina's millinery shop, only to be fired after the season. Eventually, she realizes that "she had neither the aptitude nor the moral constancy to remake her life on new lines."[30] And just like Martha's death under the wheels, so Lily's chloral overdose can be interpreted as an accident or a suicide.

In both cases, rescue seems to be at hand, but moral scruples do not allow protagonists to take advantage of it. Lily comes into possession of Bertha Dorset's compromising letters, which could help her take revenge on her nemesis and restore her fortune. Still, she refuses the gambit and decides to burn them. And while she accepts money from Gus Trenor, as soon as she receives a small inheritance, she decides to pay off the debt rather than to use the money to give herself a new start.

Whether on the labor or the matrimonial market, a woman is a commodity. Throughout the novel, Lily is referred to as an asset or an investment. She "must have cost a great deal to make," looks "as if she was up at auction."[31] Sam Rosedale pierces her "with a steady gaze of his small stock-taking eyes, which made her feel herself no more than some superfine human merchandise."[32] The language of exchange as thoroughly permeates *Marta* as *The House of Mirth*.[33] A former friend who, struggling with similar difficulties, chose to become a prostitute gives Marta a lecture: "A woman is not a human being, a woman is an object ... that one can take and throw away as one pleases ... The moment I lost faith in my humanity, my suffering ended."[34] Same as Lily, Marta eventually fails because she resists the impulse to sell herself.

Lastly, it is worth noting that in both novels, writers introduce a poignant commentary on women's creativity. In *Marta*, the heroine is contemplating a work of a female pen on a bookstore display:

> One of the names belonged to a person she had known once—a person who was suspected of having talent until she showed it by degrees, with slowly increasing success. Yet now, her name figured with honor among the many great, famous names of the nation's writers. Now this woman, who, Marta knew, had been alone and poor as she herself was, had a place in the sun. She had the respect of others, and she had self-respect.[35]

This short description is as accurate an account of Orzeszkowa's literary path as Martha's fate is a credible vision of what would happen to her had she not decided to become a writer.

In *The House of Mirth*, Wharton offers a scene with Lily as *tableau vivant*. She intentionally chose Reynold's *Portrait of Mrs. Lloyd*, a painting in which a woman is carving her name, thus constructing "an allusion that places her heroine in a tradition of representations of women writing."[36]

Lily posing herself as an allegory of poetry can be read as Wharton's self-portrait as a writer. At the same time, picturing Lily's New York, Wharton describes her own environment, reflecting on the fate that may have met her. She portrays the woman she was once destined to be, the fact underlined by the choice of name Lily that Wharton used in her early days.

Dwa bieguny and *The Age of Innocence*

Resemblances between *Dwa bieguny* and *The Age of Innocence* are even more astounding, from the plot to twofold temporality, to both works' nostalgic tone and autobiographical dimension. Both novels offer a complicated love story that starts with the male hero's meeting of an eccentric woman challenging the norms of his steady world. In *The Age of Innocence*,[37] a New York dandy's life is shaken by the sensual Ellen Olenska, who has just returned from Europe in an aura of scandal, having escaped an abusive husband. As "few things seemed to Newland Archer more awful than an offence against 'Taste,' " Ellen's otherness initially provokes his reluctance. It outrages him that she dresses defiantly, revealing "a little more shoulder and bosom than New York was accustomed to seeing." Her daring to leave the house alone, "on a day of such glaring sunlight, and at the 'shopping hour' " disturbs him as nonchalance. Countess Olenska disgraces herself in his eyes by accepting him at home ("she ought to know that a man who's just engaged doesn't spend his time calling on married women"), or by the fact that at a party, instead of "wait, immovable as an idol, while the men who wished to converse with her succeeded each other at her side," she accosts the gentlemen herself. The Countess, however, is the embodiment of all that Newland lacks in his orderly, predictable life. Therefore, to his surprise, he defends her, assuming before New York fashionable society the attitude of a rebellious free thinker.[38]

The Polish novel presents the consequences of a prodigal cosmopolitan Zdzisław Granowski meeting Seweryna Zdrojowska, a rich provincial heiress who came to Warsaw to complete her scarce education. The girl gives the impression of a modest governess. By stating that she considers the property she inherited after her male relatives' heroic deaths in the January Uprising to be nothing more but "a deposit," she evokes universal "curiosity, wonder, even scandal." Zdzisław laughs at her "idyllic braid and antediluvian dress," melodious accent, swarthy complexion, and "not very delicate hand." Her introducing herself to a man shocks him, as well as her "stubborn and penetrating gaze at little-known people." Although he was the first to joke at the "bushwoman," Zdzisław quickly surprises himself, taking the girl's defense against scoffers. Soon after, Granowski becomes convinced that "all I lacked to be happy, was to know her and be near her."[39]

A woman's otherness makes her a fascinating erotic object. At the same time, it can be repulsive. The flame of male desire tends to be extinguished by a minor thing, like "disgusting" pins in beloved's hair, her coarse clothes, inability to dance, and poor French.[40] The man's passion grows when the girl is absent, when she becomes a phantasm devoid of a flesh-and-blood woman's flaws. Newland also loves his idea of Ellen rather than a real person. At each meeting, he is surprised by her looks and needs to get used to her anew. Usually, he feels uncomfortable in her company, just like Zdzisław, whom Seweryna's presence prevents from dreaming about her.

For both men, romantic poetry is a medium of eroticism. While Granowski recites his translation of Byron's *Cain* before the ultrapractical Seweryna, Newland imagines an ideal love relationship as reading together of Goethe's *Faust*, not noticing that Olenska is an avid reader of French naturalists.

Both men feel the need to perceive their chosen ones as weak and needing help. Although Olenska is a confident, strong, resolute woman, Newland constantly finds her most vulnerable and enters into a savior's role. Zdzisław makes the same mistake. He often describes the feeling Seweryna evokes in him as "very similar to pity" or "tenderness mixed with compassion." He wants to play the role of "a fairy-tale prince destined to awaken a princess."[41]

Like Ellen for Newland, Seweryna is a flattering mirror for Zdzisław: with her, he can try to be "the man he fancies he might become."[42] Both heroes want to believe—they even base their identity on the fact—that they are different, better than others. A romance with a woman rejected by their circles is a challenge to the world they inhabit, the one where people, hidden behind masks, never show their true faces, where feelings get suppressed, and appearances determine position and reputation. What attracts both men the most is the protagonists' naturalness, spontaneity, and internal honesty.

Ellen's is the world of freedom. She has freed herself from social conventions and is not afraid to pay the highest price for following her dreams. Seweryna's value system is radically different, determined by her obligations toward the larger community, altruistic sacrifice of individual goals and desires. While Ellen's attitude exposes her class's hypocrisy in erotic matters, Seweryna's preoccupation with democratic ideals reveals the duplicity of Warsaw positivists, who do not believe in ideas they propagate, convinced that "at the lecture, in a sermon, or a book, it's all excellent, but in a jolly social gathering it is simply ridiculous."[43]

Archer and Granowski have similar readings behind them. Archer refers to "books on Primitive Man" (41) to describe his world. At his wedding, he ironizes about the "concealment of the spot in which the bridal night was to be spent being one of the most sacred taboos of the prehistoric ritual" (152). Olenska's rejection stands for a ritual sacrifice, the farewell dinner resembling a "tribal rally around a kinswoman about to be eliminated from the tribe" (279). Granowski uses his knowledge of Darwin, Lubbock, and Wallace to face the strangeness of Seweryna's world. During the ride to her property, he "feels thrown into the pre-dawn of human existence" (176). Polish villages are "rows of wigwams," "built and inhabited by savages" (176). Singing peasants terrify him as "unruly, gross, primitive, hideous" sounds coming from "some Zulu or Niam-Niam" (231). Both ultimately prove no better than the environment they ridicule. Newland is not only a critical observer but also a helpless participant in the rituals he exposes. The edge of his satire reaches Zdzisław when Seweryna denounces him as the actual barbarian, ignorant about the ultimate values of civilization.[44]

Unlike in classic romances, there are no external obstacles to lovers' path to happiness. Zdzisław could become Seweryna's husband—this does not happen only because of his indecisiveness. In the second part of the novel, the idle dandy constantly tries to convince his beloved to betray her values and abandon Krasowce, while he cannot give up any element of his hitherto life. Likewise, Newland is his own worst enemy. Disturbed by the first meeting with Ellen, he immediately makes his engagement to May public. Realizing Olenska's reciprocity, he insists on rushing the wedding. Later, he dissuades Ellen from divorcing her husband. He also decides neither to divorce nor to take her as a mistress. In the novel's finale, twenty-six years after the separation, his son takes him to Paris to meet his former beloved, who, in the meantime, just like him, became a widow. Nevertheless, Archer would not dare even to enter her house.

Dwa bieguny is an intensely autobiographical novel. Right after the January Uprising, Orzeszkowa experienced a similar heartbreak with some Zygmunt Święcicki. As usual in her works, the changes go far toward creating the ideal of a woman as a guarantor of the moral and spiritual order.[45] She exposes the shallowness of Zdzisław's environment and glorifies the values on which Seweryna stands. She makes her a better version of herself: during her romance with Święcicki, she was neither as young nor as innocent as her protagonist. She had her first marriage behind her, was in the divorce process, already made a controversial sale of ancestral property, and started a writing career. Unlike Seweryna, she did want happiness for herself, even if later, before critics holding her accountable for fulfilling civic and patriotic duties, she would confess this fact as her gravest sin.[46] Also, unlike her heroine, she was ready to change to better correspond to the ideal cultivated by her lover.[47]

Newland's romance with Olenska may be a transposition of Wharton's erotic adventure with Morton Fullerton. Still, it is even more interesting to see *The Age of Innocence* as "a retrospective act of self-confrontation."[48] Indeed, Wharton divided her past between characters. Under the masculine disguise, the writer shows what her life would have been like had she not broken out of her golden cage. Countess Olenska, in turn, is her portrait as a single divorced woman living in Europe.

For Wharton, who spent twenty-eight years in a relationship devoid of passion, shared interests, or aspirations, filing for divorce was not an easy decision. It provoked in her a great sense of guilt and personal failure. Similarly, Orzeszkowa, returning to the moment when she stood at the crossroads, tries to convince herself of the rightness of her choices—the fact that she must use so many distortions for this purpose seems to prove mainly the scale of her regret. Ruthlessly discredited, Granowski is not moving until he becomes saturated with the author's bitterness: "I never lacked anything— except happiness." Likewise, Newland's existence, full of apparent successes, turns out to be empty, as he has missed "the flower of life."[49]

Although the novels were created almost three decades away, their action is situated around the year 1870, with the narrator's voice bringing insights from the time each novel was written. *The Age of Innocence* begins in 1871, the time of the author's youth. When Archer visits Paris, he is fifty-seven years old, precisely the same age the author was when writing the novel. Wharton deliberately includes several anachronisms (like the act by Bouguereau hung at the Beauforts, although painted over ten years later). She also alludes to changes to come, as "a tunnel under the Hudson through which the trains of the Pennsylvania railway would run straight into New York."[50]

In *Dwa bieguny*, key events occur during the carnival of 1867, which is when the romance between Orzeszkowa and Święcicki took place. Zdzisław narrates his life more than twenty years later, that is, at the moment Orzeszkowa wrote her novel. She was then fifty-two—about the same as her narrator's age.

It is easy to overlook the single clue allowing for the precise setting of the time of action. Although only three years have passed since the Uprising's fall, Orzeszkowa constructs the novel as if Seweryna—for whom, as for Orzeszkowa, it was the most important experience of her short biography—remained forever stopped at this moment, Zdzisław being in her world a stranger from a distant future. Not only does Granowski try not to remember the 1864 defeat, constantly suggesting it is a long-gone history ("Who in the world can still remember such things!"), but also his personality is an obvious anachronism—just as in *The Age of Innocence*, Countess Olenska seems to New Yorkers a representative of a world to come, an avant-garde of inevitable moral changes. He is a typical neurotic of the fin de siècle, immersed in spleen and melancholy, who complains about his "extreme changeability of dispositions," discusses Schopenhauer, and dreams of establishing a magazine devoted to literature and fine arts. He stands not only for Święcicki, a man who did not understand the importance attached by his beloved to national and social matters, but also for a representative of the generation to which Orzeszkowa addresses her novel. In their eyes, Orzeszkowa was, like Seweryna, "transferred from another world and century." She portrays herself, as does Wharton, deeply rooted in an old order which, while oppressive to herself and fatal for her happiness, is nevertheless the only one she understands and can live in, even if, in the meantime, the whole world "had fallen into pieces and rebuilt itself."[51]

Both Orzeszkowa and Wharton intentionally avoided the subject of the woman writer.[52] Nevertheless, the novels are probably as honest as they could get in expressing their frustrations as female authors.

For Granowski's milieu—seemingly very sensitive to art—literature or theater is nothing more than "sandcastles to fill the void in one's soul, lest the winds of boredom and melancholy whistle in it."[53] Especially for women, artistic skills like singing or drawing have a decorative purpose solely, as they mainly serve to make a man's life more pleasant. Zdzisław is only confronted with an actual work of woman's art when Seweryna shows him her herbarium. This scene refers to the interests of Orzeszkowa herself—she kept an herbarium at the time of writing the novel[54]—while also pointing out yet another difference between the characters. With his translation of Byron, Zdzisław remains within the self-reproducing cultural cliché, while Seweryna is unable to find support in any tradition. Instead, assembling an album, she creates directly based on nature.

Like Seweryna, Ellen is not exactly an artist, but she also stands for an emblem of female creativity and independence. Her choice of living in a literary quarter is considered incriminating: for American upper classes, writers "were odd, they were uncertain, they had things one didn't know about in the background of their lives and minds."[55] The distrust and fear she provokes bring to mind American aversion to women authors, and especially Wharton's own trying (and failing) to make a place for herself in the United States. As Elizabeth Ammons puts it, there is in *The Age of Innocence* "an implication of awesome female energy and creativity that, given a chance, could explode old New York. Wharton agrees with the established order on this: Ellen Olenska, and by association Wharton herself, *is* a threat."[56]

The above also applies to Orzeszkowa, whose romance with Zygmunt Święcicki began almost precisely when she published her first piece. To the many conjectures already raised about their breakup, one can add the hypothesis that Święcicki objected to her writing and imagined her in the role of a traditional wife, for whom literature was at most "a diamond brooch on a dress." At the end of the novel, reconstructing Seweryna's fate, Zdzisław suggests that the price she paid for her choice was personal happiness: "What happened to her? I will not go into details, but you can be sure that nothing good could have happened to her."[57] On the part of the author, it may be ironic. Because what exactly happened to her? She became a writer. Indeed, according to nineteenth-century prejudices, nothing worse could have happened to her.

Conclusions

Although impressive, the resemblances between Orzeszkowa and Wharton are not entirely surprising, nor are they a pure coincidence. In large part, they result from the fact that in terms of women's writing in the long nineteenth century, the British novel determines "the Greenwich Meridian,"[58] to use Pascale Casanova's wording, or, in Mads Rosenthal Thomsen's terms, constitutes a temporary subcenter.[59]

Already at the beginning of the epoch, Polish readers indulged in French translations of English gothic and sentimental novels written by women, to the point that in 1806, Anna Mostowska felt compelled to parody Ann Radcliffe's work. From this moment on, women's writing only flourished, and its development, for all Madame de Staël and George Sand influence, correlates with that of British female literature. It had its great realist and naturalist novels in the midcentury and bold modernist experiments in the interwar period, and, like in Great Britain between George Eliot's death and Virginia Woolf's literary debut, its turn of the century was marked by the proliferation of short stories, a privileged medium for both formal and thematic innovation.

Though created in a "major" language, until the 1920s American literature was neither considered a part of world literature nor had its place in an international canon,[60] and American women's writing of the time was likewise subordinated to the dominant British model. It is clearly visible on the examples of a joint "Jane Eyre Mania," the shared vague of "Eliots" and parallel appearance of New Women writers in Poland and the United States.[61]

The same goes for the status of female authors. Admittedly, Central Europeans who complied with the requirements of emerging national movements were granted recognition not enjoyed by any woman writer in Western Europe (or Russia). Still, those who contested the traditional gender roles and would not subordinate their self-expression to patriotic endeavors were as marginalized and ridiculed as their American counterparts.

This is not to say that either Orzeszkowa or Wharton merely copied some dominant model. Instead, they dared to take it on. They appropriated and masterly remodeled it to the local context, thus becoming the major figures in their respective national fields.

Ultimately, if the biographies and works by Orzeszkowa and Wharton can be thoroughly set together, it is because the evolution of Polish nineteenth-century women's literature, regardless of its peripheral nature and nation-building task, corresponds to the common rhythm of literature written by women in the West. Once removed from the national canon and seen as a part of a transnational constellation,[62] it tends to lose its local parochialism and acquires a worldly dimension.

Notes

1   Place denied to them, curiously, by the editors of *Longman Anthology of World Literature by Women*. The seminal anthology to reveal a transnational

literary tradition includes no author from Poland or any Central European country for that matter.

2   David Damrosch, *What Is World Literature?* (Princeton, NJ: Princeton University Press, 2003), 4: "a work only has an effective life as world literature whenever, and wherever, it is actively present within a literary system beyond that of its original culture."

3   Cynthia Griffin Wolff, *A Feast of Words: The Triumph of Edith Wharton* (New York: Oxford University Press, 1977), 5.

4   Edith Wharton, "Life and I," in *Novellas and Other Writings* (New York: Literary Classics of the United States, 1990), 1069–96, esp. 1083.

5   Edith Wharton, "A Backward Glance," in *Novellas and Other Writings*, 933–44.

6   R. W. B. Lewis, *Edith Wharton: A Biography* (New York: Harper & Row, 1975), 45.

7   According to Shari Benstock, there is no proof of Wharton being subjected to the rest cure. The fact that this came to be commonly believed is, according to Benstock, related to the way we think about female authors being particularly vulnerable to a mental breakdown as they face enormous social pressure to adapt to domestic expectations about marriage and motherhood. Cf. Shari Benstock, *No Gifts from Chance: A Biography of Edith Wharton* (New York: Charles Scribner's Sons, 1994), 93–7.

8   Wharton, "A Backward Glance," 892.

9   Eliza Orzeszkowa, *O sobie*, edited by J. Krzyżanowski (Warszawa: Czytelnik, 1974), 39. As in Wharton's, in many of Orzeszkowa's novels, mothers personify a negative legacy, one from which the daughter has to liberate herself.

10 Cf. Edmund Jankowski, *Eliza Orzeszkowa* (Warszawa: Państwowy Instytut Wydawniczy, 1966), 28–9. To this day, Jankowski's is the only full biography of Orzeszkowa.

11 Orzeszkowa, *O sobie*, 38–9. Translation is mine.

12 Wharton, "Life and I," 1087.

13 Orzeszkowa, *O sobie*, 39.

14 Ibid., 108–9.

15 Cf. Gloria C. Erlich, *The Sexual Education of Edith Wharton* (Berkeley: University of California Press, 1992), 149.

16 Percy Lubbock, *A Portrait of Edith Wharton* (London: Jonathan Cape, 1947), 54.

17 Krystyna Kłosińska, "Kobieta autorka," *Teksty Drugie*, nos. 3/4 (1995): 90.

18 Grażyna Borkowska, *Alienated Women: A Study on Polish Women's Fiction 1845–1918*, translated by U. Phillips (Budapest: Central European University Press, 2001), 203.

19 *The House of Mirth* was published in Polish as early as 1908. For the English translation of *Marta*, the readers had to wait until 2018 (Eliza Orzeszkowa, *Marta: A Novel*, translated by A. Gąsienica Byrcyn and S. Kraft, Athens: Ohio

University Press, 2018). All further references to this edition will be included parenthetically in the text.

20   Edith Wharton, *The House of Mirth*, edited by S. Benstock (Boston: Bedford Books, 1994).

21   Wharton, "A Backward Glance," 941.

22   Orzeszkowa, *O sobie*, 110.

23   Cf. Maria Żmigrodzka, "Od romansu do powieści społecznej," in *Orzeszkowa. Młodość pozytywizmu* (Warszawa: PIW, 1965).

24   Cf. Dianne L. Chambers, "Competing Discourses and the Word in *The House of Mirth*," in *Feminist Readings of Edith Wharton: From Silence to Speech* (New York: Palgrave Macmillan, 2009), 49–65.

25   Elaine Showalter, "The Death of the Lady (Novelist): Wharton's *House of Mirth*," *Representations*, vol. 9 (1985): 133.

26   Eliza Orzeszkowa, *Marta: A Novel*, translated by Anna Gasienica Byrcyn and Stephanie Kraft (Athens: Ohio University Press, 2018), 160.

27   Edith Wharton, *The House of Mirth*, edited by Shari Benstock (Boston: Bedford, 1994), 62.

28   Ibid., 46.

29   Ibid., 249.

30   Ibid., 281.

31   Ibid., 27, 158.

32   Ibid., 242.

33   Cf. Wai-Chee Dimock, "Debasing Exchange: Edith Wharton's *The House of Mirth*," *PMLA*, vol. 100, no. 5 (1985): 783–92.

34   Wharton, *The House of Mirth*, 133–4.

35   Orzeszkowa, *Marta*, 102.

36   Candace Waid, *Edith Wharton's Letters from the Underworld: Fictions of Women and Writing* (Chapel Hill: University of North Carolina Press, 1991), 29.

37   Edith Wharton, *The Age of Innocence* (Harmondsworth: Penguin Books, 1984).

38   Ibid., 16, 28, 30, 56.

39   Eliza Orzeszkowa, *Dwa bieguny* (Warszawa: Książka i wiedza, 1950), 28–9, 83, 67, 61. All translations are mine.

40   Orzeszkowa, *Dwa bieguny*, 251.

41   Ibid., 108, 177.

42   Wolff, *A Feast of Words*, 317.

43   Orzeszkowa, *Dwa bieguny*, 33.

44   Ibid., 41, 152, 279, 176, 231.

45   Borkowska, *Alienated Women*, 213–14.

46 Orzeszkowa, *O sobie*, 105.

47 Cf. Jankowski, *Eliza Orzeszkowa*, 105.

48 Lewis, *Edith Wharton*, 431–2.

49 Orzeszkowa, *Dwa bieguny*, 289.

50 Wharton, *The Age of Innocence*, 237.

51 Orzeszkowa, *Dwa bieguny*, 69, 62, 18, 290.

52 Wharton's early novella *The Touchstone* (1900) being a sole exception.

53 Orzeszkowa, *Dwa bieguny*, 229.

54 Anna M. Kielak, *Zielnik Elizy Orzeszkowej. Nieznany zabytek botaniczny przechowywany w zbiorach PTPN* (Poznań: Kontekst, 2004).

55 Wharton, *The Age of Innocence*, 87–8.

56 Elizabeth Ammons, "Cool Diana and the Blood-Red Muse: Edith Wharton on Innocence and Art," in *American Novelists Revisited: Essays in Feminist Criticism*, edited by Fritz Fleischman (Boston: G. K. Hall, 1982), 220.

57 Orzeszkowa, *Dwa bieguny*, 289–90.

58 Pascale Casanova, *The World Republic of Letters*, translated by M. B. DeBevoise (Cambridge, MA: Harvard University Press, 2004), 87–8.

59 Mads Rosenthal Thomsen, *Mapping World Literature: International Canonization and Transnational Literature* (London: Continuum, 2010), 36–7.

60 Ibid., 40–4. It should be noted that Edith Wharton's consecration dates to this very moment, with her being the first woman to receive the Pulitzer Prize in 1921 and an honorary degree from Yale University in 1923. The transition of US literature from a national to a world literature (and backward canonization of American authors) also accounts for Edith Wharton being generally considered a part of the international canon while Eliza Orzeszkowa is not. Circumstantially, one could argue that the very moment of internationalizing American literature constitutes the end of this country's greatest period of female creativity.

61 I draw upon concepts presented by Elaine Showalter, *A Jury of Her Peers: American Women Writers from Anne Bradstreet to Annie Proulx* (London: Virago, 2010). See also my article juxtaposing *Noce i dnie* by Maria Dąbrowska and *Gone with the Wind* by Margaret Mitchell: Lena Magnone, "W sukurs ginącemu światu. *Noce i dnie* Marii Dąbrowskiej i *Przeminęło z wiatrem* Margaret Mitchell," in *Rozczytywanie Dąbrowskiej*, edited by D. Kozicka and M. Świerkosz (Kraków: WUJ, 2018), 180–97.

62 In Mads Rosenthal Thomsen formulation, "a challenging and realistic mapping of world literature" is only possible by studying "constellations of works that share properties of formal and thematic character, where [internationally] canonized works can bring attention to less canonized, but affiliated, works, and draw them into the scene." Thomsen, *Mapping World Literature*, 3.

6

Suitors with Their Stomachs Full of Lovers: Cannibalistic Tropes in the Texts of Polish Futurist

Agnieszka Jeżyk

"Man-eating fanatics" and "the apostles of deviations"—this is how the Lvovian *The Evening Newspaper* reacted to the publication of "A Nife in the Stomak: Futurist Speshal Ishew 2," the manifesto by Polish futurists Bruno Jasieński and Anatol Stern, on November 13, 1921.[1] Even though these labels should not be taken literally, they speak volumes about the emotions the poets' work generated among a more conservative audience. The "cannibalistic" tropes in the poems of Polish futurists have often been discussed in the context of black humor and the grotesque.[2] Relatively little has been said about the critical insights that emerge from these provocative texts, however. The main objective of this article is to treat anthropophagic tropes in Polish futurist poetry not as an example of "a slap in the face of the public taste"[3] but rather to view the cannibal as a figure who embodies the crucial problems of modernity. I closely analyze four texts: "A Barbarian Day"[4] and "Romance. Peru"[5] by Anatol Stern; "Man-Heart"[6] by Jerzy Jankowski; and "The Meat of Women"[7] by Bruno Jasieński. I am mostly inspired by the psychoanalytic tradition, particularly by the concepts of incorporation (Abraham and Török) and Freud's interpretation of primal revenge. I also refer to cannibalism and the presymbolic/symbolic order (Deleuze and Guattari), and to Bataille's insights on anthropophagy. Additionally, I draw from Marxism in the usage of commodity fetishism (Rubin), as well as feminist theory in the linking of cannibalism to motherhood (Stanford-Friedman). In this chapter, I take the visual route in following some anthropophagic images; I move from analyzing the human sacrifice to a reflection on the significance of the heart as a symbol in the offering; I discuss different representations of a meat market and problematize the issue of gendered flesh. To conclude, I analyze cannibalism and writing.

All You Can Eat: The Anthropophagite in Scholarship and Avant-Garde Culture

Traditionally, cannibalism as a trope was explored by postcolonial theoreticians, who examined this category to expose the master–slave dialectics between the colonizer and the colonized, civilization and primitivism, the cultured and the barbarian. In their anthology, *Cannibalism and the Colonial World*, Barker, Hulme, and Iverson argue that cannibalism is, above all, a discourse of identity and ideology, where the figure of the anthropophagite, the savage functioning outside of the Western world, serves as an excuse for the empire to cannibalize the subordinate territories.[8] Cătălin Avramescu emphasizes the inseparable connections the cannibal establishes: anarchy, anomie, promiscuity, incest, and communism. Avramescu further suggests that this link goes back as far as the early sixteenth century, when the first images of the American anthropophagus appeared.[9] In psychoanalysis, the anthropophagite functions as a signifier of loss. For Sigmund Freud, it designates primal revenge; Karl Abraham links cannibalism to a fixation on the oral stage.[10] Abraham and Török discuss similar concepts, incorporation and introjection, as an impossibility to work through a loss, while Julia Kristeva connects cannibalism to melancholia when analyzing the case of Hélène.[11]

The plenitude of connotations generated by the figure of the cannibal, and the shock value of the trope, attracted the attention of experimental artists at the beginning of the twentieth century. Virgine Pouzet-Duzer lists Alfred Jarry's 1902 text "Anthropophagie," which problematizes the connection between anthropology and colonialism, and Remy de Gourmont's humorous 1909 essay "Apologie du cannibalisme."[12] The author creatively uses anthropophagy as a metaphor for killing and eating the other, which was the strategy of rival avant-garde movements. Cannibalistic tropes also appear in the work of Tristan Tzara, Francis Picabia, and René Crevel. The most deliberate reference to the figure of the cannibal is the 1924 "Anthropophagous Manifesto," introduced by Oswald de Andrade, a member of the Brazilian modernist movement. Drawing its inspiration from the ancient beliefs of the autochthons, this text proved to be fundamental for the experimental artists in interwar Brazil and is now considered a proclamation of singularity.[13] The theme also appeared in Marinetti's 1932 *The Futurist Cookbook* where, among all other absurd dishes, the author discusses "Sculpted Meat created by the Futurist painter Fillìa," art perfectly suited for a cannibal's palate.[14]

In Poland, interest in anthropophagy was part of a broader fascination with exoticism, which quickly found its representations in literature. The writers of the youngest generation, such as Anatol Stern, Antoni Słonimski, or Aleksander Wat, found these motifs especially rewarding. Viewed as derivative, this trend attracted criticism from, most notoriously, Karol Irzykowski, who attacked the poets for mindlessly recycling Western trends.[15] The article triggered Stern to famously respond that "A Blackman is only an elf of modernity!"[16] Disapproving voices did not limit the common interest in primeval cultures, however. This curiosity was fueled by the fact that the newly sovereign Polish state, following in the footsteps of the Western powers, aspired to establish colonies. Anthropologist Bronisław Malinowski mocked this tendency, exposing clichéd imagery ingrained in the collective imagination of Poles and the stereotypes of exotic civilizations othering primitive "barbarians":

> Many listeners came here to see a famous anthropologist in his astonishing performance. He will surely put together a quite promising list of anticipations, namely cannibalism, couvade, avoiding one's mother-in-law, the honorable custom of killing and eating your old and decrepit parents, hunting for heads, infanticide, wizardry, trial by ordeal, human sacrifice, taboo, totem, and other professional tricks the anthropologist uses to entertain the audience.[17]

A Barbarian Day: Human Sacrifice and Polish Colonial Ambitions

These trivialities are also utilized in the satirical poems "Romance. Peru" and "A Barbarian Day" by Anatol Stern, published four years apart, in 1920 and 1924. Andrzej K. Waśkiewicz notes that in Stern's early poetry, one can observe the entanglement and tension between the biological and the social, where the former is usually privileged.[18] In "A Barbarian Day," the main focus is on the vitality of the crowd during a celebration on the streets of Warsaw. The subject makes an apparent association between the demeanor of the masses in then-modern Poland and the collective rituals performed by ancient tribes. A part of the gathering himself, the narrator begins to share the excitement of the masses: "blood rushed to my head with a screaming bludgeon/ and time ripped my body apart galloping over it viciously."[19] In the final verses of the poem, he confesses, "I yelled that it's high time to take over Tahiti / And start eating each other!"[20]

One of the possible readings of this cryptic call for common cannibalism is that the text is a mockery of Poland's colonial ambitions. These imperial appetites were represented by institutions such as The Maritime and Colonial League, founded in 1918.[21] The main objective of this organization was to promote the idea of colonial expansion. Most of its accomplishments came in the mid-1930s when the League bought land from the Brazilian state of Paraná and established cultural and economic connections with Liberia.[22] With about a million members in 1939, its popularity could be attributed to the League's mission: establishing Poland as an international superpower.[23] It also wished to confirm the state's modern status. In this line of thinking, modernity was synonymous with the subjugation and exploitation of the colonies. Poland's imperial ambitions did not go unnoticed by the foreign media. *The Pittsburgh Courier*, for example, warned its leaders with the headline "Liberia might be gobbled up by Poland's Greed."[24] In "A Barbarian Day," the vision of an insatiable Poland intending to devour exotic provinces to prove the absurd claim of its global influence is satirized. Stern shows the process of eating up both colonies and "each other," reversing the roles: the civilized colonizer becomes the barbaric anthropophagus. Imperialist ideology works like a contagion here. Once it is launched, it turns first against the other, but then against the familiar. This is especially ironic considering that for 123 years the country was partitioned and subject to its neighbors' imperial aspirations.

Another aspect of the cannibalistic repertoire is highlighted in "Romance. Peru," a narrative poem that follows a hero's efforts to rescue a princess soon destined for sacrifice. The text elaborates on clichéd Western thought patterns. The tribal ritual was taken out of context and used as a plot device to create a melodramatic narrative. This misunderstanding of unfamiliar cultures was pointed out by Malinowski, who patiently explains the logic behind the mysterious customs of the "savages": "Seriously, however, most of these peculiar and nasty customs contain rational and practical rules. ... meat is meat, and where it is lacking, a strong nervous system cannot be overly sensitive."[25] In the way that the imperialist exploiters of the colonies take advantage of conquered lands, European poetry uses the theme of human sacrifice to enhance the dramatic qualities of the story. The offering is emptied of meaning and substituted with a reference familiar to the average Western reader. "Romance. Peru" ends with a reversed genesis: the couple, who successfully fled the oppression of cannibals, is in an idyllic garden, and the savior serves apples to his visibly pregnant beloved. The plot's conclusion only reinforces the juxtaposition between the primitive culture associated with inflicting a cruel and unnecessary death and the Western civilization advocating for life. Read through this lens, the poem attempts to expose what we would now call "cultural appropriation." It presents an apt critique of how ignorant Europeans exploit exotic cultures to confirm their dominance. With this gesture of "eating up the other," they, this time metaphorically, repeat the cannibalistic liturgy.

All Lovers Are Barbarians: In Search of a Language of the Other

Stern's primary object of mockery, however, is the language that he utilizes in the text: romance. In "Romance. Peru" he suggests that erotic discourse is close to the primitive speech of barbarians. Part III of the poem describes the lovers' meeting with an archetypical glossary. It includes the princess, a tower, the hero, promises of love, and a plan to escape together. The initial encounter is followed by a conversation that consists mostly of onomatopoeias, repetitions, diminutives, and punctuation marks. Paweł Majerski points out its emotional and phatic function: "The emotional state is expressed in the set of universal words composed from soft and softened sounds: 'teeny weeny beanie weenie enie enie / teeny tiny meeny miny – miny –iny'."[26] In his meticulous analysis of the aural and visual aspects of the poem, the critic also draws attention to the effect it generates: "In Stern's poems something of the mystery of an unspecified language of Africa's inhabitants was supposed to be present."[27] The grotesque effect of the whole scene is intensified through the assemblage of diminutives, which resemble bird sounds or baby speech. For Stern, it is a means to ridicule melodrama as a genre and the type of infantile speech it produces. Yet, simultaneously, it is difficult to overlook the joy of utilizing a trope typical for the avant-gardists—a semiotic kind of speech. In *A Thousand Plateaus*, Deleuze and Guattari describe primeval language, stressing its closeness to "natural codings" that apply human corporeality: gestures, dance, and rhythm. The fundamental quality of such speech is its utilitarian character. The signifier already once used is consumed by the system itself, ensuring that it does not obtain the qualities of abstraction or become a political tool. In this context, "the meaning of cannibalism in a presignifying regime is precisely this: eating the name, a semiography that is fully a part of a semiotic in spite of its relation to content (the relation is an expressive one)."[28]

The image of language eating itself to reduce ambiguity, which could potentially allow institutions, agencies, and states to exploit it and turn it against its users, is just one of the possible ways in which Stern problematizes erotic discourse. Another phenomenon occurs when the signifier referring to something idiosyncratic and singular loses its meaning through the process of constant repetition, and the signified gets swallowed, leaving a gaping lack. In its particular manifestation, melodrama, significations are overflown by the surplus of emotions. Caryl Flinn compares this situation to Abraham and Török's notion of introjection, which "includes the instincts and desires attached to the object—the emotions, relations with it, not just the object or loss itself—an observation one might equally make about melodrama, whose worlds are inhabited by so many over-invested, overwrought 'things, not people.'"[29] Consequently, a conventionalized discourse, such as the language of love, becomes a cannibal's speech.

A Matter of Heart: On Those Who Are Offered

Stern's "cannibalistic poems" expose modern European society as a construct that can sustain its appearances only through the perpetual repression of its instinctive element. Jerzy Jankowski, the precursor of Polish futurism, presents a more existential and historiosophical perspective. Moreover, his poetic prose "A Man-Heart," from the 1920 collection *Tram Across the Street*, explores the theme of anthropophagy in at least two contrasting ways. The text begins with a mysterious tribal ritual, in which the heart is ripped out of a brave warrior's chest: "The chest was opened—and—The Butterfly flew in the direction of the ancient Sun ... A poor human heart jerked with cramps, bled with hot blood, dear kids, and was thrown to the road, into the dust, under the legs of passersby, for the dogs to devour, for the life of misery."[30] The simplified vision of the sacrifice, distilled to shock European audiences, is absent in Jankowski's text. The poet points out that the offering was made for the sun, alluding to the sacrifice's purpose. This gruesome tradition, as Bronisław Malinowski explains, had its rationale "that by eating a defeated enemy, one absorbs his features and spiritual virtues."[31] It is not accidental that the human heart, around which the text centers, is characterized as "manful." Bataille's *The Accursed Share* similarly serves to contextualize Jankowski's prose. According to an Aztec myth of origin, day and night were created thanks to the offering of the ancient gods' hearts torn out by the wind to animate the stars.[32] In the poem, the ritual is performed partially. Instead of being consumed to preserve the hero's courage in the body of his enemy, the warrior's heart is desecrated. Its callous disposal implies that this organ is useless. Interpreted through the lens of ancient practices, this gesture signifies the act of disrespect for the warrior. Only cannibalism could preserve the righteousness of the defeated. The refusal to eat the heart of the brave condemns him to exist as a waste of history and casts him into oblivion. This process is typical of constructing historical narratives, since, as Susan Signe Morrison explains, "we need to designate what is valuable and that which should be forgotten."[33]

In a crucial moment, however, the heart is saved by the magical intervention of a sorceress. With this plot twist, Jankowski draws a visible parallel between the pagan rituals of Slavs and those of shamans from the remote islands. He thereby approximates the Other to the reader. After having been brought back to life, the heart transforms into a living creature:

> The heart came alive … It expanded, it grew taking shape of a torso swollen with blood, from which hands and legs slid out like branches. The head was formed in a painful birth … The brain started working. Under the spell of the priestess from the chief's dying heart a new red man grew, gleaming with bloody muscles … and deprived of skin eternally.[34]

Then the man-heart decides to acquire the missing tissue in the neighboring town. Regrettably, the thick-skinned sellers refuse his request, explaining that the skin is: "for personal use only."[35] The language itself suggests a possible reading of this enigmatic ending. Among idioms related to human body parts, the heart is especially rich in connotations. In Polish, expressions such as "mieć serce na dłoni" [to have one's heart in a hand], "czyste serce" [pure heart], or "być z kimś sercem" [to be with someone with one's heart] designate a plenitude of positive meanings. In English, "to be all heart" conveniently signifies being considerate, generous, and courageous. The allegory of the "man-heart," who lacks skin, would indicate both virtue and vulnerability of the protagonist.

The weak position of the subject suggests another, this time pejorative, function of cannibalism in Jankowski's poetic prose. "A Man-Heart" brings in the politics and pragmatics of sacrifice and the hierarchy it generates. When discussing the previously mentioned Aztec genesis tale, George Bataille comments, "This myth is paralleled by their belief that not only men but also wars were created so that there would be people whose hearts and blood could be taken so that the sun might eat."[36] In Jankowski's text, becoming a victim was the result of losing a battle. In modern societies, social class determines who will serve as an offering for the system. Yet Jankowski's idea appears surprisingly proximate to Russian philosopher Nikolai Fedorov's understanding of cannibalism. Irene Masing-Delic, for example, discusses Vladimir Solovev's correspondence with his master, in which he elaborates on the problem of the annihilation of death, and its potential consequence: resurrecting cannibalism. Masing-Delic contends that for Fedorov, literal cannibalism was only a marginal issue: "To the anti-capitalist and anti-imperialist Fedorov, war and the slave labor of peasants and industrial workers constituted forms of cannibalism."[37] Likewise, for Jankowski, it is not literal man-eating that endangers humanity: it is the dictatorship of the thick-skinned and overwhelming consumerism that poses the real threat.

The Butcher's Chopper: Cannibalism and Consumerism

Jankowski's message is enhanced by the image of a human meat market: the ultimate objectification of the subject. The organs one might acquire are displayed as if they were just regular attire. The sellers praise the supreme quality of their goods: "—Here one can purchase heads bold of wisdom ... / —A great deal on a suit of fit legs, / —Steel calves! / —Hands! Qualified patient hands! / —Hearts! Hearts! Hearts! Very cheap!"[38] Each of the body parts on sale is advertised according to its most desired characteristics. It is the reason why the heads are wise, legs are fit, calves are steel, and hands are patient. Nevertheless, it is not the case with the organ crucial for the story's plot: the heart. In the text, the heart is valued based on its competitive price. On the contrary, skin is priceless and has to be grown independently. With such a gesture, Jankowski takes the problem of commodity fetishism to the extreme and equalizes subjects and objects. I. I. Rubin explains that our relations to things and the connection between things reflect social and class order: "revealing the illusion in human consciousness which originated in the commodity economy and which assigned to things characteristics which have their sources in the social relations among people in the process of production."[39] It is clear that the modern reality of the contemporary barbarians described in "A Man-Heart" does not value the heart's courage and generosity but, instead, privileges the callousness and cruelty presented by the thick-skinned.

Bruno Jasieński's controversial poem "The Meat of Women" published in 1921 in the magazine "The Futurists' Daily" presents a similarly gruesome and socially terrifying image of a human meat market. The poem begins with the subject seeking refuge from the heat in the shadowed arcade. Suddenly, he notices a butcher chopping up a body. The parts of meat lay on the counter. What is striking about this scene is the nonchalant and matter-of-fact depiction that enhances the overall surreal effect of the text. In his book, *An Intellectual History of Cannibalism*, Cătălin Avramescu remarks that

> In the Middle Ages, the butcher was a neighbor who carried on his activities in the communal courtyard or even in the middle of the street. Urban modernization banishes him to the abattoir, where we now find him as a wage laborer. Bleeding flesh and its production is ever more difficult to observe. As cannibalism is hard to dissociate from a perception of bodily dismemberment, the question arises whether the developments are of such a nature as to thrust anthropophagy into the shadows.[40]

Jasieński draws the butcher into broad daylight in a typically futurist gesture of destabilizing the social order. With more deliberate intent—and much like Anatol Stern—he unveils the bloodthirstiness hidden in the collective unconscious. In the poem, the anthropophagus is synonymous with the butcher, so his position is ambiguous from the start. He is both a social pariah and holds the power over the slaughtered. This fact establishes a peculiar relationship between the chopping and the chopped, because due to the butchers' act executed on the margins but still within the system, the body is transformed into the meat.

Gendered Flesh: Men Who Feed on Women

One should not ignore the context already indicated by the title of the poem. This meat is gendered: "I saw a woman chopped by a butcher / and displayed on the counter piece by piece. / ... Through the smell of female bodies sharper than smoke / rhythmic tap of the cleaver moaned."[41] In the text, the dismembered body of a woman is depicted as mute flesh. Significantly, her suffering is redirected onto an object and expressed by the rhythmic movements of the chopping knife. The paradox of this situation is that the tool of destruction becomes the means of communicating its horror. According to psychoanalytic theory, a knife is a phallic signifier, a symbol of patriarchal oppression. Carol J. Adams remarks, "The knife separates meat-eaters from vegetarians (supposedly) because it reminds them of the butchering that motivates the entire structure."[42] A knife functions here both as the epitome of unjust and senseless violence and as a marker of the universality of suffering. By this logic, the body of a woman is no different than the flesh of an animal. This type of sexism was sadly not uncommon among the avant-gardists. In certain surrealist works, for instance, women as subjects were "disfigured, reduced to an animal, to Bataille's *bassesse*, the result of the male's fear of castration and his fetishistic disavowals."[43]

In Jasieński's "The Meat of Women," the initial act of putting a woman in the position of meat is the ultimate gesture of domination, and a cliché. In the following verses of the poem, the situation becomes complicated as the subject openly calls for substituting sex with cannibalism: "Don't lick your mistress' lips lying on their bellies! / Eat them with sour cream and swallow with sugar! / ... You, Don Juan, who caresses your lady's body / and who have never eaten any of your lovers."[44] The peculiar appeal to sublimate one's sexual drive into literal consumption of female flesh was meant to shock (and entertain) the reader. But it also evokes questions concerning the relationship between the one who eats and the one who is eaten. Jane Bennett's reflections on the exchanges between different types of matter prove to be productive in this case: "Eating appears as a series of mutual transformations in which the border between inside and outside becomes blurry."[45] From this perspective, the narrator's proposal aims at establishing an ultimate connection between lovers. While sex is immediate and momentary, absorbing one's lover as food allows the separate bodies to be forever intertwined with one another. This peculiar desire exposes the subject as a melancholiac fixated on his loss. Mária Török and Nicolas Abraham define such a situation as incorporation: "When, in the form of imaginary or real nourishment, we ingest the love-object we miss, this means that we refuse to mourn and that we shun the consequences of mourning even though our psyche is fully bereaved. Incorporation is the refusal to reclaim as our own the part of ourselves that we placed in what we lost."[46] In the context of interwar Poland, "The Meat of Women" signifies the anxiety around social changes, including the transformation of gender roles in Polish society. Don Juan, who has never eaten any of his lovers, succumbs to modernization. The one who holds on to outdated forms of collective existence submits to cannibalistic fantasies.

Pregnant Men and the Anxiety of Writing

Jasieński does not stop there, however. His subject pictures a new order where repressed sexuality manifests itself in eating the other, establishing a society of melancholiac cannibals. The question becomes whether sustaining a population is possible in such a scenario. In the final lines of the poem, the subject finds a creative solution to the problem: "Suitors, you, who carry your lovers in the stomachs, / your era is approaching, new motherhood." The theme of pregnant men, though surprising, is not particularly inventive. Jasieński, who knew the Russian poetic tradition very well, must have seen such images, for example, in Burliuk's work.[47] Predating modernism, the depictions of pregnant men were present already in ancient Greek literature. The concept designated a multitude of connotations, including the problem of creation, or attempts to undermine the sexual difference.[48] In the view of Susan Stanford-Friedman, this imagery functions ultimately to the benefit of the patriarchal order. The author remarks that "the male childbirth metaphor paradoxically beckons woman toward the community of creative artists by focusing on what she alone can create, but then subtly excludes her as the historically resonant associations of the metaphor reinforce the separation of creativities into mind and body, man and woman."[49] Stanford-Friedman's reading emphasizes that the metaphor of childbirth is one of the most extreme markers of gender difference.

"The Meat of Women" introduces a particular case of male pregnancy: carrying a lover in one's stomach. Analogously to cultures that viewed cannibalism as a means of acquiring desired features of the enemy, Freud derives anthropophagy from the concept of primary revenge: "The violent primal father had doubtless been the fear and envied model of each one of the companies of brothers: and in the act of devouring him they accomplished their identification with him, and each of them acquired a portion of his strength."[50] In the poem, this valued quality is the ability to reproduce. The new type of motherhood that Jasieński proposes rests upon the transformation achieved through cannibalizing a female partner. For the subject, women signify the infinite endless artistic possibilities. It is why Jasieński presents it as an antidote to writer's block and the anxiety of writing. In this reading, the cannibalistic metaphor reflects the desire to find a previously unattainable form of creativity. However, the call for "eating your lovers" remains unanswered. Undeniably, anthropophagy cannot be equalized with giving birth to a human or a poem. The subject as a failed poet is only able to digest the potentially creative matter and discharge it as a waste. He functions like a scavenger who can just feed on a dead body to produce only more death, more copies of previously utilized material. In the end, "The Meat of Women" becomes an impression about the limits of creativity and the problem of originality and inspiration. One might wonder to what extent the poem might have been a humorous self-reflection on the status of Polish futurism that fed on its Italian and Russian predecessors and their literary conventions, which the innovative avant-gardists, paradoxically, established.

Cannibalism and Crisis: A Summary

In her insightful essay "Consumerism or the Cultural Logic of Late Cannibalism," Crystal Bartolovich interprets anthropophagous motifs in Peter Greenaway's 1989 film *The Cook, the Thief, His Wife, and Her Lover*. The author makes a point that the figure of the cannibal in Western culture has always been dependent on economic factors: "Cannibals have been, and are, obliged to be a site of negotiation of the capitalist crises in appetite (even before the dominance of the capitalist mode of production)."[51] Even though Poland was a newly independent state at the time when Anatol Stern and Bruno Jasieński first published their poetry, "the joy of retrieving one's dumpster," to use Kaden Bandrowski's phrase, was laced with economic, social, and geopolitical anxieties. As a result of military action on Polish territory, infrastructure was in ruins. A hundred and twenty-three years of partitions left law, administration, education, and the financial system in desperate need of unification. Poland was tormented by political conflicts and weakened by Silesian uprisings and the Polish-Soviet war of 1919–21.[52] These problems, directly and indirectly, are represented in literature and expressed in seemingly apolitical tropes, such as the figure of the cannibal. In "A Barbarian Day" and "Romance. Peru" by Anatol Stern, "Man-Heart" by Jerzy Jankowski, and "The Meat of Women" by Bruno Jasieński, the anthropophagite functions in a variety of manifestations, marking issues crucial for modernity. Imperial ideology and the exploitation of colonies, cultural appropriation, social injustice, changes in gender roles, and the problem of originality of art are just some of the questions addressed in the "cannibalistic poetry" of Polish futurists. By utilizing cannibalism as a figure of modernity in crisis through diverse and nuanced imagery, the seemingly ludicrous experimental poets prove the analytical and critical potential of their work.

Notes

1   Zbigniew Jarosiński, "Wstęp." Antologia polskiego futuryzmu i Nowej Sztuki. Wrocław: Zakład Narodowy im. Ossolińskich 1978. LVII.

2   Włodzimierz Bolecki, "Od potworów do znaków pustych. Z dziejów groteski: Młoda Polska i dwudziestolecie międzywojenne." *Pamiętnik Literacki*, nos. 80/1 (1989): 73–121.; Nina, Kolesnikoff, *Bruno Jasieński: His Evolution from Futurism to Socialist Realism* (Waterloo, Canada: Wilfrid Laurier University Press, 1982); Agata Krzychylkiewicz, *The Grotesque in the Works of Bruno Jasieński* (Bern: Peter Lang, 2006).

3   The quote is a reference to the famous manifesto, "Slap in the Face of Public Taste." See: D. Burliuk et al. "Slap in the Face of Public Taste," edited by Anna Lawton, *Russian Futurism through Its Manifestoes, 1912–1928* (Ithaca, NY: Cornell University Press, 1988), 51.

4   Anatol Stern, "Barbarzyński dzień," in *Wiersze zebrane* (Kraków: Wydawnictwo Literackie, 1985), 94.

5   Anatol Stern, "Romans. Peru," in *Wiersze zebrane* (Kraków: Wydawnictwo Literackie, 1985), 67–74.

6   Jerzy Jankowski, *Człowiek-serce* (Warszawa: Wydawnictwo Futuryzm Polski, 1920), 16–17.

7   Bruno Jasieński, *Nuż w bżuhu. 2 Jednodńuwka futurytuw* (Warszawa, 1921).

8   Francis Barker, Peter Hulme, and Margaret Iversen (eds.). *Cannibalism and the Colonial World (Cultural Margins)* (Cambridge: Cambridge University Press, 1998).

9   Cătălin Avramescu, *An Intellectual History of Cannibalism* (Princeton, NJ: Princeton University Press, 2009), 214.

10 Karl Abraham, *Selected Papers of Karl Abraham* (London: Hogarth Press and the Institute of Psychoanalysis, 1954), 251.

11 Julia Kristeva, *Black Sun: Depression and Melancholia* (New York: Columbia University Press, 1992), 71–9.

12 Virgnie Pouzet-Duzer, "Dada, Surrealism, Antropofagia: The Consuming Process of the Avant-garde," *L'Esprit Créateur*, vol. 53, no. 3, Old and New, Avant-garde and 'Arrière-garde' in Modernist Literature (Fall 2013): 79.

13 Ewa Kubiak, "Anthropophagy as a Concept of the Brazilian Avant-garde at the End of the 1920s: Between History, Myth and Artistic Conception." *Art Inquiry: Avant-garde and Avant-gardes*, vol. 19 (2017): 187–204.

14 Filippo Tommaso Marinetti, *The Futurist Cookbook* (London: Penguin Classic, 2015), 19.

15 Karol Irzykowski, "Plagiatowy charakter przełomów literackich w Polsce." In *Słoń w składzie porcelany (studia nad nowszą myślą literacką w Polsce)* (Warszawa: Towarzystwo Wydawnicze "Rój"), 27.

16 Anatol Stern, "Emeryt merytoryzmu. Z powodu ostatniego artykułu Irzykowskiego pt. "Plagiatowy charakter przełomów literackich w Polsce" czyli jeszcze o wiatrologii. *Głód jednoznaczności i inne szkice* (Warszawa: Czytelnik, 1972), 58.

17 Bronisław Malinowski, "Kultura jako wyznacznik zachowania się," *Ruch Prawniczy, Ekonomiczny i Socjologiczny*, vol. 17, no. 1 (1937): 117.

18 Andrzej K. Waśkiewicz, "Irrealna gwiazda": o poezji Anatola Sterna. *Pamiętnik Literacki: czasopismo kwartalne poświęcone historii i krytyce literatury polskiej*, nos. 70/4 (1979): 170.

19 Stern, "Barbarzyński dzień."

20 Ibid.

21 Józef Wąsiewski, "Dzieje polskich lig morskich 1918–2010," accessed July 28, 2021, https://web.archive.org/web/20141221214125/http://www.lmir.pl/arti cle/historia/article.php/id_item_tree/596c8167c8c2b6914a468651050559e0/ id_art/992c89a8613d978ca77c9a75d3ba9b5a.

22 The formation of Polish diaspora in Brazil is described, for example, in Lenny A. Ureña Valerio's monograph. (A. Lenny, Ureña Valerio, *Colonial Fantasies, Imperial Realities: Race Science and the Making of Polishness on the Fringes of the German Empire, 1840–1920* (Athens: Ohio University Press, 2019).

23 Tadeusz Białas, *Liga Morska i Kolonialna, 1930–1939* (Gdańsk: Wydawnictwo Morskie, 1983).

24 "Liberia might be gobbled up by Poland's Greed." *The Pittsburgh Courier* (July 17, 1937), 5.

25 Malinowski. "Kultura," 118.

26 Paweł Majerski, "O języku (w) poezji Anatola Sterna," in *Odmiany awangardy* (Katowice: EGO, 2001), 32–3.

27 Ibid., 34.

28 Gilles Deleuze and Félix Guattari, *Anti-Oedipus: Capitalism and Schizophrenia* (New York: Continuum, 1984), 118.

29 Caryl Flinn, *The New German Cinema: Music, History, and the Matters of Style* (Berkeley: University of California Press, 2004), 61.

30 Jankowski, *Człowiek-serce*, 16.

31 Malinowski, "Kultura."

32 Georges Bataille, *The Accursed Share. Volume 1: Consumption* (New York: Zone Books, 1991), 49.

33 Susan Signe Morrison, *The Literature of Waste: Material Ecopoetics and Ethical Matter* (New York: Palgrave Macmillan, 2015), 57.

34   Jankowski, *Człowiek-serce*, 16.

35   Ibid., 17.

36   Bataille, *The Accursed Share. Volume 1: Consumption.*

37   Irene Masing-Delic, "The Transfiguration of Cannibals: Fedorov and the Avant-Garde," in *Laboratory of Dreams: The Russian Avant-Garde and Cultural Experiment*, edited by John, Bowlt and Olga Matich (Stanford, CA: Stanford University Press, 1996), 18.

38   Jankowski, *Człowiek-serce*, 17.

39   Isaak Illich Rubin, *Essays on Marx's Theory of Value* (Detroit: Black and Red, 1972), 7.

40   Avramescu, *An Intellectual History of Cannibalism*, 49.

41   Jasieński, "Mięso kobiet," 225–6.

42   Carol Adams, *The Pornography of Meat* (New York: Lantern Books, 2019), 120.

43   Rudolf. E. Kuenzli, "Surrealism and Misogyny," in *Surrealism and Women*, edited by M. A. Caws, and Kuenzli et al. (Cambridge, MA: MIT Press, 1990), 25.

44   Jasieński, "Mięso kobiet," 226.

45   Jane Bennett, *Vibrant Matter: A Political Ecology of Things* (Durham, NC: Duke University Press, 2010), 49.

46   Nicolaus Abraham and Maria Török, *The Shell and the Kernel: Renewals of Psychoanalysis* (Chicago: University of Chicago Press, 1972), 127.

47   David Burliuk's famous quote, "I like a pregnant man … I like a pregnant tower; in it there are many living soldiers. And a pregnant spring field from which little green leaves protrude," can be found in Kruchenykh's study. (Kruchenykh Aleksei, *Nash vykhod: K istorii russkogo futurizma.* Moscow: Literaturno-khudozhestvennoe agenstvo RA, 1996, 80.)

48   See D. D. Leitao, *The Pregnant Male as Myth and Metaphor* (Cambridge: Cambridge University Press, 2012).

49   Susan Stanford Friedman, "Creativity and the Childbirth Metaphor: Gender Difference in Literary Discourse." *Feminist Studies*, vol. 1, no. 13 (1987): 76.

50   Sigmund Freud, *The Standard Edition of the Complete Psychological Works. Vol. XIII, Totem and Taboo* (London: Hogarth Press 1955), 142.

51   Crystal Bartolovich, "Consumerism, or the Cultural Logic of Late Cannibalism," In *Cannibalism and the Colonial World (Cultural Margins)*, edited by F. Barker, Hulme, and Iversen, 211.

52   Bolesław Winiarski, *Polityka gospodarcza* (Warszawa: Wydawnictwo Naukowe PWN, 2021), 113–24.

7

Polish Literature and/or World Literature: Bruno Schulz in English

Zofia Ziemann

Introduction

At the 2015 edition of Found in Translation, a literary festival organized in Gdańsk to celebrate translators and their work, in a panel on "Polish Literature on the English-Language Market," the American translator Jennifer Croft spoke about Anglophone readers pigeonholing foreign writing: the Hispanic/Latin American tradition stands for sex, the Polish for suffering.[1] At the 2021 edition, the translator Abel Murcia recalled first reading Stanisław Lem in Spanish, back in the late 1970s, as a representative of science fiction (alongside Isaac Asimov or Ray Bradbury) rather than Polish literature, which then hardly existed on the Spanish book market; he might not even have known that Lem, with his non–Slavic-sounding name, was Polish at all.[2] Murcia's collaborator Katarzyna Mołoniewicz emphasized that today, too, "it doesn't really matter that much to foreign publishers if something is Polish or not Polish, if it's Belarussian, Albanian or Korean … [t]he fact that a given author is able to go beyond these national connotations is very positive, because then he or she becomes more universal."[3] On the other hand, Dorota Masłowska reminisced how her translator Olaf Kühl was regularly accosted at book promotions in Germany by members of the local Polish diaspora criticizing his translation choices; these readers, she said, seemed to unwittingly regard the colloquial register of her writing as too intimate, too much their own, to be taken away from them and audaciously transformed in translation. Kühl diagnosed this as a somewhat paradoxical "anti-universalist mentality": on the one hand, Poles want their literature to be recognized in the world, but on the other, they want it to be theirs alone, untranslatable.[4] Zofia Bobowicz, the translator of Masłowska's 2002 debut novel *Wojna polsko-ruska pod flagą biało-czerwoną* and a highly experienced editor and promoter of Central-Eastern European writing in France, once explicitly stated that the title, which could be literally translated as *Polish-Russian War under the White-and-Red Flag*, would put the French reader off, inviting stereotypical associations (Poland—Russia—war). Instead, she opted for a more abstract and catchier *Polococktail Party*.[5] Poland (but not Russia!) was preventively erased from the title in most foreign-language editions of the book: the English translation appeared in the UK as *Snow White and Russian Red* (like the German, Dutch, and Spanish) and in the United States as *White and Red*. While the eponymous colors of course refer to the Polish flag, they will not be immediately identified as such by all readers.

Seemingly trivial and certainly not surprising to anyone familiar with the international book market, these examples are nevertheless symptomatic of two issues which, arguably, are not given enough consideration in academic discussions on the production and reception of translations from Polish literature, where the focus is usually on textual problems of interlingual translation, such as rendering style or cultural references. The first issue concerns representation and imagology: promoters of literature from Poland need to decide how to position a given author and/or text with regard to the Polish literary tradition and the image of Poland in the world.[6] Polish origin can be seen as irrelevant (Lem) or even potentially disadvantageous (Masłowska): associations with stereotypical Polishness should be avoided if the Western reader is to be "tricked" into reaching for a Polish author. The second issue has to do with ownership and authority (Kühl's problems with Polish *Besserwissers*): rather than following the international travels of Polish writing to learn how it resonates with foreign contexts, many Polish readers prefer to nitpick about particular translation choices, which they see as a disservice to "their" author.

Of course, both these phenomena might one day become a thing of the past. The recent success of Olga Tokarczuk, whose writing defies the stereotypical Western image of Polish literature without removing the question of Polishness from the picture, may help change the general perception—and, consequently, the book market value—of Polish writing.[7] Polish-speaking critics, too, may one day accept the fact that translation inevitably entails change, and move beyond narrowly understood linguistic analysis of the translated texts.[8] But whatever the future position of literature translated from Polish between world literature and Polish literature, I would argue that it is worthwhile to consider the problem of belonging (as representation and ownership) in research on the international presence of Polish authors through history. This perspective sheds light on the mechanisms of translation, publishing, marketing, and reception, helping to explain the fate of particular translations in terms other than their textual quality, and problematizing source text–oriented translation criticism.

In what follows, this approach will be adopted with regard to one of the relatively few Polish writers who enjoy international recognition: the Polish-Jewish modernist author of two short story collections and a handful of essays, Bruno Schulz (1892–1942).[9] I will revisit the history of the English translations of his fiction,[10] focusing on the framing and reception of Schulz as a representative of Polish, Central or Eastern European, and Jewish literature, and of literature "as such." Theoretically and methodologically, my research is situated in the area of translation history[11] and retranslation studies;[12] it combines analysis of paratextual material (book covers, forewords, afterwords, etc.)[13] and metatexts (reviews, critical essays) with archive-based investigations into the circumstances of translation production. Schulz's road to success with English-speaking readers will be presented as a departure from national literature for the sake of world literature in the Damroschian sense, that is, a mode of reading beyond source-culture contexts.[14]

Difficult Beginnings

Although it is generally believed that the first English translation of Schulz's fiction is by Celina Wieniewska, published in 1963,[15] this is only partly true: to be precise, hers was the first *published book-length* translation. As early as 1947, Zofia Tarnowska-Moss, an émigré charity worker from an aristocratic Polish family, and her husband William Stanley Moss, a British army officer, translated the second collection of Schulz's short stories, *Sanatorium pod Klepsydrą* (*Sanatorium Under the Sign of the Hourglass*, originally published in Polish in 1937). It was a spontaneous decision: the Mosses, who had literary ambitions but no previous translation experience, stumbled upon a copy of Schulz's book in the presence of the Polish author Aleksander Janta-Połczyński, who became the unofficial patron of their translation enterprise. As evidenced in their correspondence, the translators simplified Schulz's challenging, intricate style, arguing that the author "suffers from an acute form of adjectival diarrhoea [*sic*]" and thus "it is necessary to 'tone' him down a bit, or else the whole thing would be much too heavy and cumbersome."[16] However, this reader-friendly strategy was not enough to secure a willing publisher. Interestingly, among the publishing companies approached by Janta-Połczyński were two established in the 1940s by German-Jewish émigrés in New York, who published Kafka and other Jewish authors: Pantheon, founded by Kurt Wolff, and Schocken, founded by Salman Schocken, with Hannah Arendt as editor. This suggests that Janta-Połczyński sought to promote Schulz as a representative of Jewish-European rather than Polish writing—an insightful strategy, which, however, would prove successful only thirty years later, with Philip Roth's patronage of Wieniewska's translation.

Only one short story in the Mosses' translation was eventually published: in 1958, "My Father Joins the Fire Brigade" appeared in *Ten Contemporary Polish Stories*, a small anthology edited by Edmund Ordon, Polish scholar at Wayne State University in Detroit, Michigan, with an introduction by Olga Scherer-Virsky, another Polish émigré, then at Columbia. The editor's introduction makes it clear that the book was envisaged as an "occasional" piece: "In a few years Poland will celebrate its thousandth year as a nation … This selection of Polish short stories is … to make available to the American reader some of the fruits of Poland's long history."[17] Schulz is present here in a somewhat random company of lesser and more prominent authors: Maria Dąbrowska, Kazimierz Wierzyński, Michał Choromański, Piotr Choynowski, Maria Kuncewiczowa, Witold Gombrowicz, Józef Mackiewicz, Jerzy Zawieyski, and Marek Hłasko. The translation confirms William Moss's self-proclaimed strategy of "toning down" Schulz's exuberant writing: his meandering sentences are often split; his verbosity is tweaked.

Ordon's anthology received very little attention, and, in line with its profile, only in Polish contexts, then inseparable from Cold War political relations. Discussing it in *The Saturday Review*, Wacław Jędrzejewicz, a former Polish minister of education then serving as head of Slavic studies at Ripon College, Wisconsin, treated the volume as a sociopolitical rather than literary or cultural statement.[18] Robert Belknap, professor of Russian at Columbia, devoted more space to its literary value, yet his contribution in *The Polish Review*,[19] an academic quarterly of the Polish Institute of Arts and Sciences of America (PIASA), would not have reached readers interested in literature more than in Poland itself—and, arguably, only such general readership can ensure a wide reception of a foreign author.[20]

More significant in terms of volume, but as negligible in terms of efficiency in reaching foreign readers, were the translations of Schulz's individual stories printed in *Poland Illustrated Magazine*, a general interest monthly published since 1954 in several language editions and distributed internationally to legitimize the communist authorities of the Polish People's Republic in the eyes of the West. In 1958, under the joint heading *Cinnamon Shops* (Schulz's first collection of short stories, *Sklepy cynamonowe*, originally published in 1934), the magazine featured "Birds," "The Mannequins," and the three parts of "A Treatise on Mannequins," accompanied by a short note by the literary critic Henryk Bereza, who compared Schulz to Kafka, Marc Chagall, and Thomas Mann.[21] The translations were not signed, but a later reprint proves that their author was Jenny Rodzinska (Janina Rodzińska), an obscure figure who seems to have occasionally worked for state-owned publishing houses on academic (not literary) translations. Her rendering of Schulz is very literal, closely following his syntax, but of dubious artistic value. While there seem to be no deliberate cuts, one can spot some omissions, errors, and inconsistencies characteristic of hasty journalistic translation that was not given enough care. A more accurate and skillful translation, accompanied by a long, informative essay by Schulz's chief biographer, Jerzy Ficowski, was published in *Poland* magazine in 1965: "Gale winds" and untitled excerpts from "Spring."[22] It was authored by Christina Cenkalska (Krystyna Cękalska de domo Swinarska), a US-born graduate of Columbia, who settled in Poland after the war to become an experienced literary translator and longtime collaborator of *Poland* magazine. While generally following Schulzian syntax, Cenkalska's version is not as literal as Rodzinska's, and seeks to do justice to the artistic qualities of the original, for example, Schulz's use of alliterations.

In 1964, Rodzińska's translation was reprinted without changes in *Introduction to Modern Polish Literature: An Anthology of Fiction and Poetry*, edited by two Polish émigré scholars, Adam Gillon of the State University of New York and Ludwik Krzyżanowski of Columbia University, editor of *The Polish Review*. Despite their claim that it was "addressed to the general reader in English-speaking countries,"[23] the five-hundred-page hardcover volume presenting Polish late-nineteenth- and twentieth-century fiction and poetry from forty-four authors, with a twenty-page scholarly introduction covering the whole history of Polish literature, and with pronunciation guidelines accompanying Polish names, was more of a textbook.[24] The largest readership the editors could hope for were students at Slavic departments.

One may wonder why to unearth these forgotten early translations, given that they had virtually no impact on the Anglophone reception of Schulz. The answer is that they put into perspective the later success of Wieniewska's version. As Anna Cetera-Włodarczyk argued in the context of Polish nineteenth-century Shakespeare translations, "it is only by comparing successful and unsuccessful projects that we can fully assess which factors determined the success of the former and the failure of the latter."[25] If one is unaware of early attempts at introducing a given author to foreign readers, it is easy to see him or her, with hindsight, as "doomed to success," without fully appreciating the efforts of translators and other agents involved. If retranslations are compared without taking into account all elements of the sequence, this may lead to a simplified image, reducing historical development to linear progress[26] and disregarding the extratextual factors that influenced their reception.

It is noteworthy that on the textual level, the early translations of Schulz's stories covered a whole spectrum of approaches: from the readable but simplified version of the Mosses, through the largely accurate and aesthetically pleasing translation by Cenkalska, to the grammatically faithful but somewhat cumbersome rendering by Rodzinska. Schulz was not rejected by English-speaking readers because he was poorly translated; he simply did not have a chance to reach them. These early publications strongly (and somewhat randomly) inscribed his work in Polish contexts, not only literary but also socio-politico-historical, thus limiting the target readership to those wishing to learn more about Poland, rather than those keen on discovering a literary gem. The "where" (publishing outlet) and "how" (paratextual framing) precluded wider acquaintance with the "what" (the actual translated texts). Moreover, the fact that *Poland* preferred to commission a new translation from Cenkalska, and Gillon and Krzyżanowski reprinted Rodzinska's, rather than including excerpts from Wieniewska's (whose publication both the magazine and the anthology acknowledged), shows that they followed their own agendas, rather than thinking about introducing Schulz to English-speaking readers in a more systematic and coordinated manner.

Proper Start

A radically different approach is visible in the press forerunner to Celina Wieniewska's book-length translation. In late 1962, the story "Mr. Charles" was featured in *Transatlantic Review*, an illustrated literary quarterly established in 1959 as a tribute to and continuation of Ford Maddox Ford's influential monthly from the 1920s, *The Transatlantic Review*.[27] Schulz's text appeared there without any paratextual framing save for a one-sentence note announcing the publication of *Cinnamon Shops*. Moreover, apart from a few pieces by the Israeli poet David Rokeah, it was the only translation in the volume. Featured alongside an essay by William S. Burroughs, a story by Paul Bowles, and some new poetry, Schulz was to speak for himself as a new author worth knowing, rather than representing Polish literature or even foreign writing at large.

Wieniewska's translation came out in 1963, first in London with MacGibbon & Kee, under the original title, then in New York with Walker & Company, as *The Street of Crocodiles*. The starkly contrasting blurbs of the UK and US editions demonstrate how the publisher's profile and allegiances influence the way in which a given author is presented. The British edition featured a rather standard bio and note on the text, praising Schulz as "a master of the extraordinary and the commonplace" and suggesting that his humor is reminiscent of Edward Lear. The flap announced three other new books from the publisher's catalog, including one translation: novels by the contemporary American author William Gaddis, Oscar Wilde's friend Ada Leverson, and Italian turn-of-century verist Federico de Roberto.

In the American edition, the whole back cover was used to promote a novel by Maria Kuncewicz, then Chair of Polish Literature at the University of Chicago, and the blurb for Schulz's text put great emphasis on contemporary politics and ideology. After introducing Schulz as "one of the most remarkably gifted writers to be produced in Eastern Europe in this century" and repeating a reference to Kafka and Chagall from Wieniewska's preface, the final paragraph of a three-paragraph note on the flaps reads thus:

> Schulz, a Jew, was murdered by the Nazis, who anathemized his writing. After the war, the Communists of the Stalin era likewise condemned his work, but following the Polish liberalization of 1956, Schulz's reputation underwent a partial rehabilitation. As one Polish observer put it, "he is no longer overly condemned; but ... he is never written about in the official journals." In fact, the philosophical gap between Schulz and the Communists in unbridgeable. Perhaps this helps to explain his continued popularity in Poland.

Inaccuracies aside, the ideological load of this blurb, which almost suggests that reading Schulz would be an act of resistance against Communism, is striking. It becomes less so, however, when one remembers how deeply entangled in politics were East–West cultural relations at the time, and it begins to sound almost like a natural "excuse" for publishing an author from (Communist) Poland when one learns that Walker & Co. was founded by Samuel Sloan Walker Jr., former vice president of the CIA front organization Free Europe Committee, who continued to receive CIA funding for his publishing activity.

Both editions contain Wieniewska's short preface, which, apart from giving biographical facts—including the information, since disproved, that Schulz translated *The Trial*[28]—presents the author as one of a kind:

> Attempts were made to place his oeuvre in the mainstream of Polish literature, to find affinities, derivations, to explain him in terms of one literary theory or another. The task is well-nigh impossible ... Polish and other critics have drawn attention to the influence that Thomas Mann, Freud and Kafka exercised on him. This may or may not be true."

Rather than seeking literary parallels, Wieniewska chooses to explore the visual power of Schulz's writing. She concludes her preface as follows: "The magic touch of a poetic genius, in a proses as memorable, powerful and unique as are the brush strokes of Marc Chagall."[29]

The book had a limited but very favorable critical response on both sides of the Atlantic. It was reviewed in the biggest newspapers, by authors who had no connection to Poland or things Polish, which was reflected in the associations and references they made, for example, to the American humorist James Thurber.[30] Most reviews echoed Wieniewska's preface, mentioning Kafka, but also emphasizing Schulz's uniqueness. Readers of *The Guardian* learned that Schulz "will inevitably be compared to Kafka,"[31] but in *The Spectator*, B. S. Johnson wrote about this analogy that "the Pole possessed a lyrical quality that his fellow Jew never had."[32] A similar view was expressed in *The New York Times*: "Although Schulz is most often compared with Kafka, ... there is nothing imitative in these stories."[33] To Kafka and Chagall, an American critic added the key figure of contemporary Jewish-American fiction: "One might also think ... [of] Isaac Bashevis Singer; but his voice, his world, remain uniquely his own."[34] Some weeks later, Singer himself published what was the longest review of Schulz's work at that time, first in Yiddish in *Forverts*, then in English. Admitting that he hadn't heard of this author when still living in Poland (until 1935), in his thousand-word essay, Singer reinforced both the Kafka comparison and admiration for Schulz's originality: "Schulz cannot be easily classified. He can be called a surrealist, a symbolist, an expressionist, a modernist ... He wrote sometimes like Kafka, sometimes like Proust, and at times succeeded in reaching depths that neither of them reached."[35] The latter sentence was to become the most quoted endorsement in the history of Schulz's English translations.

The transatlantic reach of Wieniewska's translation and the critical accolades Schulz received, of which only a portion has been referenced above, were incomparably more effective than the earlier attempts at introducing his fiction to English-speaking readers. Yet even such response in major UK and US press outlets did not ensure sales figures that would encourage the publishers to follow with the second volume of Schulz's stories, which Wieniewska had ready to print.

Impetus

The tables turned when *The Street of Crocodiles* was rediscovered by Philip Roth: in 1977, Wieniewska's translation—with slightly amended, that is, Americanized, spelling and vocabulary but without revisions—was reissued in his popular Penguin series *Writers from the Other Europe* (1975–87). Its self-declared aim was to bring to the American reader "outstanding and influential works" from "literature that has evolved in 'the other Europe' during the postwar decades," and Schulz stood out in the seventeen-volume series as one of two authors (the other was Géza Csáth) who did not live past the Second World War; others—for example, Milan Kundera, Tadeusz Konwicki, György Konrád—engaged more or less directly with the postwar political reality. Although Roth's series automatically placed Schulz in the contemporary Eastern European context, at the same time it emphasized his Jewishness: Schulz was given a seal of approval from the most prominent Jewish-American authors, the series editor himself and Singer, whose 1963 endorsement quoted above appeared on the back cover of the Penguin edition, effectively shaping the reception of Schulz in the following years. This was especially true in the United States, where Schulz became known as a representative of Jewish rather than Polish literature.[36]

Roth not only published *The Street of Crocodiles* in an accessible paperback edition but also launched a successful promotional campaign with lasting effects. *The New York Times Book Review* featured his conversation with Singer about Schulz, next to a long and very favorable review by Cyntia Ozick (the lead: "With Babel and Singer and Kafka"), who thus joined the triumvirate of Schulz's committed Jewish-American patrons (and went on to write a novel inspired by his work, *The Messiah of Stockholm*, 1986).[37] Over the next months, Schulz's name regularly appeared in *The New York Times* and *The New York Review of Books*, and *The New Yorker* printed three stories announcing the second volume—a rare distinction for translated fiction.[38] *Sanatorium under the Sign of the Hourglass* premiered in 1978, and was reviewed on page 1 of *The New York Times Book Review* by Singer (soon to be Nobel Prize winner), who called Schulz "one of the most remarkable writers who ever lived" and sealed his fate as "A Polish Franz Kafka."[39] Bruno Schulz became a household name among Jewish-American intellectuals, a trend still present in the twenty-first century, as testified by admiration from contemporary authors such as Jonathan Safran Foer, Nicole Krauss, or Rivka Galchen.

Alongside this strong reception paradigm, Schulz's growing international fame also took on a more dispersed form. Since the late 1970s, Wieniewska's translation has had sixteen book editions, and individual stories were reprinted in twenty magazines and anthologies, which inscribed his work into multiple contexts. Penguin included Schulz in the *Twentieth Century Classics* series in early 1990s, in 2008—in *Penguin Classics*. The twenty-first century brought two retranslations of Schulz's work, by John Curran Davis and Madeline G. Levine, which can be seen as both results of his success and instruments of its furthering.[40] Schulz has entered world literature in three ways. First of all, critics have repeatedly put his name next to the greatest figures of the Western canon—predominantly Kafka, but also Proust, Mann, Conrad, Joyce, Dostoevsky, Sterne, Borges, and Nabokov. Secondly, and, in my view, more importantly, since the 1990s his work has appealed to readers with different ethnocultural backgrounds, including some acclaimed authors—Schulz has always been "a writer's writer." Salman Rushdie alluded to his work in *The Moor's Last Sigh* (1995), the Lebanese-American author Rabih Allamedine made the title protagonist of his novel *An Unnecessary Woman* (2012) translate Schulz into Arabic (alongside other works from the Western canon), the Pakistani-born British writer Nadeem Aslam called *The Street of Crocodiles* his "book of a lifetime,"[41] the Kenyan author and LGBT+ activist Kenneth Binyavanga Wainaina listed Schulz among his three favorite writers, the other two being African.[42] Thirdly, his work became a point of reference for English-speaking critics disusing greater or lesser literary figures around the world: from the Lebanese Canadian author Rawi Hage[43] and Cuban Reinaldo Arenas,[44] through the Greek Margerita Karapanou[45] and Israeli Yehudit Katzir,[46] to Haruki Murakami.[47] That Schulz's work is not only read and discussed for its own sake but also spontaneously mentioned in discussions of other authors is, I believe, an unmistakable sign of genuine assimilation into the Anglophone critical discourse.

Conclusion

As follows from this inevitably hasty overview, in the mature phase of reception, Schulz, like Lem, has "effectively sidestepped or transcended 'Polishness' and its attendant marginalizations in the anglophone world."[48] Yet despite this success, Polish Schulz scholars have shown little interest in comparative, "world" readings of his work, and Polish critics of Wieniewska's translation tend to focus on its shortcomings, rather than appreciating its role in the development of Schulz's international career.[49]

Benjamin Palloff once rightly observed that "Polish literature" and "literatura polska" are not equivalent; it is unrealistic to believe that the canon of authors and texts known to foreign readers (and, to some extent, even to scholars of Polish literature) will ever be the same as the domestic one.[50] This is a gentle way of putting it; to literary critics with no Polish connections and to general readers, Polish authors read in English need not be seen as representatives of "Polish literature" (let alone "literatura polska") at all. Perhaps this is the fate of all major authors from minor literatures. From this point of view, translation appears as liberation from domestic contexts, and the inevitable obverse of international success is losing control over one's "own" author—which should not mean losing sight of his or her adventures overseas.

Notes

1   Program available at http://odnalezionewtlumaczeniu.pl. Croft's *bon mot* has since circulated in several versions; it was recently echoed, for example, in the interviewer's question to Antonia Lloyd-Jones, another eminent translator from Polish: "Does Polish literature have the problem of being stereotyped about only being about misery and suffering?"; Ben Koschalka, "The Challenges of Bringing Polish Literature to the World: An Interview with Translator Antonia Lloyd-Jones," *Notes from Poland* (May 10, 2021), https://

notesfrompoland.com/2021/05/10/the-challenges-of-bringing-polish-literat ure-to-the-world-an-interview-with-translator-antonia-lloyd-jones/.

2   Similarly, Bill Johnston noted, "It has been pointed out that in the only print version of *Solaris* currently available, there is no mention of the fact that Lem is Polish or that the book was originally written in Polish" (315); See Johnston, "Translated from the Polish: The Fates, Feats, and Foibles of Polish Literature in English," in *Being Poland: A New History of Polish Literature and Culture since 1918*, edited by Tamara Trojanowska, Joanna Niżyńska, and Przemyslaw Czapliński (Toronto: Toronto University Press, 2018), 308–26.

3   https://www.youtube.com/watch?v=NbGn3eHHW3Y.

4   https://www.youtube.com/watch?v=bcORB0r4z3s.

5   Personal telephone conversation, June 2021. Cf. Benjamin Paloff, "Czy fraza 'Polish literature' oznacza 'literaturę polską'? (Problem teorii recepcji i nie tylko …)," *Wielogłos*, vol. 2, no. 4 (2008): 61: "If I were to point out the main weakness of the promotion of Polish literature and culture abroad, I would emphasize the adjective 'Polish'."

6   Cf. Luc van Doorslaer, Peter Flynn, and Joep Leerssen (eds.), *Interconnecting Translation Studies and Imagology* (Amsterdam: John Benjamins, 2015).

7   That the question of Polish identity is important for Tokarczuk is manifested both on the textual level, in her critical, unapologetic approach to national history, and beyond, in her public statements, triggering uncomfortable and often hate-ridden reactions from Polish conservatives.

8   A promising sign of this evolution is the publication of two edited volumes internationalizing Polish literature: *Being Poland: A New History of Polish Literature and Culture since 1918*, edited by Tamara Trojanowska, Joanna Niżyńska, and Przemysław Czapliński (Toronto: Toronto University Press, 2018) and *Światowa historia literatury polskiej*, edited by Magdalena Popiel, Tomasz Bilczewski, and Stanley Bill (Kraków: Wydawnictwo UJ, 2020). Still, their editors did not go as far as to invite contributions from scholars who read Polish authors only in translation, that is, represent the actual target readership of translated literature from Poland.

9   See, for example, Johnston, "Translated from the Polish," 308, 310.

10 Spanning more than seven decades, here this history can be discussed only selectively and hastily; I focus on the lesser known facts from its early stages. For context, see my other publications on the topic, for example, "The Good Bad Translator: Celina Wieniewska and Her Bruno Schulz," *Asymptote* (September 20, 2017), https://www.asymptotejournal.com/blog/2017/09/20/ the-good-bad-translator-celina-wieniewska-and-her-bruno-schulz/; "Translating Polish Jewishness: Bruno Schulz in English," *Translatologica*, vol. 1 (2017): 209–29; "Extratextual Factors Shaping Preconceptions about Retranslation: Bruno Schulz in English," in *Perspectives on Retranslation: Ideology, Paratexts, Methods*, edited by Özlem Berk Albachten, Şehnaz Tahir Gürçağlar (New York: Routledge, 2019), 87–104.

11 E.g. Anthony Pym, *Method in Translation History* (Manchester: St. Jerome, 1998); Lieven D'hulst, "Translation History," in *Handbook of Translation*

Studies, edited by Yves Gambier and Luc van Doorslaer (Amsterdam: John Benjamins, 2010), 397–405; Jeremy Munday, "Using Primary Sources to Produce a Microhistory of Translation and Translators: Theoretical and Methodological Concerns," *The Translator*, vol. 20, no. 1 (2014): 64–80.

12 E.g. Outi Paloposki and Kaisa Koskinen, "A Thousand and One Translations: Revisiting Retranslation," in *Claims Changes and Challenges in Translation Studies*, edited by Gyde Hansen, Kirsten Malmkjær and Daniel Gile (Amsterdam: John Benjamins, 2004), 27–38.

13 Şehnaz Tahir Gürçağlar, "What Texts Don't Tell: The Uses of Paratexts in Translation Research," in *Crosscultural Transgressions. Research Models in Translation Studies II: Historical and Ideological Issues*, edited by Theo Hermans (Manchester: St. Jerome, 2002), 46–60.

14 David Damrosch, *What Is World Literature* (Princeton, NJ: Princeton University Press, 2003), 6, cf. *How to Read World Literature* (Chichester: Wiley-Blackwell, 2008), 46–104.

15 Bruno Schulz, *Cinnamon Shops and Other Stories*, translated by Celina Wieniewska (London: McGibbon & Kee, 1963), *The Street of Crocodiles*, translated by Celina Wieniewska (New York: Walker and Co., 1963).

16 While the manuscript of this translation remains lost, Janta's archive at the Polish National Library contains a number of letters pertaining to this project.

17 Edmund Ordon (ed.), *Ten Contemporary Polish Short Stories* (Detroit: Wayne State University Press, 1958), 2nd ed. 1974.

18 Wacław Jędrzejewicz, "Affirmations of Freedom," *Saturday Review* (August 9, 1958): 26–7.

19 Robert Belknap, "*Ten Contemporary Polish Short Stories* by Edmund Ordon," *Polish Review*, vol. 4, nos. 1/2 (1959): 148–50.

20 Cf. Johnston ("Translated from the Polish," 310), who mentions two most typical, relatively small readerly "constituencies: the academic world, where [Polish authors] often appear on course reading lists; and those of Polish descent who yearn to reconnect with their cultural heritage."

21 Bruno Schulz, "Cinnamon Shops," *Poland*, vol. 50 (October 1958): 25–8.

22 Bruno Schulz, ["Cinnamon Shops (Gale Winds)"] and ["Sanatorium under Water Clock (Excerpts),"] trans. Christina Cenkalska, *Poland*, vol. 134 (October 1965): 29–31.

23 Adam Gillon and Ludwik Krzyzanowski (eds.), *Introduction to Modern Polish Literature: An Anthology of Fiction and Poetry* (New York: Twayne, 1964), 7 (2nd ed. 1968, 3rd, expanded ed. 1982).

24 Danuta Bieńkowska, "Anthologies of Contemporary Polish Prose in English Translation," *Canadian Slavonic Papers*, vol. 8 (1966): 243–49.

25 Anna Cetera-Włodarczyk, "'It Takes a Genius to Set the Tune, and a Poet to Play Variations on It': Some Remarks on the Irksome (Im)Possibility of Editing Shakespeare in Translation," translated by Zofia Ziemann, *Przekładaniec*, special issue "Translation History in the Polish Context" (2019): 46–62.

26   Palopolski and Koskinen, "A Thousand and One Translations," 36.

27   B. Schulz, "Mr Charles," trans. Celina Wieniewska, *Transatlantic Review*, vol. 11 (Winter 1962): 84–6.

28   In fact, the translation was done by Schulz's fiancé, Józefina Szelińska, and edited by him. They agreed that since Kafka was little known in Poland, and Schulz was already an accomplished author, his name on the cover would help promote the book.

29   Schulz, *Cinnamon Shops*, 8, 9, 10.

30   Christopher Wordsworth, "A Private Individual," *The Guardian* (April 11, 1963): 7.

31   Ibid.

32   B. S. Johnson, "Short Stories from Four Countries," *The Spectator* (March 29, 1963): 30.

33   Paul Hamel, "Realities in Illusion," *New York Times* (March 29, 1964): 26.

34   Robert L. Stilwell, "Suffering and Sea Change," *Saturday Review* (October 26, 1963): 45.

35   Isaac B. Singer, "Burlesquing Life with Father," *Herald Tribune* (December 22, 1963) [newspaper cutting from Singer archive at the Harry Ransom Center, University of Texas; page number missing].

36   It is ironic that at the time of Schulz's debut, in 1930s Poland, Jewish literature was considered peripheral to Polish (alongside Lithuanian or Belarusian), and the first critics who embraced his writing had to defend him from anti-Semitic attacks.

37   Cyntia Ozick, "*The Streets of Crocodiles*," *New York Times Book Review* (February 13, 1977): 2.

38   Bruno Schulz, "Loneliness," translated by Celina Wieniewska, *New Yorker* (November 14, 1977): 43; "Sanatorium Under the Sign of the Hourglass," trans. Celina Wieniewska, *New Yorker* (December 12, 1977): 44–54; "Father's Last Escape, translated by Celina Wieniewska, *New Yorker* (January 2, 1978): 24–6.

39   Isaac B. Singer, "A Polish Franz Kafka," *New York Times Book Review* (July 9, 1978): 34.

40   See Zofia Ziemann, "Extratextual Factors Shaping Preconceptions about Retranslation: Bruno Schulz in English," in *Perspectives on Retranslation: Ideology, Paratexts, Methods*, edited by Özlem Berk Albachten and Şehnaz Tahir Gürçağlar (New York: Routledge, 2019), 87–104.

41   Nadeem Aslam, "*The Street of Crocodiles* by Bruno Schulz," *The Independent* (February 23, 2013): 28–9.

42   "Binyavanga Wainaina, Gay Kenyan Author, Hopes to Boost LGBT Rights with Coming Out," *HuffPost* (January 28, 2014), https://www.huffpost.com/entry/binyavanga-wainaina-lgbt-rights-_n_4677847?guccounter=1.

43   Sara Dowse, "Memory and Regret in a Cold Climate," *Canberra Times* (July 25, 2009): 12.

44 James Sallis, "Irreverent and Spiteful, Arenas' *Assault* Attacks Senses," *Orlando Sentinel* (July 20, 1994): E3.

45 John Updike, "Bruno Schulz, Hidden Genius," *New York Times Book Review* (September 9, 1979): 1.

46 Robert DiAntonio, "A Fresh, Distinctive Voice from Israel," *St. Louis Post-Dispatch* (June 14, 1992): 5C.

47 Steve Yarbrough, "Short-Story Improv: Murakami's Masterful Riffs," *The Oregonian* (October 15, 2006): O15.

48 Johnston, "Translated from the Polish," 315.

49 See Ziemann, "Translating Polish Jewishness: Bruno Schulz in English." Translatologica 1 (2017): 209–29.

50 Paloff, "Czy fraza 'Polish Literature," cf. Johnston, "Translated from the Polish," 309.

8

Polishness Revisited: Witold Gombrowicz and the Question of Identity

Jacek Gutorow

The work of Witold Gombrowicz (1904–1969) is neither particularly popular nor critically acclaimed among the Anglophone readers. The writer, whose oeuvre belongs to the strict canon of the twentieth-century Polish/ European literature and who was a strong candidate for the Nobel Prize at the end of the 1960s, is hardly read, let alone discussed, in English. The existing English translations of his works are mostly of poor quality, at least in comparison with the original text. They certainly do not give justice to the truly resplendent greatness of Gombrowicz's language and style, or rather styles—the Polish novelist was a virtuoso of changing tones and registers, a master of syntactical pranks and capers, a tireless caricaturist of literary conventions. Like Joyce, Gombrowicz is a protean and infinitely resourceful writer, rarely satisfied with standard usages and literary etiquettes. The analogy with Joyce is surely worth following; it may help us see why Gombrowicz's texts are so elusive and immune to the efforts of the translators. The trouble with the author of *Ferdydurke* and *Trans-Atlantyk* is that he wrote in a minor European language embedded in rich cultural history—and it is not so easy to cope with the profusion of cultural references and cross-references understandable in the local context but almost completely cryptic outside of it.

Gombrowicz's inimitable and idiomatic style is a considerable challenge even for the most careful and competent translators. Lillian Vallee's translation of his *Diary* is a case in point. The *Diary*, considered by many critics (especially Polish ones) to be one of the greatest monuments of Polish artistic prose in the twentieth century, comparable to the canonical works of Baroque and Romantic periods, is a linguistic and stylistic tour de force. Gombrowicz the diarist writes in many registers and idiolects, shifting between meditative and expressive tones, fusing all kinds of Polish oral and literary diction, experimenting with conventions and clichés. It should be noted at once that Vallee's rendering is accurate and precise; as a matter of fact, it might be the best English version of Gombrowicz to date. Still, the translation lacks the most essential component of Gombrowicz's idiom—its indebtedness to various nonstandard idiolects and variants of Polish speech, to the inimitable music of subtle vocal tonalities as well as the many rhythms of colloquial jargon. The musical and rhetorical aspects of Gombrowicz's prose are contextual and require that the reader knows and is able to detect, even intuitively, the range and diversity of the *Diary*'s many styles and registers; this in turn requires familiarity with the Polish language in its historical and cultural perspective, something not immediately present in the text and thus "invisible" to the non-Polish reader. No wonder that the English readers may feel disappointed by the existing translations of Gombrowicz's works, not finding in them the enthusiastic praises offered by the Polish critics.

Gombrowicz's main concern was the enigma of individual and collective identity. Understandably, the writer laid emphasis on the dilemmas and ambiguities of Polishness in general (the word *polskość* is one of his catchwords, recurring in many essays and letters) and his own Polish background in particular. We have here yet another paradox that makes him a highly problematic figure for many readers. On the one hand, the author of *Ferdydurke* was questioning the significance and legitimacy of national or communal narratives, viewing them as constructed and fictional. On the other hand, he persistently referred to the idea of Polishness, finding in it a metonymical figure embracing his own personal identity. The tension between skepticism and a sense of belonging can be felt in most of his prose works and many diary entries. Strong individuality was for him the agent capable of demystifying all social and cultural codes and conventions. In a truly dialectical fashion, the opposite is true as well: one's identification with such "grand tales" as the narrative of Polishness is not only a guarantee and insurance of one's identity but also a threat to it.

The concept of *polskość* is highly ambivalent with Gombrowicz. It is definitely a limiting force, capable of imposing stereotyped (and fictional) identities on individuals. Once overcome, however, it may provide a basis for a heightened sense of identity. Not that Gombrowicz believed in such a thing as identity—after all, his main contention was that the notion of the self is a fiction. At the same time, though, he gladly subscribed to the Nietzschean imperative of "overcoming oneself"—but laid emphasis on "overcoming" rather than "self." Gombrowicz approached Polishness as a sort of contagious disease that helps acquire immunity from further infections. It was for him something to be absorbed and only then rejected. He felt he could question his own background only at the moment when—and to the extent that—he also validated it. Thus, his brilliant parodies of the standard narratives of Polishness are always indebted to those narratives. For this strongly self-conscious and self-styled artist, parody is after all a double-edged sword as it carries in itself a mute acknowledgment, and even appreciation, of what is being parodied. This is the truly dramatic aspect of his work—and its latent paradox.

Still, it is rather the deconstructive aspect of Gombrowicz's novels, avant-garde plays, and autobiographical writings that attracted the readers' and critics' attention, especially in the decades following the writer's death. His multivocal and multilayered prose, as well as his constant emphasis on the heterogeneity and dissemination of the narrative voice(s), encouraged the readings informed by the poststructuralist agenda (it is worth remembering that the late 1960s, the heyday of Gombrowicz's popularity in Europe, was also the time of the rapidly growing fascination with the new ideas of Barthes, Foucault, and Lacan). The tenor of such interpretations is not surprising. Tomislav Z. Longinović discovers in Gombrowicz's *A Kind of Testament* the "radical divestment from the essentialist conceptions of the self" and describes the Polish writer's autobiographical voice as a "floating signifier." Ewa Płonowska Ziarek argues that Gombrowicz's notorious "me" (which proudly opens the *Diary* and is repeated in a conspicuously parodic way, putting the authority of the speaking voice/self in question) is "an enigma, a titillating cipher, a carefully orchestrated puzzle to which there is no one solution." And George Gasyna speaks of Gombrowicz's "scriptive selves and personae," which add up to create the narrative I, in itself a "fictive figuration," textualized and constantly at play.[1]

Such assertions are no doubt justified. From the very beginning of his career, Gombrowicz questioned the essence and validity of the very notion of identity, both individual and collective (stereotyped Polishness being his favorite target). In *Ferdydurke*, his sensational novelistic debut, which was published in 1937 and quickly became a manifesto for many young people in Poland, the narrator's personal identity is seen as a somewhat nebulous category resulting, directly and indirectly, from social interactions, class divisions, and sometimes even speech acts. The ideas of the interhuman (*międzyludzkie*) and in-betweenness (*pomiędzy*), crucial for the understanding of Gombrowicz's view of the self as merely derivative, determined the main direction of his artistic development. The two concepts found their mature expression and elucidation in the *Diary*, begun in 1953, when Gombrowicz, then almost fifty, was still looking for an adequate—and persuasive—literary form to articulate the apparently inarticulate puzzle of the self. The diaristic convention became an outlet for his ambivalent feelings about himself ("that official Gombrowicz whom I built with my own hands"[2]) as well as his controversial views about the idea of Polishness. One of the strongest effects produced by the *Diary* is a sense of the dissolution of the autobiographical subject. Importantly, however, the I does not disappear. Instead, it is challenged in the course of the narrative, which often flips over and contradicts itself in a never-ending cycle of affirmations and cancellations.

Gombrowicz recapitulated the *Diary*'s tale of the contorted self in *A Kind of Testament*, written shortly before his death. The *Testament*, which might have been modeled on Nietzsche's *Ecce Homo*, provides us with the writer's final evaluation as well as reinterpretation of his artistic biography and his work. It is both confessional (in its somewhat intimate tone) and anti-confessional (in its many paradoxes and denials). First of all, though, it is highly dramatic. At one moment Gombrowicz writes, "I don't know who I really am, but I suffer when I am deformed. So, at least I know what I am not. My 'self' is nothing more but my will to be myself." The identity of the writing/speaking "I" is constantly questioned, and this takes on the form of impatient cross-examination and interrogation: "If I am always an artefact, always defined by others and by culture as well as by my own formal necessities, where should I look for my 'self'? Who am I really and to what extent am I?" Gombrowicz's answers in *Testament* are usually dark and troubled:

> I was an agglomeration of different worlds, neither one thing nor the other. Indefinite. If I were followed step by step and spied on, my every contact with people could easily show just how much of a chameleon I was. According to the place, the people, the circumstances, I was good, stupid, primitive, refined, taciturn, talkative, self-effacing, arrogant, superficial or profound ... What was I not? I was everything.[3]

Such statements anticipate what the poststructuralist critics have described as the "death of the author": the dissolution and disappearance of the authorial voice that is perceived as a function of language and a rhetorical trope. Yet the author of *Ferdydurke* can be also portrayed as an unprogressive, conservative writer whose views and inclinations were sometimes astonishingly conventional and reactionary. Many readers are surprised when they discover that Gombrowicz was critical of the twentieth-century artistic and literary avant-gardes. More often than not, he was overly disapproving of the modernist idea of the autonomous work of art with its imperative of examining the minutest movements and hidden layers of the human mind. He was, to take one example, fault-finding and derogatory in his remarks about such writers as Proust or the representatives of the French *nouveau roman*, accusing them either of exhibitionism or of tedious formal experimentation (and forgetting that in his own novels and plays he likewise experimented with innovative formal patterns and devices). At the same time he admired and publicly praised such writers as Henryk Sienkiewicz, a conservative author of epic historical novels and a staunch critic of modernity, or Thomas Mann. One can also find in Gombrowicz's texts a lot of derogatory remarks about contemporary painting and music. As it were, the writer reserved his praise mainly for traditional artists of the bygone centuries, although even with them he could be harshly discriminating (his critique of Dante's *Divine Comedy* drew sharp condemnation from Leopardi). All in all, Gombrowicz was highly suspicious of all kinds of aesthetic, introspective, and self-conscious art. "I consider myself a dedicated realist," he stated in his conversation with Dominique de Roux, and this terse declaration seems to summarize his literary aims and aspirations.[4]

More importantly, the problem of identity was for Gombrowicz, especially in his later works, a kind of malaise resulting from weak will, inertia, and lack of clear self-consciousness. True, he was constantly and quite radically questioning his own sense of himself, especially as far as its existential and metaphysical legitimacy was concerned. As it has just been shown (see the quotes provided above), the writer acknowledged and admitted the multiplicity of selves, and claimed that the problem of the self is of illusory nature while self-identity is no more than a useful—although very convincing—fiction produced in the social environment (it was clear to the Polish writer that the human being placed outside of the social context could not be properly termed human). At the same time, though, Gombrowicz was addressing the drama of the self in the surprisingly combative, even militant terms. Many passages in the *Diary* and the *Testament* read like a kind of psychomachia. We get the impression that each time the author of *Ferdydurke* reveals and castigates the ambivalences of identity, he does so not as a minimalist concerned with the idea of disappearance and absence— say, in the Beckettian mode—but as a maximalist not satisfied with what is customarily called the self and attempting to raise its stakes. Gombrowicz's violitionist and activist language is conspicuous and may give us a pause. The imperatives of transcending oneself and overcoming one's cultural and social environment are frequent in his work—they imply the vision of a strong self to be attained in the process of dissolving the old and untrue (because imposed) identity. It is difficult to overlook this moment: the writer is rejecting his socially constructed "I" with such vehemence that the gesture unexpectedly becomes a sign of confident, self-assured personality.

How to reconcile these two conflicting aspects of Gombrowicz's oeuvre? The question has been bothering Polish critics in recent years. In a seminal study of the narrative strategies used by the Polish writer in the *Diary*, Katarzyna Chmielewska proposes the category of the supra-subject (*nadpodmiot*) who oversees both the narrator of the *Diary* and its main protagonist. Despite the fact that the *Diary* is outwardly a personal journal, its author often employs the third-person singular narrative, transforming himself into an apparently fictional character (this effect is strengthened by the fact that from time to time the name Gombrowicz is inserted into quotation marks). One of the *Diary*'s dominant gestures is the stratification and dislocation of the authorial voice—the latter can be self-ironic, self-questioning and is sometimes markedly italicized. As already noted, most of the critics have emphasized the carnivalesque aspect of the work and pointed to its playful dimension, seeing in it an anticipation of the postmodern aesthetic of the replenishment of selves and personae. Such an interpretation is valid—Gombrowicz is openly mocking the institution of what Philippe Lejeune called the autobiographical pact—yet, as Chmielewska convincingly demonstrates, this is by no means the whole story. The point is that the *Diary*'s deconstructive and distancing effects are just elements of the writer's strategy of authorial resistance and dominance. Chmielewska comments on this in the following way: "the *Diary*'s subject, although hierarchical, is non-essential. But it does not mean that it is devoid of a center or can be reduced either to a mere display of flickering fake images or to a carefree play of signifiers ... at the center of its agency is a strategy and a will to be oneself."[5] She summarizes her analyses with two important statements that pave the way for a revaluation and reinterpretation of Gombrowicz's project. First, Gombrowicz's idea of the subject (self) may be said to be based on the paradox of inconclusiveness: "The subject is a task to be completed, not a distinct being. It can become a subject only in confrontation with the external pressure."[6] Second, it has to do with the problem of identity. Toward the end of her book Chmielewska combines the *Diary*'s program of the self as the "will-to-be" with a broad perspective on what she calls the "post-traditional identity." The latter is neither a "simple negation of the past" nor a "rejection of social roles and attitudes." On the contrary, it willingly embraces its own cultural and social past, yet at the same time it defies being absorbed by it—a classic example of the Nietzschean will to power, with its combative, indeed agonistic, resistance to history and tradition.[7]

And then we have the problem of national identity. Starting with *Trans-Atlantyk* and the first volume of the *Diary* (both published in 1953), the writer mockingly and mercilessly questioned the narratives of Polishness. However, his sweeping criticism of the stereotypes and clichés of Polishness was conveyed in a strangely ambiguous language that both condemned and intensified the very idea of the national identity. We feel that what Gombrowicz tries to achieve is not so much an outright rejection but rather a paradoxical strengthening and saving of one's sense of ethnic and social bonds. In a few important fragments of the *Diary*, Gombrowicz forcefully articulates this point of view. After presenting his principal thesis—that Polishness is something to be overcome—he writes (referring probably to the fierce controversies around his satirical presentation of the Polish émigré circles in *Trans-Atlantyk*),

I did not feel at all that I was striking at Polishness; on the contrary, I had the impression that I was rousing and enlivening it. How could that be? After all, didn't I want to liberate them from their Polishness? Yes, indeed ... but this challenge really had a strange feature, thanks to which a Pole became more of a Pole the less he was devoted to Poland.

The ensuing series of arguments and counterarguments leads to the inevitable conclusion: "My desire to 'overcome Poland' was synonymous with the desire to strengthen our individual Polishness."[8] It has to be added that in the later phase of his career Gombrowicz shifted the emphasis from "individual Polishness" to Polishness as a complex of collective and nationalistic sentiments—a very important change that intensified Gombrowicz's paradoxical "take it and leave it" stance and let him eulogize such authors as Sienkiewicz.

At stake is also a vision of the Polish literature, art, and culture as areas of an individual and collective struggle for independence. As it is, the author of *Ferdydurke* starts with an acknowledgment of the secondary or even provincial status of modern Polish literature, which in his view results in the repressed inferiority complex discernible in virtually all works produced in Poland in the twentieth century. Gombrowicz touches upon one of the consequences of this situation—the Polish artists instinctively try to adopt and imitate the Western literary models in order to absorb and make them their own. This path, though, only deepens a sense of dependence and secondariness. As it has already been hinted, it is an axiom in Gombrowicz's agonistic anthropology that identity is something constructed and man is shaped by others. Thus, the only chance to win identity is through opposition and resistance. In the context of literary history this usually means that writers should write against themselves, transcending and at the same time rejecting themselves. This gesture is translated by Gombrowicz into the following aesthetic and existential agenda articulated in the *Diary*: "the only means by which I, a Pole, could become a fully valuable phenomenon in culture, was this one: not to hide my immaturity, but to admit it; and with this admission to break away from it; and to make a steed out of the tiger that was devouring me up to now."[9] The writer stresses the imperative to be stronger, more independent, and effective. This need, though, can be met only through contradiction, denial, and negation. Again, it should be repeated that such a negation has nothing to do with nihilism. Writing against others and oneself implies inventing a new form and a new consciousness that elevate the writer and make him or her sovereign and self-reliant. This is particularly true in reference to the cultures usually seen as secondary and derivative. In an important letter to Czesław Miłosz, included in the *Diary*, Gombrowicz explains why his radical critique of Polishness and contemporary Polish culture is not just an aesthetic program: "I attack Polish form because it is my form, because all of my works desire to be, in a certain sense ... a revision of the modern man in relation to form, to form which is not a result of him but which is formed 'between' people."[10] There is a paradoxical double bind here (often overlooked by critics writing about Gombrowicz). On the one hand, the writer rejects his Polishness in strongest possible terms, attacking the whole cultural, indeed civilizational, context of contemporary Polish literature. On the other hand, he does so in the name of the maximally enhanced sense of Polishness that turns out to be not only a figure of self-will (self-construction, self-reliance, self-definition) but also a manifestation of the will to power. This is Gombrowicz's mantra: to overcome Polishness is to redefine and reactivate it.

Hence his preference for specific literary epochs (Polish sixteenth- and seventeenth-century works) and conventions (particularly private memoirs and diaries). In his novels and plays, especially those written in the last two decades of his life, Gombrowicz followed those traditional literary genres that embraced linguistic artificiality and ambiguity. Typically, the writer turned to the works with the first-person narrative that was a guarantee of the presence of strong and distinct identity, both in its individual and national—ethnic, linguistic, communal—dimension. He was especially fascinated with the Baroque aesthetic of ornate, convoluted syntax based on fancy vocabulary and eccentric phraseological units. In her pioneer study of Gombrowicz's oeuvre, Ewa M. Thompson accurately characterized the rhetorical and stylistic peculiarities of his prose (the quote refers to *Trans-Atlantyk* but her statements may be easily generalized):

> The narrator ... tells the story in a manner similar to that used by *raconteurs*, as opposed to writers. His sentences are spoken sentences, full of exclamatory words, unfinished phrases and the spelling which follows pronunciation instead of orthography ... This kind of narration brings forth the elements of intonation and natural turns of phrase which often disappear from written texts. The speaker ... is an actor as well as a narrator: his rhythms of speech and abundant colloquialisms require reading aloud.[11]

It is not easy to assess Gombrowicz's own attitude to the overblown, bombast, and highly declamatory style of the historical oral and narrative genres. Many critics and readers have come to the conclusion that the writer simply wanted to mock the traditional Polish styles in what might be termed the postmodern frame of mind, with parody, pastiche, and playful imitation as sanctioned (and favored) rhetorical strategies. On such a reading, the *Diary* is standardly interpreted as a carnivalesque travesty of the personal memoirs popular in sixteenth- and seventeenth-century Poland, while *Trans-Atlantyk* is perceived as a deliberately exaggerated caricature of the Polish Baroque genre of *gawęda* (spoken, colloquial, free-flowing narrative with elements of the picaresque convention). According to this view, Gombrowicz deconstructed the traditional Polish literary narratives as well as the ideological programs sometimes conveyed by them, including the rhetoric and ideology of Polishness.

Let us repeat that such a view of Gombrowicz's works is appropriate but definitely does not give justice to all its ambivalences and dilemmas. While obviously critical in spirit, the body of his fiction—particularly the later texts—lends itself to a different interpretation in which the writer may be seen as conservative, reactionary, and strangely nostalgic in his stubborn withdrawals to past standards and traditional models—these are mocked but also preserved, uplifted, and glorified. Actually, some of his best works—*The Marriage, Operetta, Trans-Atlantyk*, or the *Diary*—read like teasing celebrations of the Polish literary heritage and its canonical styles. By force of the same paradox, the author of *Ferdydurke* does emphatically distance himself from the world's prevailing literary systems and traditions (his prime example being the history of French literature which in Gombrowicz's view is *the* example of world literature). The problem with the so-called great national literatures, goes the argument, is that they provide writers with ready models and strong identities that apparently do not need to be examined and questioned, and this is the main reason of their paradoxical, and usually unacknowledged, immaturity, and naivety— when not challenged and opposed (and finally overcome), the identity is an empty signifier with a zero or minimal potential of meaning. For the Polish writer, immaturity can be exorcized only when it is addressed and cross-examined, and this is usually done by the artists unsure of their identities and questioning them. On the rhetorical (literary, stylistic, even purely linguistic) level this exorcism takes on the form of parody that, surprisingly but logically, reinforces the parodied manner, reduplicating and reactivating the model it mimics. This double effect is discernible almost everywhere in Gombrowicz. Accordingly, one has to read him on two levels, so to say, with an awareness of an undercurrent of irony that constantly reverses the meanings, messages, and even morals of his work.

Let us take a closer look at *Trans-Atlantyk*. This novelistic fantasy, based in part on Gombrowicz's gloomy experiences in Argentina, is a frontal attack on the idea of Polishness, expressed in the satirical portraits, most often caricatures, of the Polish officials and petty diplomats met by the narrator in the capital city of Buenos Aires. Gombrowicz reveals the subsequent layers of Polish nationalistic chauvinism, xenophobia, and skin-deep patriotism, displaying the characters' hypocrisy and pretense. This is accompanied by a truly distinctive style, a mixture of the bombastic Polish Baroque language and contemporary peasant idiolects, the former prevailing and shaping the peculiar tone of the narrative. Here is the novel's opening paragraph in Danuta Borchardt's translation:

> I feel the need to convey to my Family, to my kin and friends, this the beginning of my adventures, now ten years long, in the Argentinian

capital. I'm not inviting anyone to eat these old noodles of mine, the turnips that may even be raw, because they're in a common pewter bowl, Lean, Paltry, even Embarrassing withal, cooked in the oil of my Sin, of my Embarrassments, these my heavy grits, Dark, together with this black gruel of mine, oh, you better not put them in your mouth, unless 'tis for my eternal damnation and degradation, on my Life's unending road and up this arduous and wearisome Mountain of mine.[12]

As already mentioned, in *Trans-Atlantyk* Gombrowicz uses the style and rhetoric of the old Polish genre of *gawęda*—the free-flowing oral tale characterized by mannerisms and archaisms—as well as the Baroque convention of the personal memoir describing the extravagant and colorful life of the seventeenth- and eighteenth-century Polish nobility. In particular, Gombrowicz refers to Jan Chryzostom Pasek's *Memoirs* (*Pamiętniki*, written in the 1690s and published in 1836) and Henryk Rzewuski's *Memoirs of Seweryn Soplica, Esq.* (*Pamiątki Imć Pana Seweryna Soplicy*, 1839) as his favorite models. The result is a dense prose full of repetitions, unusual idioms, and colloquial phraseology, with bizarre turns, odd phrases, and capitalized words (awkward also to the Polish ear). It is hard not to agree with Danuta Borchardt when she calls *Trans-Atlantyk* "his [Gombrowicz's] most untranslatable work."[13]

The ironic dimension of Gombrowicz's Argentinian novel is quite evident. By reactivating the Baroque codes and conventions of the Polish diaspora in Buenos Aires at the outbreak of the Second World War, the author of *Ferdydurke* produced (as Ewa Płonowska Ziarek notices) the "parodic repetition of an obsolete and degraded cultural formation, no longer in service of the preservation of the national identity."[14] Both the narrator and the Polish expatriates portrayed in the novel use an archaic and pretentious language, turning to phrases from the canonical works of classical Polish literature. The effect is perverse: "When Gombrowicz turns to the provincial and parochial prose of seventeenth-century memoirs, he intends not to lend them a new veneer of nobility or nostalgia in the manner of Mickiewicz or Sienkiewicz, but, on the contrary, to intensify their ugliness—to turn them into the unworkable caricature of national literature."[15] The same refers to the narrative and language of national identity—they are shown to be artificial and highly rhetorical, products of inferiority complex that are hardly hidden behind pompous words, truisms, and clichés.

What many critics have failed to notice (or have decided not to notice), however, is that the old Polish convention of *gawęda*, so central to *Trans-Atlantyk*, is in itself self-ironic and self-conscious. Like most Baroque literature, it is sharply aware of its conventionality and rhetoricity, turning upon itself and offering contradictory statements. What one often finds in the memoirs of the Polish Baroque authors is the carnivalesque spirit manifesting itself in the form of the spontaneous flow of narrative that, in its oral capacity (constantly stressed), exaggerates and mocks its own gestures; as a matter of fact, the moments of exaggeration, extravagance, and excess define the character of *Trans-Atlantyk*. So when Gombrowicz turns to parody and pastiche, he simply imitates and thus confirms (and affirms) the rhetoric of *gawęda*. He by no means writes against the Baroque conventions and artistic sensibility. On the contrary, he recognizes their validity and unlocks their potential. In the same way, one cannot say that the Polish novelist just dismisses the idea of Polishness. Rather, he raises its stakes and asserts its latent power in the strongest possible terms.

A sense of affirmation is present in Gombrowicz's prefaces to the first three editions of *Trans-Atlantyk*.[16] These short texts are agonistic and belligerent. However, they also offer a program—and each program is by definition positive. Here, as elsewhere, Gombrowicz's project involves overcoming Polishness: "to reveal, legalize another dimension of feeling which orders a human being to defend himself against his nation as against any collective force."[17] The idea is clear, and it finds its manifestation in the plot of the novel. Less clear, and surprising to many readers, is the writer's appeal to the nation as the base for a revaluation and redefinition of Polishness: "to find oneself both in the nation and outside of the nation—even above the nation. Outside and above—so that we can create a nation in our image and likeness."[18] Significantly, when the novelist writes about a "national self-examination" and a "revision of our relationship to the nation," both phrases point to the idea of the nation (with its history, tradition, and heritage), the idea desperately in need of reformulation but still valid and legitimate. This is stressed in the 1957 preface: "to obtain—this is most important—freedom from the Polish form, while being a Pole to be someone larger and higher than a Pole!"[19] Thus, although Gombrowicz seems to reject the idea of identity, at the same time he wants us to rethink and reaffirm it. All in all, the novelist attacks the idea of Polishness in its name and (so to say) under its banner, which makes it both a critique and an act of veneration. One can say that Gombrowicz deconstructs the narrative of Polish national identity (*polskość*) in order to immunize and thus strengthen it.

It is by now clear that the program of overcoming Polishness and winning a new (heightened and doubly secured) sense of collective identity, while ostensibly turned toward the future, was in fact strongly influenced by the writer's pure nostalgia for the golden age of the Polish history, in particular the sixteenth and seventeenth centuries when Poland was a multinational kingdom and a major European player. Gombrowicz's is a bizarre example of the conservative and retrograde utopia: a criticism of the contemporary, a yearning for the distant past, and a vision of the reestablished identity. Importantly, this utopia is paradoxical and antagonistic. It is based on the premise of a constant struggle for Polishness—*polskość* is for Gombrowicz a challenge, an act of resistance and a ceaseless interrogation of oneself and one's relationship to the collective context (ethnic group, nation, language, race). It is as if one was proclaiming two contradictory truths, not in order to arrive at some synthesis but, on the contrary, to accentuate the inevitable ambiguity of denial becoming affirmation and vice versa. It should not come as a surprise, then, that in the last months of his life Gombrowicz wrote, "Some of my compatriots regard me as an exceptionally Polish author— and I may well be both very anti-Polish and very Polish—or perhaps Polish because anti-Polish; because the Pole comes to life in me spontaneously, freely, to the extent in which he becomes stronger than I."[20] While tentative, these words contain Gombrowicz's final credo—or perhaps a mock-credo.

The author of *Ferdydurke* has often been called a cosmopolitan writer. The label is hardly appropriate. Throughout his whole career, Gombrowicz was interested almost solely in the Polish culture, seen by him as a minority culture struggling for recognition. As a matter of fact, he rarely referred to other cultures and the concept of world literature would mean nothing to him.[21] In his view, a literary/cultural framework can emerge as distinct and "authentic" (the word was always of relative value to the writer and should be put in quotation marks) only in direct opposition to other ones. This refers in particular to minor, peripheral and secondary cultures dominated and shaped by the major ones. As it has already been hinted, such an agonistic vision of a culture overcoming its limitations mirrored Gombrowicz's belief that individual identity, constructed and inescapably distorted by the "interhuman church," is something to be created, affirmed, and imposed on others. Accordingly, a national literature has to battle for its sovereignty and defend its uniqueness. What we find in Gombrowicz, especially in reference to the problem of identity, is the language of power and domination. This adds to the piquancy of his prose but at the same time leaves the reader dumbfounded. All in all, the writer provides more questions than answers. Maybe this is what he intended—ambivalent about the issues of individual and national (Polish) identity, Gombrowicz maintained his ironic stance and kept on multiplying paradoxes.

Notes

1   Tomislav Z. Longinović, "I, Witold Gombrowicz: Formal Abjection and the Power of Writing in *A Kind of Testament*," in *Gombrowicz's Grimaces: Modernism, Gender, Nationality*, edited by Ewa Płonowska Ziarek (Albany: State University of New York Press, 1998), 33. Ewa Płonowska Ziarek, "Introduction," in *Gombrowicz's Grimaces*, 7. George Z. Gasyna, *Polish, Hybrid, and Otherwise: Exilic Discourse in Joseph Conrad and Witold Gombrowicz* (New York: Bloomsbury, 2013), 3–4.

2   Witold Gombrowicz, *A Kind of Testament*, edited by Dominique de Roux, translated by Alastair Hamilton and with an introduction by Maurice Nadeau (London: Calder and Boyars, 1973), 154.

3   Ibid., 77 (the first two quotes) and 51.

4 Ibid., 31. It should be noted that the original (Polish) version of *Testament* is presented as a conversation with the French critic Dominique de Roux (in fact, Gombrowicz was approached by de Roux but wrote all the questions and answers himself); in the English translation there is no information about the interviewer, and the text has a form of a series of autobiographical fragments.

5 Katarzyna Chmielewska, *Strategie podmiotu. Dziennik Witolda Gombrowicza* (Warszawa: IBL PAN, 2010), 170.

6 Ibid., 31.

7 Ibid., 172.

8 Witold Gombrowicz, *Diary*, translated by Lillian Vallee (New Haven, CT: Yale University Press, 2012), 297–300.

9 Ibid., 207.

10 Ibid., 19.

11 Ewa M. Thompson, *Witold Gombrowicz* (Woodbridge: Twayne, 1979), 80.

12 Witold Gombrowicz, *Trans-Atlantyk: An Alternate Translation*, translated by Danuta Borchardt (New Haven, CT: Yale University Press, 2014), 1.

13 Danuta Borchardt, "Translator's Note," in Witold Gombrowicz, *Trans-Atlantyk*, vii. Similar remarks were articulated by Carolyn French and Nina Karsov, the first English translators of the novel, who write, for example, that *Trans-Atlantyk* is "too Polish to be Englished" ("Translators' Note," xxii).

14 Ewa Płonowska Ziarek, "The Scar of the Foreigner and the Fold of the Baroque: National Affiliations and Homosexuality in Gombrowicz's *Trans-Atlantyk*," in *Gombrowicz's Grimaces*, 218.

15 Ibid., 224.

16 Actually, two book editions and a journal edition. Several fragments of *Trans-Atlantyk* were first published in the literary journal *Kultura* in 1951—Gombrowicz added an introductory note. The first full edition of the novel appeared two years later in Paris (Paris: Instytut Literacki, 1953). In 1957 it was published for the first time in Poland (Warsaw: Spółdzielnia Wydawnicza Czytelnik, 1957) with still another (third) preface from the novelist. Only this last one has been translated into English (included in Witold Gombrowicz, *Trans-Atlantyk. An Alternate Translation*).

17 Witold Gombrowicz, "Preface to the 1957 Edition," in *Trans-Atlantyk: An Alternate Translation*, xvi.

18 Witold Gombrowicz, "Przedmowa do *Trans-Atlantyku* (1953)," in *Trans-Atlantyk* (Kraków: Wydawnictwo Literackie, 1993), 139.

19 Gombrowicz, "Preface to the 1957 Edition," xvi.

20 Gombrowicz, *A Kind of Testament*, 105.

21 There are references in Gombrowicz's texts to several non-Polish writers like Montaigne, Kafka, or Mann, but these are mainly brief acknowledgments. More typically, the *Diary* includes fierce criticism of such authors as Dante or Proust as well as ironic comments on Gombrowicz's contemporaries.

9

Beyond Identity: John Ashbery's and Frank O'Hara's Impact on Polish Poetry

Kacper Bartczak

The early 1980s in Poland saw the cracks in the communist regime's monolith grow deeper and wider, which ultimately led to its collapse at the end of the decade. Subsequently, the 1990s became a troubled scene of social and economic changes. Poland joined the West, and—for better or worse—the precariousness of capitalism. One of the key literary developments of this period was the reception of the New York poets, primarily John Ashbery and Frank O'Hara, in the Polish literary culture. The extended process in which New York poets were received in the 1980s, 1990s, and beyond ranks among the most important facets of Poland's cultural transformation. Even though today's political winds in Poland are very different, the traces of the New York School's influence are a lasting and evolving presence.

The story of this American import is a tale of poetic communication beyond linguistic and cultural barriers. It involves international friendships, artistic dialogues, daring translation efforts, heated domestic debates, and questions of influence. It reveals feats of theoretically advanced scholarship, where questions of translatability touch on the intertwined concepts of linguistic communication, identity, subjectivity, and originality.

In Poland of the mid-1980s the ground for encountering the New York avant-garde was ripe. Coupled with a sense of political exhaustion was a parallel crisis in the poetic culture. The Nowa Fala movement, the most exciting poetic novelty of the 1970s, had not managed to resolve the aesthetic dilemmas that defined its initial rebellion against the dominance of the great masters. Postulating a return to everyday diction in connection with critical analysis of the propaganda, the Nowa Fala poets were stopped short of drawing far-reaching consequences from their own diagnoses. The towering presence of the central tradition prevented them from moving beyond the paradigm defined by the postwar Polish poetry. As a result, the dominance of Zbigniew Herbert's hieratic style of moral austerity and Czesław Miłosz's formula of universalized witness to history still held fast, pushing the major representatives of Nowa Fala to metaphysically underpinned heights—a stylistic whose imperviousness to historical change equaled its antiquated vacuity.[1] This retreat cut off the Nowa Fala impulse from novel ways of engaging the political-vs-the private divide.[2] In short, there was a growing sense of the exhaustion of the all-too-local debates. Polish poetry on its own was unable to see how a widening of the register variety—already apparent to the New Wave—could lead to a rethinking of the status of the speaking subject, its originality, its intertextual and political entanglements.

The situation was ripe for a much-needed external impulse. It is precisely in the ways in which the New York aesthetic artifice repositions the private/public, blurring the boundaries between language in general and the poetic subject's "personal" utterance, that the styles of New York poets proved—in the long run—capable of nourishing the Polish poetry. Together with models of lyric subjectivity, they radically changed the Polish poem's approach to communication in language. Language itself, as an indeterminate and opaque medium, became an object of exploration, an endeavor in which Polish poetry and critical discourse joined discussions over the legacies of international modernism. In short, the New York influence—both at its reception and in continuations—amounts to a paradigm shift in the Polish thinking about the place and mode of poetic expression in the dynamic and globalized world of the late twentieth century.

The New York poetic influence revolves around the reception of two poets, Frank O'Hara and John Ashbery. The famous "blue" issue of *Literatura na Świecie*[3] did contain poems by Kenneth Koch and James Schuyler, and they were also translated later, but it is the translated work of O'Hara and Ashbery that has commanded the bulk of poetic and critical interest. However, it must also be observed that any closer perspective soon reveals crucial differences between the reception of O'Hara and Ashbery. It is precisely in those differences that the story of the entire import is revealed in its entirety, presenting its host of actors—poets, translators, critics, editors, and readers. In the end, it is the various ways in which they translated, interpreted, and misinterpreted their American colleagues over the period of more than thirty years that amounts to an ultimately unified process within which Polish poetry has received a tremendous boost that pushed it toward a newly emergent globalized world.

Frank O'Hara and the Polish "O'Harists"

The story of O'Hara's initial impact in Poland is a strangely productive comedy of errors, harsh poetic polemics, and a general upheaval of a poetic community in search for renewed self-understanding. This general "vigorous mudslinging"[4] amounts to a mixture of gains and losses, the former related to poetry's return to everyday detail while the latter constituting a not so productive misreading of O'Hara himself. This initial phase of the story, revolving around an unexpected career of a largely misinformed, polemically coined term "O'Harism," has by now been very well researched. In this section, I will review the main findings of the critical commentary and expand them with a view on what it was that the young Polish poets were trying to do, what they feared, and what, perhaps unavoidably, they missed.

Piotr Sommer, one of the fathers of the change, tells how he came across Frank O'Hara in the early 1980s and how he "instantly knew what O'Hara was doing."[5] Sommer's instinctual response brilliantly saw O'Hara as just the right kind of remedy to the deadlock of the Polish poetics in the mid-1980s. In the "blue" issue Sommer presented a selection of his translations of O'Hara's poems from the 1950s and 1960s, although this initial presentation did not feature such titles as "The Day Lady Died" or "A Step Away from Them." These, together with O'Hara's other characteristic urban and social peregrinations, were found in an independent collection titled *Twoja pojedynczość*. Tadeusz Pióro has observed how the two presentations gave the Polish reader a "Sommer's O'Hara"—a selection that favors O'Hara the peripatetic realist at the cost of the poet's longer and more surrealist poems.[6] Nevertheless, these early presentations, supported by fragments from Perloff's *Frank O'Hara: A Poet Among Painters*, Sommer's own insightful essay, O'Hara's mock manifesto "Personism," and his essay on American art, did get the Polish reader in touch with an ample, valid, and representative group of titles, bringing into the Polish language a distinctive formal and aesthetic proposal.

It must be noted at this point that the "blue" issue was not devoted solely to O'Hara. This richly composed book-length collection also contained poems by Ashbery, Schuyler, Koch, Ashbery's intro to O'Hara's *Collected Poems*, a long interview with Ashbery conducted by Sommer, as well as work by other representatives of the New York avant-garde milieu. Nevertheless, the early phase of the New York poets' reception in Poland revolved around O'Hara. Over the years, O'Hara has inspired a wide spectrum of Polish poets, but the initial moment of reception involves poets associated with the Kraków-based *bruLion* magazine. Born mostly in the 1960s, these predominantly male and urban poets were the first generation of Polish postwar poets who strongly felt the need to operate on more private and individualist terms, beyond the formula of the opposition toward the communist regime. Oppositional they were for sure, although their rebellion went far beyond a particular historic political struggle, for they aimed at scandalizing the entire spectrum of the Polish cultural and spiritual mindset, not sparing the highest ideals of Poland's religious paradigms. Marcin Świetlicki and Jacek Podsiadło, the two key poets of the group, felt cramped within antiquated schemes of value derived from the mid-century national, political, historical, and religious debates, and they were ready to transgress all sorts of taboo lines.

Strange as it sounds from today's vantage point, one of those taboos proved to be writing exactly the kind of apparently directionless, spur-of-the moment poem-as-report from loosely planned pleasures of the quotidian—what Frank O'Hara famously called "I do this I do that poem," and what some of his academic commentators called the "walk poem."[7] There is no regular evidence of any extensive perusal of O'Hara's output by the major representatives of the *bruLion* formation. Rather, we have to do with an authentically hectic, pleasure-oriented pursuit of a poetic novelty that nevertheless must have been generally liberating and inspirational for what Marcin Świetlicki, Jacek Podsiadło, and other poets of the group were trying to do. And it seemed to some that what they were trying to do was nothing short of striking a treacherous blow at the heart of the national poetic culture.

"O'Harism" was the title of a harshly polemic piece against Świetlicki, published in a *bruLion* issue in 1990 and authored by Krzysztof Koehler, a young poet from Kraków. Koehler did not bother to give justice to any poems by Świetlicki, much less O'Hara, and felt justified in a defiant bashing of Świetlicki on the grounds that the latter naively dared to forgo poetry's conventional and thus more objective side, dabbling in the privately trivial, thus wasting everyone's time. The piece denied the poet's freedom to deal with everyday contingency, thus accusing Świetlicki of "boring [readers] with pronouncements" concerning worthless trivia.[8] Świetlicki quickly responded in kind, standing firmly by his right to experiment, not just with convention but with the very notion of what is important. Świetlicki brilliantly pointed out the general artistic necessity of experimenting in order to identify "that obscure, undefined side," related to either the reader or a general interlocutor, a "distant someone" the communication with whom might be healthily uncharted by any sort of economies of importance.[9]

Symptomatically for that phase of the New York influence, Koehler did not mention O'Hara even once. His term—which sounded a bit like the name of a disease—had no substance, as the author never said what he thought of the Świetlicki–O'Hara connection, yet its frequent use in ensuing debates secured it a sort of a working definition.[10] Importantly, at the moment of its coinage, the term signaled anxiety: for Koehler "O'Harism" was a specter encroaching on the uncertain future of Polish poetry's sovereignty. Sadly, fear and bias precluded any familiarity with the source. However, what about the *bruLion* poets' familiarity with O'Hara?

It is instructive to note the differences between the tough *bruLion* existential stances and Frank O'Hara's poetry. Świetlicki, Podsiadło, Baran, Jaworski, Śliwka, and others were angry iconoclasts on the lookout for viable positions amidst a spreading collapse of the Polish reality. As critics observed, their gritty masculine negation of received ideas was not only an anti-ideological outcry but also a sign of disorientation.[11] On the brink of the 1990s, Świetlicki and Podsiadło were finding allies in American poets, predominantly O'Hara, in reaching toward isolated everyday episodes, delineated in opposition to systemic hypocrisies, not just communist but also Polish Catholic and neoliberal ones. Theirs was a radical "privatization" of poetic dealing with experience,[12] a loathing of ideologies realized as heroic separateness within a more palpable and authentic "now."

Their dominant mode was a turn to the individual self, seeking authenticity of experience. "Personality was the true main hero of the '90s," wrote the critic Piotr Śliwinski much later.[13] It is here that the paths of those poets divert from a much more subtle and complex compositions of the personal and the biographical found in O'Hara. Where he is offering an expansion of the self whose identity is playful and communicative, in his remote Polish cousins the subject formation undergoes a condensation. Joanna Orska, commenting on these erratic exchanges, noted how the *bruLion* poets, later also identified as "barbarians" caught in a duel against "classicists,"[14] won a battle for the everyday detail overthrowing the ethos of the anticommunist tradition, while unknowingly embracing a deeper traditional layer, a Byronic archetype afforded by Polish Romanticism.[15] Such maneuvering effectively left O'Hara out of the picture. Whatever stood behind the devastations of tradition, in Świetlicki's eyes the gesture was cathartic, ushering in the first truly twentieth-century Polish poetry. Paradoxically though, the impetus itself may have contained a preclusive conservatism. According to Joanna Niżyńska, by lowering the register of poetry and thus performing a Bloomian "kenosis" in relation to the dominant traditions—a separation and "emptying out" of the predecessor's power—the *bruLion* poets overrated their status as radical novelty and overlooked what was truly new in O'Hara himself, "removing O'Hara from O'Hara."[16]

But perhaps it was too early. At the heart of O'Hara's poetics lies the common ground for all New York School poets: a pluralistic subjectivity— always in the process of dynamic, nonessentialist self-formation—merging with the artificially arranged environment of the poem, no matter if this environment consists of realistic detail (O'Hara), bravado linguistic eccentricity (Ashbery), or aestheticized diarism (Schuyler). Central to those constructions is an experimental subjectivity that simply annuls the dominance of the biographical fact, not renouncing it but making it open to the poetic intrusion.[17] And the true bonding element of the poetic and the biographical, something that separates New Yorkers from their confessional colleagues in America, is an improvised composition of the present moment based not on the cumulative contents of the past—biography, history, tradition—but on a still adamic faith in a now always slipping into a future. There is a renouncing of knowingness, an amateurish program of believing in an uncharted present, what both O'Hara and Ashbery carry out from their nonspecialist interaction with the visual arts, that constitutes the basic bloodstream of their poetry.[18] Immersion in the moment, as immersion in a work of abstract expressionist art, will push back embittered analyses of one's personal past, cancelling the idea of the subject as a site of insulated authenticity.

It is a characteristic omission that Piotr Sommer, whose perceptive early essay on O'Hara was part of the "blue" issue, fails to draw any clear separation lines between the author of *Lunch Poems* and Robert Lowell.[19] But Sommer's brilliant instinctive feel for O'Hara in that essay did point out a feature that puts serious distance between O'Hara and the *bruLion* group: while the Polish poets were individualists of angry separateness, Sommer shows how O'Hara's urban peregrinations are in fact drafts for inclusivity, not wanderings of a lonely rebel. Sommer spots brilliantly that O'Hara's notorious name-dropping, his flirt with a coterie aesthetic, is a form of invitation for others to join the crowd.[20] It is this opening, ultimately leading to a renewed interaction with communal subjectivity, that was more fully engaged in those Polish poets who were able to read O'Hara next to his friend John Ashbery.

John Ashbery, Bohdan Zadura, Andrzej Sosnowski

If the recoil from the communal toward individual subjectivity was a measure against disorientation, what stood behind this situation was a tectonic shift in the understanding of history. Even without Francis Fukuyama's debatable thesis, the Polish literary culture needed to confront a serious historical change that could be considered on three levels: first, it affected the status of literature and the condition of literary magazines and literary publishers; secondly, the function of the writer was also altered: from a shepherd of the community to a more privately oriented author of poems;[21] finally, history itself—its mechanisms and rationality—required a revision. The iron grip of the former system provided the Polish poet with a sense of order to the world—the poet stood as witness to an oppressive regime. Its demise signaled the evacuation of exactly the thing that the Polish poetry had on offer in the ongoing twentieth-century Polish-American poetic commerce. Writing in 2004, Charles Altieri commented soberly how there had been a time when the Polish poets' sense of history provided just the means for stabilizing one's understanding of experience the American poets may have needed.[22] Now, the tables got turned. The rigid structures vanished, and the Polish poet stood amidst a sense of unprecedented uncertainty. Jamie Fergusson captured that atmosphere when he asked, "What's a poet to do when the pressure of political censorship is removed and everything can be said?"[23]

The New York School influence worked as a midwife for Polish literature joining the aftermath of modernism, with pressures put on the notions of truth-as-reference, communicative intention, authorial identity, and translation and translatability. It is this cluster of concepts that also inform the poetics of John Ashbery, and the New York stylistics understood as a collective phenomenon. Properly understood, Polish poetry was changed not by O'Hara or Ashbery taken separately but by a wide cultural undertaking that involved those poets, their New York friends, their translators in Poland, and an enormous bulk of publications—including many later issues of *Literature na Świecie*, not to mention an impressive body of academic research.[24] It is true, however, that it is the mercurial poetics of John Ashbery, a poet who had challenged the poetry discourse in America, that is the nucleus of the New York School's pushing the Polish poetry on to novel tracks. In this section, I will discuss how Ashbery's poetry nourished two distinctive Polish poets, Bohdan Zadura and Andrzej Sosnowski, who paved the way for many others.[25]

Bohdan Zadura met John Ashbery in May 1980. Ashbery and other American writers were invited by *Literatura na Świecie*, and besides Warsaw they also traveled to several other Polish cities, including Zadura's hometown, Puławy. Zadura met with Ashbery at that time and later revisited him in New York. The exchange resulted in Zadura's trying his hand at translating poems from Ashbery's *Houseboat Days* and *Shadow Train* in which he was greatly helped by Piotr Sommer.[26] Together with Sommer's work on O'Hara's poems in the early 1980s, those translations constitute the historical beginning of the New York School's presence in Poland.[27]

At the end of the 1970s Bohdan Zadura had already been a recognized poet, using the classicist stylistics but also searching for approaches to the quotidian, independently of the Nowa Fala poets. A great example of this search is a poem entitled "August 1st, 1979, 7:45 a.m.–22:45 p.m.; 14 hours with Piotr Sommer," which appeared in Zadura's 1983 volume *Zejście na ląd*. The piece is a record of the meeting announced in the title. Had it been published after 1986, the poem would have certainly been tagged "O'Harist." There is a need to chronicle an important event by noting the minutiae of the day, a classicist poet's attempt to merge the rational communicative level with everyday contingencies. Zadura goes for modulated naturalness of everyday speech, achieved within controlled free verse, and displays attentive intelligence that Frank O'Hara would certainly have appreciated.

The poem also shows that reading Ashbery in the early 1980s was just the boost that Zadura had been ready for. The key issue here was communication as translation. Zadura's attempt at translating Ashbery at that moment was one of those episodes making literary history in which fascination and poetic craft overcome the language barrier. But the fact that Zadura's English was not perfect worked in his favor. The Polish poet took all the famed Ashbery difficulties in his stride, treating them as part of the task. Translation becomes an exercise in close reading, an ongoing negotiation between languages and interlocutors. Zadura consulted native users of English and found that they were also baffled by Ashbery's poems. It was an encouraging and illuminating news: there is a difficulty to communication even in one's own language. Advanced linguistic exchanges involve a slipperiness of meanings and understanding requires much more than automatic following of the principle of equivalence. It turns out that a poet from a different linguistic area may be a better interlocutor of a poem than a native speaker.[28] Language comes to the fore as a nonessential and opaque medium of interaction.

I imagine Zadura was thrilled to discover the messiness and accidentality of communicative encounters overtaking the very place of the "topic" of the poem. This is the case with Ashbery's "Paradoxes and Oxymorones," one of the poems Zadura translated for No i wiesz. As we remember, this poem imitates an entire environment of communication, including its distractions and gaps. What matters is staying with the very process of pursuing the trail of connections and disconnections, an exasperating chase that surprisingly amounts to a proximity with oneself and the reader/interlocutor: "And the poem / Has set me softly down beside you."[29]

What Zadura found was liberation through the embrace of linguistic impurity. As he comments in an essay, the immediate attraction was the use of the marginal parts of speech, especially conjunctions, and the discovery that a playful approach to their syntactic positioning produces logical twists and turns that expand the poem. Commenting on their use in Ashbery, Zadura wrote, "[Ashbery's poems] opened me to a completely new way of speaking, to a new kind of linguistic energy."[30] He goes on in the essay to quote from the title poem of the volume Shadow Train—"the banana shakes on its stem, / but the strawberry is liquid and cool"[31]—which leads him to a refreshing discovery of what Ashbery had called, early on in his career, "the logic of strange position."[32] This idea, which in Ashbery reaches back to Gertrude Stein and the surrealist poets and painters, was what actually saved Zadura as a poet, by loosening up the strictures of the classicist perfections he had already achieved.

To Zadura, the "logic of strange position," far from a call for abandoning logic, is a return to the capacities of syntax. The poem as a testing field of dialogic communication remains at the center of his interest, and in fact dialogue is precisely what Zadura is having with Ashbery. The volumes in which Ashbery's presence is most clearly felt are *Starzy znajomi* (*Old Friends*, 1986) and *Prześwietlone zdjęcia* (*Overexposed photographs*, 1990). The former contains a much-discussed poem "John Ashbery i ja" ["John Ashbery and I"]. Commenting on Ashbery's metaphor that brings together a train cutting through a landscape and a zipper, Zadura's poem notes, "I know more than I am able to name / in this case it is the other way around."[33] The sentence points to Ashbery's own interest in the limits of expression, as well as to the Polish poet's friendly bafflement at the surprising logic contained in the surrealist metaphor. At another layer, it merges perfect Polish syntax and logic with the possibility of their collapsing, the second clause raising the case for linguistic redundancy, so much trusted by Ashbery and so much shunned by the Polish central tradition.

This kind of playfulness was used to exhilarating effects in *Overexposed Photographs*. Most poems here record events of the poet's visit to Hungary in 1986. They are displays of linguistic adherence to the spontaneous messiness of everyday episodes. Importantly, the poems are set in a foreign language reality, which again foregrounds questions of communication and translation.[34] Light is thrown back on the Polish language, as the poems expose its polysemic capacities. Also, the witty meanders show communication and the speaker's identity to be inextricably related to the language's capacity for error, as well as accurate reference. Garrulity meets silence in these poems, as words and understanding keep missing each other, almost as in Ashbery's poems. And yet, the entire volume amounts to a discussion with Ashbery. Zadura clearly wants his "photographs" to be precise, despite the impinging blurriness, more precise and disciplined than Ashbery's wildly discordant habitats of thought. In Zadura, the language's centrifugal side remains in constant and palpable check by the exigencies of form (the sonnet) and the contours of the actual biographic episode. In the end Zadura will comment, "A poem is patient / That's true But not a donkey However hard /you drive it it won't bear everything."[35]

In his dialogue with Ashbery, Zadura remodeled his classicism and transferred it to late twentieth-century conditions in response to the increased rate of information exchange. The line that Zadura refused to cross was a more radical cancellation of reference. The closest he comes to the Ashberian degree of forsaking reference is in some poems in *Overexposed photographs*, like "Gliders" or "Nieznany szczegół" ["An Unknown Detail"]. Both are loose compositions in which the makings of a landscape engage accidental detail, personal reminiscence, or abstract reflection. The latter poem's case is instructive—opening the volume with this lyric, Zadura decides to follow it up immediately with a poem-footnote on the next page. "Korepetycje dla Wacka" ["Make-up Lessons for Wacek"] functions as additional context decoding the indeterminacies of the former poem whose loose threads are now reconnected to anchor it in a specific moment of public history—the catastrophe of the Challenger Space Shuttle.[36]

That step back was a display of artistic honesty. In the dialogue with Ashbery, Zadura finds out what kind of poetics simply does not belong within the scope of his creative self, which is especially admirable given the fact that he was clearly attracted to the withdrawal of reference. We see this attraction in his comments on Andrzej Sosnowski's second volume, his Rousselian prose *Nouvelles impressions d'Amerique*. In his enthusiastic review, Zadura focuses on the complications of reference: the referential layer does not vanish completely, it is traceable—with contexts ranging from academic discourse to personal moments—though admittedly the sources are fantastically difficult to reach. Zadura prepares the Polish recipient for a new reading experience in which interaction with the text shifts from its "understanding" to the appreciation of its erudition and deriving pleasure from noticing how reference, although somehow implied, is highly blurred or forever inaccessible.[37]

We are clearly in the realm of Andrzej Sosnowski's exchange with John Ashbery. The great topic of this exchange is the status of the original, a conceptual cluster that involves such questions as the construction of truth in language, the ontology of the text, authorial identity, and intention. It is no less than that formidable philosophical–theoretical caliber that Sosnowski engages, as he is realizing two tasks: making himself into a poet under a flooding influence of a foreign voice, while at the same time making room for a new Polish "now."

The pleasure of the text, hinted at in Zadura's review, is a trademark of the New York School poets in general and, as Tadeusz Pióro observed, it is precisely this side of O'Hara's poetics—his nonchalant preference for trivia—that struck the conservative critical nerve in Poland.[38] Now, in reference to Sosnowski, stakes are raised higher, as pleasure becomes part of a more complex philosophical argument. As has been well noted by critics, Sosnowski ushers in the excess of rhetoric, activating the Derridean idea of the inaccessibility of the absolute signified, thus bringing into the Polish critical discourse points heavily argued by Derrida's and de Man's divergent readings of Nietzsche. On the reader's end this translates to a joyful experience of a "stylistic softness" that removes declarative proclamations of truths.[39] Sosnowski's style demonstrates the deconstructive *j'accepte*, the Derridean version of Nietzsche's affirmative stance toward the absence of the logos.[40]

Before encountering Ashbery in the mid-1980s, Sosnowski had done research on Pound, which allowed him to discover a crack in the modernist project. Will the enhanced rhetoricity of language in Pound or Stevens always cave in under the pressure of the politically or metaphysically conceived foundation, as Pound himself seems to have assumed, or will it eventually amount to saving Pound against his own intentions? The second option is what Sosnowski sees in Perloff's battle for stylistics getting the better of ideology.[41] An even more vital source of this message is Ashbery's great long prose poem, "The System," with its beautifully indeterminate opening declaration: "The system was breaking down,"[42] which stands as an indispensable interactive source for Sosnowski's long poem "Konwój."

Sosnowski's encounter with Ashbery does contain then, as was the case with Zadura, a liberating moment. Siding with Perloff's indeterminacies and de Man's definition of irony against any political ideology (including de Man's own youthful infatuation with fascism), as well as against homogenizing readings of modernism, Sosnowski found in Ashbery a powerful ally enabling him to return to his beloved Pound on new grounds, thus opening his entire poetic self, as a poet writing in Polish, to the continuously vibrant legacy of Western modernism. The first Polish poet to do so on this scale, Sosnowski brings this anti-identitarian and anti-essentialist heritage to bear on his duel with the Polish poetry's normative preference for the big lettered alliance of Truth, Identity, and History. A new "now" is needed in the Polish (poetic) culture, and Sosnowski carves out space for it by nothing less than turning himself into a medium for an alien force, amazingly never forsaking the richness of the Polish language.[43] However, this deep identification with the aesthetic and theoretical program of the strong predecessor does raise a critical question: who, or what, has Andrzej Sosnowski been in relation to his great foreign predecessor, John Ashbery?

The initial impression of reading Sosnowski is of overhearing Ashbery. In some cases the proximity is an obvious and intended effect of working with an Ashbery original, sampling it or playing with it. Cases could be made for close interaction between many individual poems by Sosnowski and Ashbery.[44] At first glance, the basic challenge for anyone reading a poem by Sosnowski will almost be the same as in the case of reading Ashbery. Meandering syntax, unexpected breaks or twists of dream-like plots, a constant sense of being in *medias res*, mixtures of the concrete with the abstract, phrases intercepted from the public domain, passages reminiscent of lectures, the quotidian merged with the sublime, bizarre compositions of objects and philosophical concepts, wild surrealist similes—all those features, so typical of Ashbery's indeterminacies, are profusely found in Sosnowski.

But the parallels go deeper than the normal literary allusiveness. Often a rhetorical construct of a Sosnowski poem will bring in a remote echo not just of a phrase but of an entire Ashberean thought-formation. Consider a fragment in *Nouvelles Impressions d'Amerique* that discusses a "lack of any center of meanings," instead offering "a twisted dance of the local clusters of sense, subject to rapid continuous metamorphoses."[45] How far from or how close is this to a passage in Ashbery's "And Ut Pictura Poesis Is Her Name," in which "desire to communicate" is played out "for the sake / Of others and their desire to understand you and desert your / For other centers of communication."[46] In any case, the freedom with which diverse multivocal echoes float in Sosnowski decisively transgresses the boundary that Zadura refused to cross: a thoroughgoing rejection of reference, which results in the erasure of the lyrical subject. The nagging question that hovers above the text by Sosnowski is the same as in the case of Ashbery. With language imploding under the pressures of its redundancies, we are left wondering—who is speaking?[47]

What then makes Sosnowski a legitimate poet in his own right? First, his is the late twentieth century's task of a poet who abandons the idea of the authenticity of the original. I have argued elsewhere how some of his poems undertake series of rhetorical condensations in which the poetic influence itself becomes the very material of the poem. Such is the case at the beginning of "Zoom," where the poem whips itself into existence by quickly surveying images the common theme of which is the willed erasure of the original image or record, or the destruction of the technology of record, with some images bringing to mind other images from Ashbery's "Syringa."[48]

A different way to theorize this feature in Sosnowski is to treat his poetics as a radicalization of Ashbery's response to modernism. It is the Ashbery text already that puts pressure on the idea of the original, pointing toward an overarching literary/textual experience in which individual works live in constant communication and interaction with one another. Jacek Gutorow proposes to read Sosnowski's later volumes as presenting a "progressing spectrality of language."[49] On this argument, Sosnowski's combined readings in Pound, Stevens, and, most importantly, Ashbery push the meditation on the hauntological element of the literary text, already inherent in these poets, to a greater level of self-awareness where the spectral layers of language—and the late capitalist reality with it—become the main topic of the poem.

But perhaps the best way in which to understand Sosnowski's exceptionality is to see his project as a radical argument for the generalized idea of the poem as an artifact whose very identity is inextricably enmeshed with the project of translation. For Sosnowski, poetry is the literary discourse that makes a living example of the generalized Derridean argument: the original is impossible without its other; thus, every original text exists as an anticipation of its readings or readings-as-translations. This idea is inscribed at the basic level of Ashbery's text: while its indeterminacy confounds authorial intention, thus making full translatability a serious problem, its own status is not the traditional one of the original but of a translation of an original that has been lost. Sosnowski utilizes the same principle, which, paradoxically, allows him to reopen the experience of Polishness. His poetic activity, having so much to do with foreign traditions, of which Ashbery is a condensation, brings to the fore the very heart of the Polish idiom.[50]

The richest commentary on the deep connection between translation and Sosnowski's poetics comes from Joanna Orska. Discussing the complex exchanges between Roussel, Ashbery, and Sosnowski, Orska presents a close reading of Sosnowski's long poem "Konwój" and demonstrates how the stylistic makings of that work are impossible to think about without bearing in mind a rich textual network made up by Roussel's works, Ashbery's long poems, and Sosnowski's own translations of Ashbery. Orska argues that all of those texts remain in relation of a literary language game that she calls "translation-transition."[51] In it, meaning is inextricable from a constant movement, a passage of the linguistic signal that plays things forward, which is also a kind of ongoing translation, a decoding or a response to the earlier signal. Sosnowski's "Konwój" is an element of such a network, a "conversation-in-translation."[52] It is a tribute to his predecessors—Roussel, Ashbery, Rimbaud—but also a saving of their impulse, a keeping alive of the formula. The ontological status of such a text, its identity, is an unheard-of anomaly on the map of the Polish literature. And so is the identity of the author. Not dead, the author himself becomes a speaking anomaly, a being that is very far from the idea of any narrowly defined cultural or national identity.

At some point in "Konwój" the text dreams up a "perfect evacuation … a pointless one, as there is nowhere to evacuate, so there is only the action of vacating, vacuity, an emptying out." But this apocalyptic diagnosis is also "an unheard of chance."[53] A poem that remains in constant transition-translation is a heroic effort to bypass heavy essentialities of history and subjectivity. The textual movement of this poem cuts across all kinds of boundaries and limits, questioning any totalizing reading of the historical progress as well as any essentialist approaches to identity. Sosnowski grappled with the same pressures of disorientation that afflicted Świetlicki and Podsiadło, but his solution is the opposite of theirs: a textual reset of the received essences of personal or national identity—a necessary condition for a rewriting. With this, Sosnowski's legacy remains a greatly debated issue in present-day Polish poetry.[54]

Notes

1 Tadeusz Pióro has observed, "The New Wave … had retrenched from politically motivated linguistic experiments to a more elevated and conventional diction." See Tadeusz Pióro, "The Influence of the New York School on Contemporary Polish Poetry," in *Exorcising Modernism*, edited by Mikołaj Wiśniewski (Wrocław: SWPS, 2014), 186–203.

2 Piotr Sommer spoke about the generally unconvincing ways in which the Nowa Fala engaged the public languages that "eventually left some people … distanced." Piotr Sommer, "An Interview with Piotr Sommer" by W. Martin, *Chicago Review*, vol. 46, nos. 3/4 (2000): 194.

3 *Literatura na Świecie*, nr 7 (lipiec 1986).

4 Rod Mengham, "Introduction" to *Altered State: The New Polish Poetry*, edited by Rod Mengham, Tadeusz Pióro, and Piotr Szymor (Todmorden, Lancs: Arc, 2003), 11.

5   Sommer, "An Interview with Piotr Sommer," 193.

6   Pióro, "The Influence of the New York School," 190.

7   For a full discussion of this term, see Roger Gilbert, *Walks in the World: Representation and Experience in Modern American Poetry* (Princeton, NJ: Princeton University Press).

8   Krzysztof Koehler, "O'Harism," *Chicago Review*, vol. 46, nos. 3/4 (2000): 281.

9   Marcin Świetlicki, "Koehlerism," *Chicago Review*, vol. 46, nos. 3/4 (2000): 284.

10 P. Dunin-Wąsowicz and K. Varga, "Definicja 'o'haryzmu'," *Parnas bis* (Warszawa, 1995), 63.

11 Ostap Sływynski, "Źródła i metamofrozy poetyki personizmu: szkoła nowojorska—polski o'haryzm—poezja ukraińska XXI wieku," *Postscriptum Polonistyczne*, no. 1 (2009): 25.

12 Piotr Śliwiński, *Przygody z wolnością. Uwagi o poezji współczesnej* (Kraków, 2002), 135.

13 Piotr Śliwiński, "Fermentacja kanonów," *Teksty Drugie*, no. 5 (2020): 140.

14 This division was proposed by Karol Maliszewski, and developed in a number of publications. For a more comprehensive gathering of those discussions see Karol Maliszewski, *Nasi klasycy, nasi barbarzyńcy: szkice o nowej poezji* (Bydgoszcz: Instytut Wydawniczy Świadectwo, 1999).

15 Joanna Orska, "Co to jest o'haryzm—próba krytycznej rewizji pojęcia," *Kresy*, nr. vol. 3, no. 35 (1998): 55.

16 Joanna Niżyńska, "The Impossibility of Shrugging One's Shoulders: O'Harists, O'Hara, and Post-1989 Polish Poetry," *Slavic Review* vol. 66, no. 3 (Fall 2007): 479.

17 For an extended discussion of how in Ashbery the poetic layer intrudes upon the biographical one, thus shaping it, see Kacper Bartczak, "Autokreacja wielościowa w poetyce Johna Ashbery'ego," in *Poeci Szkoły Nowojorskiej*, edited by Kacper Bartczak (Warszawa: Wydawnictwo UW, 2018), 170–97.

18 For a great discussion of how O'Hara and Ashbery remained at odds with academic art criticism, retaining the freshness of their capacity to get their poetry writing inspired by art, see John Yau, "The Poet as Art Critic," *American Poetry Review* 34, no. 3 (May/June 2005): 45–50.

19 See Piotr Sommer, "'O krok od nich': szkic do portretu wierszy Franka O'Hary," *Literatura na Świecie*, no. 7 (1986).

20 Ibid., 207.

21 Orska, "Co to jest 'o'haryzm'," 50.

22 Charles Altieri, "Polish Envy: American Poetry's Polonising in the 1970s and 80s," *Metre* (Spring 2004): 81.

23 Jamie Harmon Ferguson, "Whose Turn Is It Anyway?," *Chicago Review*, vol. 46, nos. 3/4 (2000): 219.

24 The successful "blue" issue was the first item on a long list of publications cocreating the phenomenon. These include a substantial number of subsequent issues of *Literatura na Świecie* devoted in part or exclusively to New York School poets. They were supported by numerous issues that included the work of artists who are vital to the New York avant-garde: Mathews, Stevens, Bishop, Tate, Roussel, Rimbaud. Ashbery's poems, translated by Zadura, Sommer, and Sosnowski, appeared as an independent book publication. See John Ashbery, *No i wiesz*, translated by Piotr Sommer, Andrzej Sosnowski, and Bohdan Zadura (Duszniki: Zdrój, 1993).

25 While Bohdan Zadura, Piotr Sommer, and Andrzej Sosnowski are the undisputed fathers of the change, they have over the years been followed by many others. Tadeusz Pióro, Jerzy Jarniewicz, Miłosz Biedrzycki, Maciej Melecki, Krzyszof Siwczyk, Adam Wiedemann, Darek Foks, Jacek Gutorow, Julia Fiedorczuk, Paweł Marcinkiewicz, Przemysław Owczarek, Kacper Bartczak—this is just a narrow sample of relevant names, poets, translators, and editors who should be mentioned when discussing the general transformative thrust in the Polish rethinking of the ontology and epistemology of the poem.

26 See Bohdan Zadura, "John Ashbery i ja. Poezja spójników?," *Literatura na Świecie*, no. 3 (1992): 111–12 (footnote 1). In this footnote Zadura mentions Piotr Sommer's "wild editorial" contribution to the final outcome.

27 In his afterword to *No i wiesz*, Andrzej Sosnowski reports that the first poem by Ashbery ever to have appeared in Polish was an anonymous translation in issue 63 of "Kultura Amerykańska" from 1969 (see Sosnowski, afterword to *No i wiesz*, p. 67). This is inaccurate. The publication is not a poem but a translation of Ashbery's 1967 essay on Joseph Cornell, "The Cube Root of Dreams."

28 Zadura, "John Ashbery i ja," 112.

29 John Ashbery, "Paradoxes and Oxymorons," in *Collected Poems 1956–87* (New York: Library of American, 2008), 698.

30 Zadura, "John Ashbery i ja," 110.

31 John Ashbery, "Shadow Train," in *Collected Poems*, 728.

32 Zadura, "John Ashbery i ja," 111. The quote is from Ashbery's "Le livre est sur la table."

33 Bohdan Zadura, "John Ashbery i ja," in *Wiersze Zebrane*, vol. 1 (Wrocław: Biuro Literackie, 2005), 388 (my translation).

34 Andrzej Sosnowski provides a useful comment when he says that in the 1980s Zadura developed conversational poetics, which involves ironic exchanges between variously imagined interlocutors. See Andrzej Sosnowski, "50 lat po Oświęcimiu i inne sezony," interview by Mariusz Maciejewski and Tomasz Majeran, in *Trop w trop: rozmowy z Andrzejem Sosnowskim*, edited by Grzegorz Jankowicz (Wrocław: Biuro Literackie, 2010), 26.

35 Bohdan Zadura, "Overexposed Photographs," translated by Piotr Sommer and M. Kasper, *Chicago Review*, vol. 46, nos. 3/4 (2000): 185.

36 Bohdan Zadura, "Nieznany Szczegół" and "Korepetycje dla Wacka," in
    Wiersze Zebrane, vol. 2 (Wrocław: Biuro Literackie, 2005), 5–6.

37 Bohdan Zadura, "Otwarcie," Twórczość, no. 10 (1994): 113.

38 Pióro, "The Influence of the New York School," 189, footnote 4.

39 Dariusz Sośnicki, "Fortuna i fatum," Czas Kultury, no. 3 (2008): 98.

40 This idea was explored first by Jacek Gutorow. See Andrzej Sosnowski, "Trop
    w trop," interview by Jacek Gutorow, in Trop w trop, 51.

41 Andrzej Sosnowski, "Big Bang, jak to się czasem mówi," interview by Grzegorz
    Jankowicz, in Trop w trop, 118.

42 John Ashbery, "The System," in Three Poems (New York: Ecco, 1972), 53.

43 Grzegorz Jankowicz has showed how Sosnowski's engagement with what John
    Ashbery has called "other traditions" allows him to dodge the universalizing
    modernist tendencies and push poetry "beyond the subject." See Grzegorz
    Jankowicz, "Sosnowski i nowoczesność," in Lekcja żywego języka: o poezji
    Andrzeja Sosnowskiego, edited by Grzegorz Jankowicz (Kraków: biblioteka
    Studium, 2003), 36. This argument meets Marjorie Perloff's ongoing campaign
    for the contemporaneity of the modernist avant-garde, a "now" of modernism,
    which for Sosnowski becomes a vehicle for a new "now" of the Polish
    literature.

44 Grzegorz Jankowicz discusses the intertextual relation between "Wiersz dla
    Francoise Lacroix" and "Self-Portrait in Convex Mirror." See Jankowicz
    "Otwarcie: hasos," in Lekcja żywego języka, 9–11. I have discussed
    elsewhere the direct allusions to Ashbery's "Syringa" and "A Wave" in
    Sosnowski's "Zoom." See Kacper Bartczak, "Końce kodowania: Andrzej
    Sosnowski i John Ashbery," in Dialog międzykulturowy w (o) literaturze
    polskiej, edited by Marta Skwara, Katarzyna Krasoń, and Jerzy Kazimierski
    (Szczecin: Wydawnictwo Uniwersytetu Szczecińskiego, 2008), str. 105–22.

45 Andrzej Sosnowski, Nouvelles impressions d'Amerique (Wrocław: Biuro
    Literackie, 2004), 38 (my translation).

46 John Ashbery, Houseboat Days (New York: Farrar, Straus, and Giroux), 46.

47 For language imploding in Sosnowski—severing referential connections and
    erasing speaker's identity—see Jacek Gutorow, Urwany ślad (Wrocław: Biuro
    Literackie, 2007), 143–60.

48 Bartczak, "Końce kodowania," 110–13.

49 Gutorow, Urwany ślad, 197–8.

50 Jamie Fergusson called his translations of Sosnowski into English a
    "self-portrait in a post-communist mirror," hinting at the symmetries
    between Sosnowski and Ashbery. He also points out how the work on
    those translations sends one to intense idiomatic energies of the Polish.
    See Ferguson, "Whose Turn," 121. Similarly, Inez Okulska noted how the
    Polish poet's dialogue with Ashbery results in a kind of diction that she
    calls strong Polishness, which, in the Derridean fashion, "is begging for
    translation." Inez Okulska, "Miłość i fetysz a spotkanie języków," in Wiersze
    na Głos: szkice o twórczości Andrzeja Sosnowskiego, edited by Piotr Śliwiński

(Poznań: Wydawnictwo Wojewódzkiej Biblioteki Publicznej i Centrum Animacji Kultury, 2010), 168.

51 Joanna Orska, "Podróż poematu (tłumaczenie jako tranzyt)," in Poeci Szkoły Nowojorskiej, 309.

52 Orksa, "Podróż poematu," 309.

53 Andrzej Sosnowski, Konwój Opera (Wrocław: Pomona, 1999), 32.

54 I am referring to attempts by younger Polish critics who read Sosnowki's later volumes as a return to reference, by which they want to include the poet in their neo-Marxist critique. It remains to be discussed if Sosnowski needs to be seen as returning to reference in order to be part of such a critique. See Marta Koronkiewicz, I jest moc odległego życia w tej elegii: uwagi o wierszach Andrzeja Sosnowskiego (Wrocław: Fundacja im. Karpowicza, 2019).

10

The Collective Constipation of the Polish/Israeli Subject: Lipski, Levin, Warlikowski

Andrzej Brylak

Polish-language literature in Israel has generated a fair number of academic works devoted to the question of belonging of that peculiar literary phenomenon. Eager to move away from visions of literature and literary studies delimited by ethnonational boundaries, scholars have looked at Polish-language literature in Israel as a "third state of being." In 1994 Polish literary historian Jacek Leociak wrote,

> One cannot call the Polish literature that came into existence on Tel-Avivian pavements émigré. … Polish Jews in Israel are Israelis. They are in their own country, over which they fought often with guns in their hands. Polish-language literature in Israel, between the one created in Poland and the other in emigration, constitutes a third state of being. Maintaining its unique identity of Polish-Jewish experience, at the same time it is an integral part of the entirety of Polish literature due to the shared language and cultural traditions.[1]

Attempts to classify Polish literature in Israel have pursued several directions. They can be read vis-à-vis the "mainland" Polish one, as we discuss, for example, the influence of the Polish Romantics on Polish/Israeli writers;[2] alternatively, they can be analyzed vis-à-vis Israeli literature from the period, as we compare, for example, the images of Israel or the

Holocaust produced in such works.[3] Another important and popular strand of research sets out to juxtapose Polish literature in Israel against the works of Polish émigré writers, but, as we can see from Jacek Leociak's quote, such juxtapositions are rife with their own problems.[4]

If we subscribe to a rather positivistic treatment of Polish literature in Israel, that is, as an incomparable, autonomous entity, we may devote our hypothetical exegesis to numerous literary journals in Tel Aviv, describing relations between writers in that milieu and struggling to recreate the world of local Polish-language bookstores, cafés, and newspapers.[5] An opposing strategy would be to inscribe Polish literature in Israel into the broader European modernist tradition, and to position authors such as Ida Fink or Leo Lipski alongside Kafka or Celine.[6] All of these approaches have certain risks of their own, as they toggle between the parochialisms of excessive hermeticism and the dilutions of overgeneralization.

In this chapter, I propose a different angle, one that focuses not on capturing the essence of a particular phenomenon, such as Polish-language literature in Israel, but rather on illuminating the mechanism of circulation between various works of literature and theater in the cultural arenas of Poland, Israel, and Europe. I also emphasize the multidirectional character of said circulation. Instead of prioritizing Polish influences on Israeli writing and vice versa, or demarcating what lies in between, I show the dynamic relationship between three elements—Polish literature in Israel, Israeli literature, and Polish theater—insofar as all of them are deeply embedded in a larger European modernist tradition (in which the legacy of the Holocaust, we might add parenthetically, plays quite a prominent role). The three works I have selected as my case studies are Leo Lipski's 1960 novella *Piotruś*, first published in Polish in Tel Aviv, and Hanoch Levin's 1972 drama *Krum* and its 2008 staging by Polish director Krzysztof Warlikowski.

Although representative of the cultural spheres in my purview, all three defy simple categorization, as they operate, even thematically, on the level of abstraction and universalization. The Tel Aviv portrayed in Lipski's novella, in his own words, could easily stand for any modern city with its "often terrifying, often grotesque elements."[7] Levin's play, dealing with complicated family affairs, hardly ever betrays its Tel Aviv setting, either, and thus, as we read in the prologue to the English translation, "could take place anywhere."[8] Warlikowski's adaptation, as well as his theater work at the time in general, is also distinguished by a high degree of universality, as it inches away from the traditional role of the Polish theater as a "national stage"—as a hub, that is, of political and social debates. It is also worth mentioning that Warlikowski, before *Krum*, had worked multiple times in Tel Aviv and Beer Sheva adapting Kafka and Shakespeare, which further complicates his work's "exclusively Polish" status and allows to include him in the realm of Polish/Israeli art. According to the renowned Polish theater critic Grzegorz Niziołek,

Warlikowski repeatedly stressed the need to search for a myth, for primordial sources of evil. He pointed at connections between Greek tragedy and the Bible. He was trying to pose the question of evil and "values" outside of a framework associated with political debate, especially the debate which took for granted and invigorated the clash of "values" with modernization, tradition with progress, the left with the right. Perhaps that is why he took great pains to avoid the areas of Polish literature inherently marked by such disputes. He was reading the religious experience against pre-Christian sources, particularly Judaism and the theology of Greek tragedy; all of that in order to escape the conflation of religion with national and political issues, characteristic of Polish culture.[9]

It is the universal nature of the three texts that makes possible a productive comparison that, in the spirit of World Literature, goes beyond the confines of national lines. However, as I prove in this chapter, such a comparison, paradoxically, can reveal some previously hidden aspects of the Polish, Jewish, and Israeli collective subjectivity, which only manifest themselves when anti-Semitism, nationalism, Zionism, and the Holocaust linger in the unconscious instead of being addressed head-on.

Leo Lipski's *Piotruś*, set in the British Mandate Palestine after the Second World War but before the Israeli independence of 1948, serves in my analysis as a forgotten *urtext*. As such, it provides a conceptual matrix for discussing the post-Holocaust, Polish/Israeli subject defined by constipation and melancholia—a subject later on developed by Levin and Warlikowski. The lineage between *Piotruś* and the latter two is not direct. We can assume with great certainty that Levin had not read the novella, as it was never translated into Hebrew or English and remains virtually unknown in Israel to this day. Among the substantial number of ephemera regarding Warlikowski's production of *Krum*, including interviews with the director himself, we do not find any mention of Lipski, either.

I am borrowing the concept of *urtext* from the field of biblical studies, where it denotes the original, uniform text of the Hebrew Bible. *Urtext* is believed to be the original source of both Septuagint and Masoretic Texts. The theory of a single text from which had sprung both Greek and Hebrew versions of the Bible was particularly popular in the nineteenth century, although nowadays it is widely disputed.[10] For my purposes, I nominate *Piotruś* as an *urtext* in a more abstract way. It is the first text that introduced a melancholic, constipated, post-Holocaust Polish/Israeli subject into intellectual history and the global circulation of ideas. The fact that it was not a conscious source of inspiration for either Levin or Warlikowski does not mean that it cannot be theorized within the parameters of intellectual history as that from which their works stemmed.

Opening on the Tel Aviv market, Lipski's novella immediately invokes distinct biblical imagery: "It was in Palestine, in the Holy land, sometime in spring 194. ... That was the time when I was forced, by circumstances and moral debts, to put over my head a huge signboard in German, Hebrew, and English. Piotruś—For Sale—clothing included—the signboard read."[11] Soon the protagonist is purchased by the demonic Mrs. Cin, who in the following words explains his role from hereon:

> Let's discuss our thing. You ought to look unappetizing. Actually, the way you look now should suffice. The crucial thing. We do have roommates here. He an alleged engineer—to hell with him, she has gonorrhea she contracted in the army. But anyway. The thing is, Mr. Piotruś, for you to occupy the restroom. From morning to evening. I am providing the food. I will be locking you, just to make sure. ... In the evenings you can go out. It is the only way. Blocking the toilet if one wants them to move out.[12]

As noted by Polish literary critic Antoni Zając, Piotruś's job effectively impedes the processes of assimilation and inhabitation of Palestine by new Jewish immigrants, who are Mrs. Cin's tenants.[13] From that point of view, the "toilet plug" hired by Cin effectively prevents the Zionist project from functioning smoothly. If we consider that access to water and sewage, from the beginning of Zionist settlements up to now, is one of the main sticking points in the Israeli-Palestinian conflict, the seemingly funny premise of the novella discloses much deeper political implications.[14] One should also keep in mind that Mrs. Cin disappears toward the end of the novella, summoned by the British administration to embark on a secret mission. Can it be that she represents the faction among the Brits who opposed the establishment of a Jewish state? Additionally, in the novella's time frame, various Jewish terrorist groups, such as the Lehi, are active in Palestine fighting the British whose support for the fully independent Israel is far from settled.

Piotruś, despite living in the bathroom, is unable to use the toilet for its original purposes. Constipated throughout the novella, he lives on his "private Golgotha," where he is supposed to "suffer for all of us": "suffer for the entire unfortunate generation." For all his rich intellectual life, vast correspondence, and substantial library ranging from Greek classics to contemporary philosophy, Lipski, due to his disability (aphasia and paralysis), was unable to transform his education into a larger number of literary work, his entire oeuvre stalling out at around three hundred pages. Not only does Piotruś's constipation evoke this biographical detail, but it also represents the larger problem of blockage in the symbolic economy. In many ways, Lipski's aphasia can be read metaphorically as constipation, in which the intellect is intact, yet one cannot express one's thoughts through language. Likewise, in constipation, digestion is happening, but defecation is inhibited.

We know from Lipski's correspondence that he was familiar with the writings of Freud.[15] In view of that, he might say that the toilet seat in the novella stands for the development of an anal personality, which, according to Freud, is the result of harsh "potty training" in early childhood. The anal personality is characterized by an inflated feeling of guilt, domination of the super-ego, immoderate orderliness, and meticulousness.[16] Such personality traits spring from the efforts to control bowel movements undertaken by a child. The development of the anal personality often brings about such symptoms as constipation and neurosis, but this development is far from particular to Piotruś—indeed, it takes place also on the collective level. "Such is this nation—I thought—chosen by God, also through that. One big neurosis, one big conundrum, which ramifies like an artery and ends with picking and peeping. It is contagious, I thought, while picking and rummaging wherever I could."[17]

The collective neurosis diagnosed by Piotruś gestures to the larger issue of the Yishuv (Jews living in Palestine) attitude toward Holocaust survivors. In my interpretation, the collective constipation and the trope of blockage, on both symbolic and literal levels, mark an inability to enfold the Holocaust into the narrative of the nascent Jewish state. As phrased by Haim Yahil, one of the Jewish Agency envoys sent to the DP camps after the war in order to transport the survivors to Palestine,

> Our attitude toward the remnant was determined not by humanitarian motives alone but, above all, in accordance with an evaluation of the role they were to play in our struggle. For this reason, we were not always gentle. Despite all our sympathy for the survivors' plight and their fundamental demands, we kept a certain distance between us and them ... We did not declare that the remnant and the Land of Israel were one and the same; rather, we emphasized that the remnant must exert a great mental and physical effort in order to unite with the Yishuv.[18]

Indeed, the Zionist leaders grappled with a peculiar paradox in relation to the Holocaust survivors. On the one hand, the survivors did not fit the template of the so-called muscular Jew: a strong pioneer and idealist who embraces the agricultural lifestyle, connected spiritually and physically to the Land of Israel, and is willing to fight and sacrifice for the bright future. The Jews murdered in the Holocaust were often accused of "going to gas chambers like sheep to the slaughter."[19] The newly arrived survivors in the Yishuv slang were often called *sabon*, "soap," due to the commonly held, albeit erroneous, belief that soap was produced from human fat during the Holocaust.[20]

The survivors were also routinely accused of collaboration and of having survived through immoral deeds. In the words of the first leader of Israel Ben Gurion, among them "were those who, had they not been what they were—harsh, evil and egotistical people—would not have survived, and all they endured rooted out every good part of their souls."[21] On the other hand, it was precisely the Holocaust that gave the moral argument for the establishment of a Jewish state after the war. Moreover, the dire situation in the DP camps allowed the Zionist leaders to advocate for the only solution of moving the displaced to Palestine, as they were often unable to reestablish their lives in Europe. In the immediate postwar period, the Jewish Agency would often assist Jews from Eastern Europe in placing them in the DP camps, with the goal of increasing the number of DPs. That, in turn, was supposed to create a situation in which Western powers would have to approve their relocation to Palestine. The loss of six million Jews in the Holocaust was viewed by the Zionists as an existential threat to their state-building project. The fear was that not enough Jews had survived in Europe to join the Yishuv. At the same time, moving those who did remain was seen as a vital mission of providing necessary numbers of Jews in Palestine. In short, Holocaust survivors turned out to be at the same time unwelcome and crucial.

The language of the Jewish Agency envoys' reports is rather telling as it illustrates a particular context in which Lipski's Israeli, post-Holocaust narrative was written. As analyzed by Israeli historian Tom Segev, the DPs in those reports, repeatedly called "human debris," "scum," and "a huge community of beggars," overall constituted undesirable "human material" whose arrival would have turned Palestine into "one big madhouse" and deprived the country of its agricultural, collective kibbutz ethos (so it would have become "one big Tel Aviv"). The envoys were particularly appalled by the sexual mores prevalent in the DP camps—a feeling expressed in a language that mirrors Lipski's descriptions of Tel Aviv, where the city's oversexualized atmosphere comes to the fore. One of the envoys wrote, "At first I thought they were animals … there were families that lived five, six couples in a room, their entire sex life and everything together … for them it was natural."[22]

During the same time period, Lipski depicts the conditions of living in Tel Aviv as such:

And then I went to the room. The four of us lived there. A forty-year-old German woman sat on my bed and was trying to prove for a long time that because of her back pain she could only do it with her mouth, tongue. Then a man, who had lost all his limbs, including his prick, to the Arabs and who because of that constantly smelled like piss, entered the room. He would go on a rampage and was a poet.[23]

Another envoy recalls his journey on a ship to Palestine as follows: "We had to be policemen. The boys would go to girls' bedrooms in the evenings and at night. We kicked them out, but they came back. The girls went around with sailors and soldiers and showed no sense of virtue, and it was not easy to do our job of preserving certain standards."[24]

The quote above, once again, bears a marked similarity to Lipski's narrative:

O prostitutes. Together with the dawn they descend on the city and our courtyard. Those two, and the third one, very young. They tore out her earring together with a part of her ear. (It was a long time ago, when she was 10.) The work in the courtyard and men are waiting in the street, in silence. Focused, antisocial. The gaze into one spot, the entrance to the courtyard, attentively, not lowering their eyes for a second. They look like dogs. Wolves perhaps. They are circling, restless, they approach and walk back. There aren't many women here.[25]

Putting these quotes side by side, we can clearly see that the Tel Aviv experience of a postwar narrator, which most critics viewed as dark parody, profanation, and provocation, is indeed firmly grounded in the historical reality of the time.[26] Lipski's fantastical language, absurdist plot, and elaborate metaphors distance the reader from reality, but, overall, the novella serves up a surprisingly accurate portrayal of the city in the aftermath of the war.

Among the sexual perversions mentioned in Lipski's book are erotic asphyxiation, necrophilia, sadism, masochism, groping, zoophilia, coprophilia, masturbation, exhibitionism, and voyeurism, all of them packed into a mere sixty pages. When it comes to identifiable mental illnesses, we have schizothymia, schizophrenia, hysteria, and neurosis. Add to the mix some physical disabilities, missing limbs, hepatitis, impotence, and let us not forget that the only major character who actually does live in a kibbutz, rather than in the degenerate city, is the teenage prostitute Batia— an antithesis to the idealistic pioneer. Toward the end, she moves to Paris.

As we look at Israeli literature from the same period, it is easy to label Lipski's account of Tel Aviv as a phantasmagoric tale. Israeli prose at the time is dominated by monumental novels of armed struggle, state building, brave and hard-working kibbutzniks and soldiers. The so-called third generation of Israeli writers—Moshe Shamir or S. Yikar, for instance—were not interested in describing "one big madhouse," "one big Tel Aviv."[27] Unlike Lipski, for this Palestine-born generation, it was not the Second World War but the 1948 Israeli-Arab war for independence that amounted to a formative experience. Zionist literature could not assimilate the writings of Lipski for the same reason that the Zionist project at the time was incapable of assimilating the Holocaust into its national narrative. What Zionist leaders feared that the arrival of European Jews from the DP camps would cause was precisely what shaped Lipski's Tel Aviv.

At the end of the novella, the constipated Piotruś teleports himself into an archetypically Polish universe—the Eastern Borderlands, also known as "Kresy"—where he is finally able to relieve himself. However, shortly after that he is suddenly kicked out into the streets of Tel Aviv. Piotruś walks along the promenade taking in the city with its prostitution, gambling, moisture, shopkeepers, smells of the sea, and drunk soldiers, realizing he belongs to neither of the worlds. Considering that the toilet is a central point for both the Polish and Israeli universes, and taking into account the historico-political context outlined earlier, we can metaphorically say that in Lipski's narrative Israel is a toilet into which one cannot defecate, while Poland is a place where one can, or at least could, defecate but is unable to stay. To use scatological language as a historical metaphor for Zionism, Israel absorbs all the sewage, "human debris," "scum," and downtrodden remnants of the Holocaust but fails to include their trauma into the flow of the symbolic exchange. The state, at first sight well-equipped to do so, turns out to be a place where, due to its inability to process the collective trauma, constipation is not only a physical but also a psychological condition. Excrement, instead of being sent down the pipes, stays in the guts.[28]

It was in that context that Hanoch Levin published in 1972 his highly psychological drama *Krum*—in my view, the first major work of modern Hebrew literature to tackle the themes foregrounded by Lipski twelve years earlier. Levin's play tells the story of a prodigal son named Krum, who returns to his hometown and meets his distressed mother.

> I had no success overseas, Mother. I didn't make money and I didn't become happy. I didn't have fun, I didn't get ahead, didn't get married, didn't get engaged, didn't meet anyone. I didn't buy anything, didn't bring anything. In my suitcase there is dirty underwear and toiletries. That's all, I've told you everything, and I want you to leave me in peace.[29]

Despite Krum's wish to be left alone, the plot revolves around him, his mother, and a group of his friends, all stuck in the same town. Most of the main characters experience various form of constipation-like syndromes, either physiologically or psychologically: from Krum himself, who struggles with writer's block, to his best friend Gloomer who cannot make himself cry because he cannot "open his diaphragm." Gloomer also suffers from hypochondria and general neurosis, which drives him to obsession over timing his exercise:

> Let me give you the arguments last time, and then you give me a last and final answer. It's no secret that the problem with my health is that to this day I can't decide if I should exercise in the morning or the evening. If I do it in the morning, before work, there's risk that the exercising will wear me out and I'll be tired at work; and if I exercise in the evening, before bed, there's a chance it'll be refreshing, and then I'll have trouble falling asleep. And midday is out of the question, because I am not a man of compromise: with me it's either the start of the day or the end. There

are other problems involved, like showering for example. If I decide to exercise in the morning, I take shower afterwards, and then, what happens after work? Do I shower again? That's not realistic, especially in the winter. And if I exercise at night, before bed, of course there's no point in showering in the morning, but then the question arises again: perhaps water is refreshing, so the morning would be better. Fifteen years I've been dealing with the problem, and every time I make up my mind, I read an article in the newspaper that proves the opposite. Why don't they, once and for all, hold an international medical conference on this issue and make a final decision? Honorable doctors: you are killing us. Now tell me your final answer, on condition that you've considered all the arguments.[30]

Toward the end, Gloomer falls ill and dies, blaming, to no-one's surprise, the exercise dilemma. Gloomer's neurotic discourse stands as far apart as possible from the once-dominant Zionist narrative of "the muscular Jew."[31] Levin's Tel Aviv, both in *Krum* and elsewhere, is a place of the weak and the tormented—and yes, the constipated—all of whom are unable to stay but also to leave.

Gloomer is not the only character with a telling name. Another friend of Krum's, who eventually marries Gloomer for lack of a better choice, is called Doopa—the Polish word for "ass," phonetically transcribed. Levin's parents emigrated to Israel from Poland in 1935, which explains his familiarity with that word. And yet, we have to bear in mind that in Israel, Poland's main connotation is the Holocaust. Therefore, it would not be out of place to ponder potential connections between an ass and the Shoah; and here, once again, we return to Lipski's trope of a melancholic, constipated, post-Holocaust subject in Israel. This is how Doopa characterizes her condition: "I am frisky and cheerful, and I chirp like a bird, and I have no one. I am closed up inside. I am exploding. So many things I could give a man, devotion and love, infectious laughter, and I have no one."[32]

Doopa's affliction is quite peculiar: seemingly full of cheer, she is at the same time addled by resignation and sadness. Much like Gloomer who cannot make himself cry, Doopa cannot make herself laugh. Considering that the play was written in the 1970s, Krum and his friends can be associated with the so-called second generation—children of the Holocaust survivors—who on the surface live in a free Jewish state, yet cannot celebrate their daily lives as they are haunted by the intergenerational trauma. This interpretation would suggest that the constipation of the collective Israeli subject will last for generations, until the trauma has been processed.[33]

The first public reckoning with the Holocaust did not take place in Israel until after the 1961 Eichmann trail, which spotlighted an issue that could no longer be ignored. Levin published *Krum* eleven years later when the problem of collective constipation due to the Holocaust trauma could already be diagnosed but only emerged in literature in a veiled manner. Indeed, just like in *Piotruś*, the Holocaust is never mentioned in Levin's work directly, so the pregnant silence around the topic signals a certain melancholic condition, where the object of grief cannot be located or spoken of.[34]

> Grief appears explicitly in the play's last lines, when Krum learns about his mother's death: No, there will be time for such terrible grief, and I am not yet ready. Later. One has to prepare, to gather strength, to eat well, sleep well, exercise every morning. One has to ripen, to shore oneself up in preparation. For that day, and that day will arrive, and I will burst out in a huge tempest of emotion, and a massive wave of tears will wash over me and every crevice of my soul will open, and I will cry and cry, about everything, about my mother and my life and my loves, and about all wasted time that will never return, and I will break through the suffocation once and for all, and then will be pure and fresh—on that day which I believe is yet to come—pure and fresh and finally ready for life.[35]

What is striking here for a reader familiar with Lipski's writing is the repeated use of "and" as the opening of a new sentence, each ushering in the things to come. This literary device is borrowed from the Bible and gives the speech an air of biblical prophecy. At the same time, it brings the lofty biblical language down into the carnal realm of "eating well," "sleeping well," and "breaking through the suffocation." The result is a recognizably Lipskian mixture of registers in which the biblical prophecy of ultimate release is fulfilled through physiological, and not eschatological, processes.

The most important intervention Krzysztof Warlikowski makes in his staging of *Krum* is moving the monologue to the beginning and setting it in a public bathroom.[36] That move places Warlikowski's poetics incredibly close to that of Lipski's. Krum's monologue is broadcast as a prerecorded video on a big screen hanging above the stage. The bathroom and the monologue are thus presented as a meta-space outside of the narrative's frame. Unlike in Levin, where it logically follows the mother's death, here the monologue is imagined as the overarching message. Concluding a show that revolves around an inability to grieve—and therefore to express, write, breathe, and, last but not least, defecate—the monologue furnishes a manifesto of hope that a time for proper grief will arrive yet (but as of now, grief is unfeasible).

Actor Jacek Poniedziałek, who plays Krum, speaks with palpable confusion and unrest. Most importantly, his stare is directed not at his character's mother, as the text would suggest, but at the audience. Alternating between looking the viewer straight in the eye and averting his gaze, Poniedziałek implies, through his performance, that the problem of unresolved grief is not a family affair between Krum and his mother but a challenge extended to the collective subject. In his 2009 show *(A)pollonia*, which deals with the Holocaust openly, Warlikowski installs a public restroom on the stage again, this time in the background and partitioned off by a transparent plexiglass sheet. In both shows, the restroom is a space where the action of the show is placed in symbolic brackets and runs parallel to the main narrative. The choice of a public restroom, as a supposedly intimate yet partially exposed space, whose metaphorical potential is underlined by the use of a closeup in the *Krum* video and plexiglass in *(A)pollonia*, bespeaks a blurring between private and public, individual and collective. The character's intimate failure to grieve his mother's death instantiates a larger, collective foreclosure of grief, which has its roots in Israel's post-Holocaust condition.

On July 3, 2021, Krzysztof Warlikowski received the Golden Lion for Lifetime Achievement from La Biennale di Venezia, thus securing his status as a bona fide of European, rather than merely Polish, theater. Likewise, Hanoch Levin enjoys international popularity as an Israeli playwright whose texts are staged all over the world. Why, then, has not Leo Lipski, a forerunner of both these artists, achieved a similar level of recognition? The answer lies, as I have demonstrated, in the broader historico-political context. Both in Israel and Poland, interpretations of the Holocaust through carnal imagery were too much of a taboo in the immediate postwar era. The assimilation of the Holocaust into Israel's national narrative after the Eichmann trial, as well as ongoing discussions on the multigenerational trauma, eventually made space for plays like Levin's. In the Polish case, it was a gradual process that started in 1989, simultaneously enveloping Jewish narratives in public debates and art, and acknowledging the complete reorganization of social structures after the Holocaust (a phenomenon dubbed by Polish philosopher Andrzej Leder as "Dream-State Revolution").[37] The processing of this collective trauma both in Poland and Israel resulted in an increased demand for works of arts responsive to it, but in doing so this growing demand obfuscated the fact that such works already existed.

Notes

1 Jacek Leociak, "Na obu brzegach," *Nowe Książki*, vol. 3 (1994): 70.

2 See Eugenia Prokop-Janiec, "Literatura polska w Izraelu: pomiędzy pamięcią Europy a nowym życiem," *Roczniki humanistyczne*, vol. 64, no. 1 (2016): 63–74.

3 See Piotr Paziński, Jagoda Budzik, and Bartłomiej Krupa, " 'Tam jest życie, a tu już jakby nie-życie': Z Piotrem Pazińskim o hebrajskiej literaturze Zagłady rozmawiają Jagoda Budzik i Bartłomiej Krupa," *Narracje o Zagładzie*, no. 4 (2019): 15–40.

4 See Jagoda Wierzejska, *Retoryczna interpretacja autobiograficzna* (Warszawa: Wydawn. Elipsa, 2012).

5 See Karolina Famulska-Ciesielska and Sławomir Jacek Żurek, *Literatura polska w Izraelu* (Kraków [u.a.]: Wydawn. Austeria, 2012).

6   See Marta Cuber, *Trofea wyobraźni. O prozie Leo Lipskiego*, 1st ed. (Katowice: Uniwersytet Śląski, 2014).

7   Lipski Leo, "Jak powstawał Piotruś," *Kultura*, vol. 9 (1998): 143.

8   Levin Hanoch, "Krum," in *Selected Plays One* (London: Oberon Books, 2020), 1–67.

9   Grzegorz Niziolek, *Warlikowski: Extra Ecclesiam* (Krakow: Homini, 2008), 64.

10 G. W. Bromiley, *The International Standard Bible Encyclopedia* (Grand Rapids, MI: Eerdmans, 1979), 405.

11 The exact year is purposefully cut off, which adds to the general atmosphere of the temporariness but also universality. However, there are numerous markers allowing us to establish that the novel is set after the Second World War; the narrator reflects on his wartime spent in Russia, before the Israeli Declaration of Independence in 1948. Leo Lipski, "Piotruś," in *Powrót*, edited by Agnieszka Maciejowska. (Paryż: Instytut Literacki Kultura, 2015), 201.

12 Lipski, "Piotruś," 207.

13 Zajac Antoni, "Maksimum wyganania: Marginalne parodie i marańskie rozszczepienia Leo Lipskiego," in *Marani literatury polskiej*, edited by Bogalewski Piotr and Lipszyc Adam (Kraków: Austeria, 2020), 45.

14 "Introduction to The Politics of Verticality," April 23 [cited 2021]. Available from https://www.opendemocracy.net/en/article_801jsp/.

15 Piotr Sadzik, "Zdrobniałe jąkanie: Teologia afatyczna w "Piotrusiu" Leo Lipskiego," *Wielogłos*, 40, no. 2 (2019): 76.

16 Freud Sigmund, "Three Essays on the Theory of Sexuality," in *The Freud Reader* (New York: W.W. Norton, 1989), 293.

17 Lipski, "Piotruś," 205.

18 Tom Segev, *The Seventh Million: The Israelis and the Holocaust*, 1st ed. (New York: Hill and Wang, 1993), 139.

19 Yael S. Feldman, " 'Not as Sheep Led to Slaughter'? On Trauma, Selective Memory, and the Making of Historical Consciousness," *Jewish Social Studies*, vol. 19, no. 3 (2013): 139–69.

20 Segev, *The Seventh Million*, 183.

21 Ibid., 119.

22 Ibid., 121.

23 Lipski, "Piotruś," 203.

24 Segev, *The Seventh Million*, 118.

25 Lipski, "Piotruś," 215.

26 See Antoni, "Maksimum wyganania," 417–63.

27 Segev, *The Seventh Million*, 120.

28 On dynamics between physiological and psychological aspects of modernist literature see: Michał Paweł Markowski, *Czarny nurt*, Wyd. 1. (Kraków: Wydawn. Literackie, 2005), 301–95.

29 Hanoch, "Krum," 5.

30 Ibid., 9.

31 See Todd Samuel Presner, *Muscular Judaism: The Jewish body and the Politics of Regeneration* (London: Routledge, 2007).

32 Hanoch, "Krum," 16.

33 See Erin Heather McGlothlin, *Second-generation Holocaust Literature Legacies of Survival and Perpetration* (Rochester, NY: Camden House, 2006).

34 See Leticia Glocer Fiorini, Thierry Bokanowski and Sergio Lewkowicz, eds., *On Freud's "Mourning and Melancholia"* (London: Karnac, 2009).

35 Hanoch, "Krum," 66.

36 Warlikowski Krzysztof, *Krum*, Anonymous (Warszawa: Teatr Rozmaitości w Warszawie w koprodukcji ze Starym Teatrem w Krakowie, 2005).

37 Andrzej Leder, *Prześniona rewolucja* (Warszawa: Wydawnictwo Krytyki Politycznej, 2014).

11

Swimming Queer: Moving with Contemporary Polish Queer Literatures

Ela Przybyło

In queer world literature and film across cultural contexts, water is a common anchoring element, often used to symbolize transformation and sexuality, lust and the erotic, the unknown and the feared. On the one hand, water can be worked to render indeterminacy and the flow of desire and identities. On the other hand, proximity to water is often announced by partial or full nudity providing a vehicle for gay gazing and queer touch. Writing on Brazilian queer cinema, Fernando G. Pagnoni Berns writes that "queer desires can be tested outside the boundaries of the 'dry' socially regulated world without fear of reprisal."[1] Queer literatures often play with the depths of that unseen space, under the surface of the water, to bring queer worlds into being.

Such is the case in Tomasz Jedrowski's breakthrough novel *Swimming in the Dark* (2020), set in the dark of the repressive and revolutionary Poland of the late 1970s and early 1980s, when state socialism, under mounting pressure from Solidarity activists, revealed its cracks.[2] In Jedrowski's novel, a river and a lake in the woods are the sites of the building romance between the two main characters, Ludwik (or Ludzio) and Janusz—the latter a supporter and rising star of the state socialist party and the former a staunch anti-totalitarianist. It is through swimming together that they build intimacy despite their political differences. Not fully comprehending their queer identities, at a time when Polish gayness was not only frowned upon but when gay men were persecuted by the Party, the two men *step in*, so to say, into their romance and desires. *Swimming in the Dark*, I argue in this chapter, provides a compelling case for the need to not only read queer literature as world literature but also read Polish queer literature as world literature.

The twenty-first century is a remarkable time for lovers of queer literature and culture, with the expansion of literary canons across cultural and geopolitical locations. Challenging the too-frequent US exceptionalism of LGBTQ+ (lesbian, gay, bisexual, transgender, queer, plus) literary canons, full-length queer literary works such as Niviaq Korneliussen's *Last Night in Nuuk* (2014) set in Greenland, Pajtim Statovci's *Crossing: A Novel* (2016) set in Albania and Finland, Wanuri Kahiu's film *Rafiki* (2018) set in Kenya's capital, and the translation into English of works such as Qiu Miaojin's *Notes of a Crocodile* written in 1990s Taiwan—to name just a few—contribute to the development of a queer world literature that is diasporic and multilingual.[3] In Poland itself, queer and LGBTQ+ literatures have taken off across genres even as the right-wing has come into power, with political parties such as Prawo i Sprawiedliwość—PiS (Law and Justice) fueling homophobia and transphobia in many forms including through attempts at preventing Marsze Równości (Pride Parades) and efforts to create LGBT-free zones in southeastern Poland.[4] Works such as Izabela Filipiak's *Absolutna Amnezja* in 1995, Michał Witkowski's *Lubiewo* (*Lovetown*) in 2004, Krzysztof Tomasik's *Homobiografie* ([2008] 2014) anthology chronicling Polish queer figures, the *Dezorientacje: Antologia Polskiej Literatury Queer* (2021) anthology of Polish queer literatures, Natalia Osińska's queer and trans Young Adult (YA) series (2016, 2017, 2019), and many others partake in what queer theorists Lauren Berlant and Michael Warner (1998) and José Esteban Muñoz (1999) term "queer worldmaking" or the dreaming of queer worlds into being through "establish[ing] alternative views of the world … oppositional ideologies."[5]

In this chapter I argue for queer literature as world literature and for Polish queer world literature as vital to world literatures. While world literatures are too often imagined as heterosexual and still pervasively cisgender male, Debra Castillo argues for the importance of centralizing women, queer, and of color authors in world literature since the world is "51 percent female and 10 percent LGBT, and Caucasian men are a distinct minority everywhere."[6] I centralize Polish queer literature through focusing on Jedrowski's novel *Swimming in the Dark* (2020), which provides a unique entry point into thinking about Polish queer literature as *worldly* queer literature, because of its uniquely diasporic positioning.[7] For one, the book experienced immediate popularity in ways that most queer Polish works do not, because it was written in English, published with HarperCollins, and promoted internationally. Further, Jedrowski himself writes from the diasporic standpoint of someone born in Germany to Polish parents but who continues to be invested in Polish culture and identity. While some might argue that this makes the book less representative of Polish queer literatures, I argue that it makes the case for thinking of Polishness globally. Finally, the book itself creates textual migration through making central to its plot James Baldwin's renowned gay novel *Giovanni's Room* (1956)—a book by a Black queer US author censored during state socialism in Poland.[8]

I will undertake this analysis using the metaphor of water to theorize Polish exile, diaspora, and queerness. I adopt the phrase "analytics of water"/water analytics from Tiffany Lethabo King's *The Black Shoals* (2019), where she uses the metaphor of the shoal—the place in the sea where water and land meet—to place Indigenous and Black diasporic work in conversation with each other in ways that "ruptures normative thought and European discourse."[9] In addition to water being a common trope in queer literature and film, "water analytics," following King, serve as a powerful form of analysis for working through liminal zones of encounter. Upon reading King I was compelled by the work that water analytics could do for theorizing Polish identity in relation to histories of colonization, occupation, and recent right-wing weaponization of these themes against marginalized subjects such as queer people in contemporary Poland. Using an analytics of water, I suggest that contemporary Polish queer literatures, such as *Swimming in the Dark*, are fruitfully understood through a poetics of water that pays attention to movement, moves to LGBTQ+ liberation, and stirring the canon of a heterosexualized Polish nationalism.

Polish Queer Literatures: Context and Importance

Despite frequent heterosexist narrativizations of Polish literature, queerness has historically been part of the Polish canon. When Poland was partitioned and colonized by the three empires of Russia, Austria–Hungary, and Prussia (1772–1918) and arguably "the homosexual was [not yet] a species" in Poland—to adopt Michel Foucault's framing—Maria Konopnicka (1842–1910) wrote her patriotic literature.[10] Either bisexual or lesbian, though it might be impossible to determine which, Konopnicka is most widely remembered for authoring *Rota* (*The Oath*) (1908), a patriotic poem that came to be Poland's early anthem.[11] Living openly in a lesbian relationship, Konopnicka's work is memorialized in Poland never as queer but rather as fundamentally heterosexual and nation-building, and her figure has been fantasized as a mother of the Polish nation, since she had six children before leaving her husband.[12]

Several decades after Poland's reemergence as a nation-state in November 1918, Poland became one of the first countries in the world to decriminalize homosexuality in 1932. Many Polish modernists exhibited queer desires in their literatures and personal lives. Witold Gombrowicz (1904–1969), for instance, included queer themes in *Trans-Atlantyk* (1953), queering traditions of old Sarmatism from Poland's great epoch of the sixteenth and seventeenth centuries to turn Polish patriotism on its head.[13] Jerzy Andrzejewski (1909–1983), acclaimed author of *Ashes and Diamonds* (*Popiół i Diament*) (1948)—which was made famous by Andrzej Wajda's film (1961) by the same name—was also a central figure of Polish literature after the Second World War and also gay.[14] Even Nobelist Czesław Miłosz (1911–2004), memorialized as a staunch Polish heterosexual, was part of a community of queer cisgender male writers who "homoinfluence[d]" him and he might have experimented sexually with men.[15] I bring up these very few examples spanning over a century to suggest, as others also have, that queerness is not on the edges or margins of Polish literary canons and Polish literary formation, but that it is central, informative, and galvanizing.

Too often, movements including literary, feminist, and queer movements are framed through a temporal narrative of progress.[16] Yet these models are often based on Western and colonial fantasies of improvement that can only clumsily be applied to other geopolitical and cultural contexts. Joanna Mizielińska and Robert Kulpa (2011) argue that the queer narrative of liberation focuses on US contexts, prioritizing narratives of progress that include the Stonewall uprising, AIDS activist struggles against the state, and the legalization of same-sex marriage.[17] Not only does such a historical trajectory often neglect transgender involvement in US LGBTQ+ struggles and erase the racism and settler colonialism often entangled in queer histories, it also presents a too-readily applicable model of struggle that is assumed to apply to other contexts. Narratives of queerness emerging in a historically colonized, occupied, and war-torn country simply do not align with a temporality of improvement, necessitating a different model.

In Poland, the legalization of homosexuality occurred decades before that of other nation-states, yet conditions for gay and transgender people arguably got worse over the years and into state socialism such as with the 1985 to 1987 Hiacynt (Hyacinth) state inquisition into gay men's lives.[18] Even into the current decades—the 2000s, 2010s, and 2020s—conditions have not improved for LGBTQ+ people in Poland. Multiple right-wing parties render permissible discrimination against LGBTQ+ people, framing them as a "gender ideology," fostering "LGBT-free zones" (*Strefy wolne od LGBT*), attempting to ban Pride Parades, and endorsing transphobic and homophobic hate speech and hate crimes.[19] To build on this, Poland has had robust queer literatures and literary figures for over a century, as I mentioned earlier. Narratives of linear progress thus simply are not applicable to Polish queer struggles. Rather than tautologies of progress and improvement, LGBTQ+ struggles and movements in Poland require more robust models to account for what Mizielińska and Kulpa refer to as a "'knotting' and 'looping' of time," a "queer time."[20] One possible model to challenge Western temporalities and to make sense of the centrality of queer literature to Polish literature is the metaphor of water flowing and transforming, its change and impact slow and persistent, undulating and cycling.

Tomasz Jedrowski's Novel *Swimming in the Dark*

Jedrowski's novel *Swimming in the Dark* (2020) offers us an effective site for analyzing the value of centralizing queerness in Polish literature and in world literature more broadly. I identify three flows in Jedrowski's novel that are centrifugal to Polish literature as well as enhanced by queer writing. The first of these is water as movement of bodies across boundaries of border imperialism that demarcate nation-states. The second movement I will touch on, closely tied to the first, pertains to the intersection of sexuality and national identity, reimagining Polishness through queerness, rather than in spite of it. Finally, the third movement involves the central role that James Baldwin's *Giovanni's Room* (1956) plays for the characters Janusz and Ludwik, and the ways in which it gestures toward a worldly and transnational queer literature that adds complexities to notions of the relationship between "the West and the rest" or the West and the not-quite West of Poland.[21] In all these ways, *Swimming in the Dark* elucidates a movement to broaden understandings of Polishness and of what can count as Polish literature.

Polishness across Borders

Jedrowski's path to writing, like many Polish authors, is one of migration and displacement, his parents having emigrated to Germany during the turbulent 1980s. His parents' story is visible throughout *Swimming in the Dark*, which is set in the late 1970s and early 1980s and during the declaration of Martial Law in late 1981 and which provides a close account of the injustices of state socialism. In addition to drawing on his parents' story, Jedrowski develops his own unique positionality in the novel as a queer member of the Polish diaspora. Feeling alienated from his Polishness and from Poland throughout his upbringing, at twenty-seven Jedrowski "move[s] to Warsaw to write a novel" out of a need for "reconciliation."[22] Feelings of immigrant displacement are often intensified when one is queer, for as Adi Kuntsman puts it, "the lives of ... queer immigrants [... cause] rage and violence ... within and outside our émigré communities."[23] Heckled in Poland at age six as a "faggot," Jedrowski developed a complex positionality in relation to Poland that precipitates his novel: one of being Polish and also of feeling the sensation of being denied the right to one's nationality. "But who gets to decide who you are and where you belong?" Jedrowski asks.[24]

As a Polish queer novel written in English and published by HarperCollins, the novel has had opportunities few other Polish queer authors are warranted, being internationally promoted and sold, for instance. As Ann Steiner argues, "world literature is conditioned by sale systems, publishing traditions, translations, government support, taxes, and everything else related to the economy of literature."[25] And yet the choice of writing Polish literature in a language other than Polish is itself political, challenging the supposed monolingualism of Polish literature.[26] Part of the queerness of *Swimming in the Dark* is its commitment to rendering the reality and high stakes of crossing borders. The novel opens with the protagonist, Ludwik, in Greenpoint, Brooklyn, having emigrated from Poland due to evidence indicating his homosexuality. He awakes alienated, remembering "the gray-blue eyes the same color as the Baltic Sea in winter" of his love, Janusz.[27] Jedrowski himself lived in Greenpoint, where the "neighborhood's Polish diaspora came as a revelation" and where walking down the streets no one noticed his "foreignness," since most people were also from "neither here nor there," likely speaking varying versions of both Polish and English.[28]

In the novel, Ludwik (or, in diminutive, Ludzio), growing up in 1960s and 1970s Wrocław, in a modest income family consisting of his mother and grandmother, is alerted to how his city is marked by displacement, with "everyone—the people who'd lived here before and then the people who replaced them—ha[ving] been forced to leave their homes."[29] He also observes the ways in which the nation-state, under a totalitarian government, enforces the eradication of non-Polishness, including through the extraction of his Polish-Jewish friend and first love interest, Beniek, who disappears from his home overnight and it is only through unofficial murmurs and gossip—"unofficial secret counterknowledge, transmitted usually through family ties and the links of friendship"—that Ludzio is able to uncover why.[30] As we learn in the novel, Beniek and his family move to Israel in 1968 because student protests and civil unrest lead the Party to find a scapegoat in Jewish people, firing many from their jobs and labeling them traitors of the state.[31] "One day your country is yours, and the next it isn't," as the protagonist relates.[32]

Borders appear in Jedrowski's novel as painful scars etched into the land, with water often functioning as a respite from them. Yet even as monuments to border imperialism, borders are crossed by Ludwik himself throughout the novel, as he moves from Wrocław to Warsaw, and later from Poland to the United States. In this sense, Ludzio emerges as a character swept by the tide of his queerness to move as he needs to in order to survive. In a broader sense, *Swimming in the Dark*, through challenging Polish language primacy in Polish literature and being authored by a diasporic gay man born to Polish parents, also provides a sense of water-based movement and circulation, not toward a "better tomorrow" per se but to a realization of one's erotic potential.

Kbirness and Nationality

Another border that demarcates the life that Ludwik is able to lead is of course that between acceptable heteronormative family structures and so-called "perversion"—or queer desire.[33] While still a youth in Wrocław, alienated and looking to find other gay kin, Ludwik goes to Staromiejski Park near the river (presumably the Fosa Miejska or moat) where "the 'inverts' went" to engage in public sex.[34] After fellatio with a stranger, Ludwik experiences himself as without a home, having crossed another border and having moved away from the heterosexuality so at the core of normative ideas around Polishness. While homosexuality was technically legal in the 1970s and 1980s, homophobia intensified during this time, with police raids on public parks and washrooms, where gay men hung out, and the detention and interrogation of those deemed to be gay to extract names from them, such as during the Hiacynt (Hyacinth) action in 1985 to 1987. These interrogations led to the creation of an estimated 11,000 files incriminating gay men for reasons not entirely clear, though scholars have suggested it might have been due to increasing Polish gay rights activism and Solidarity activism or in response to the HIV/AIDS epidemic in the United States.[35] Earlier in state socialist Poland, French philosopher Michel Foucault, who visited Warsaw in the late 1950s and whose theories of surveillance are arguably shaped by his time in Poland, was expelled from the country for his homosexuality.[36] In the novel, Ludwik, having shared his name and personal information with the stranger in the park, emerges as a character who "has a file on him," a fact that rises to the surface when later in the book he begins to undertake activist actions against the state and becomes inconvenient for Janusz.

The interconnection of sexuality and nationality is evident especially in the symbolic use of water throughout the book. The relationship between Beniek and Ludwik, as young boys, is overflowing with watery erotics—like when they run through the rain together, undress together to take a bath, or swim together in the Baltic Sea during a school trip. Janusz and Ludwik's relationship is also overflowing with water metaphors that both unite and divide them. They are divided by the Atlantic Ocean after Ludwik emigrates and by the Vistula River while in Warsaw (living on opposite ends of the city) but also by their divergent political commitments, life goals, and relationships to queerness. It is water that also joined them together when they first met at an obligatory work education camp for youth and swam in a nearby stream and then in a lake in the woods. Together they swim in a river, a lake in the pine woods, and, later when they return to Warsaw, at the swimming pool.

Ludwik's intoxication with Janusz is near instantaneous. One evening at the work camp, Ludwik goes for a walk past the fields where they are required to labor picking beets and on to the nearby small river where "tall grasses moved in the wind" and he sees Janusz swimming.[37] While reluctant to enter the water initially and hesitant of his desire for Janusz's glistening body, Ludwik begins meeting Janusz by the river. Although Ludwik continues to be overwhelmed by the ease with which he is drawn to Janusz, he agrees to go with him on a camping trip to the lake district, where after walking through a pine forest they come to "a clearing filled with a large, brilliant lake, lined by high grasses like a secret" and their love affair deepens.[38] To quote more extensively from the moment in the book when Ludwik enters the lake and swims toward Janusz,

> I looked at the water. I couldn't see though its body, couldn't assess its contents. But I stepped in. And the water embraced me completely, softly and coolly. I felt myself anew, as if something in me had been switched on after a long time. It was a sensation of lightness and power and total inconsequence. I began to move, and every movement propelled me forward … I was conscious of the unknown underneath … My body moved in your direction, and you looked at me, suddenly calmed too. With your arms outstretched to the sides, you were like a ballet dancer hovering in flight. Under the surface of the water something warm rattled in my belly. I approached, until I could see the drops of water on your forehead and on the tip of your nose and in the corners of your mouth. We didn't say a thing. We looked at each other, already beyond words. You were there, and I was there, close, breathing. And I moved into your circle.[39]

As this passage suggests, Ludwik and Janusz's time at the lake is a manifestation of their sexual desire for each other, and Ludwik's coming into his own body and erotic presence. Water is frequently used in literature and film to symbolize self-transformation as well as intimacy with others. "It demonstrates the incessantly changing matter of our own essential being, of an identity in constant becoming" as well as porosity and intimate engagement with others.[40] In relation to gay masculinity, water is a space one can "probe and hide, without the risk of being punished," already naked or half naked and feeling the ripples of another's movements in the water.[41] We can understand Ludwik's swim in the dark lake as one of both coming into one's power and a challenge to Western temporalities of queer progress and liberation. Rather than swimming toward a "better future," Janusz swims into his erotic presence, lingering in an expanded present he will always dwell in, a moment of lightness and power. I understand Ludwik's swim also by way of the work of Black lesbian US author, Audre Lorde, who loved to swim and is photographed doing so. She theorized an erotic realization of one's self-worth as entailing "sharing deeply [a] pursuit with another person," as well as coming into one's strength and power.[42] In this sense, Ludwik's swimming toward Janusz, his willingness to overcome "the unknown underneath" is a giving over to sensations and to the lapping of water, to the unknown future, and the fully embodied present.[43] For Ludwik, this sensation alters the course and shape of his life, leading to continued displacement and border crossing.

Finally, water in *Swimming in the Dark* is also caught up in familial and intergenerational trauma and national be/longing. About halfway through the novel we discover that it was Ludzio's mother who taught him to swim after his father had left them, and that when she died of cancer, he stopped going to the public swimming pool. In this sense, water flows through Ludwik as a marker of his life and traumas, reminding him of the fundamental disparities of life under state socialist Poland.

While Ludwik is passed over for a doctorate because he is not Party-supporting, Janusz quickly rises in the Office of Press Control (dedicated to censorship). Committed to the ideals of socialism yet unable to see the class struggle in his own country, Janusz exudes beauty and youth and soon begins to date the daughter of a high Party official, granting him proximity to a life of abundance unknown to most people in Poland at the time. As a more sexually fluid character, he continues to date Ludwik in secret while also pursuing a heterosexual relationship that is of great benefit to him. Yet playing two sides, he remains a character affixed to Poland and to the lies of state socialism, unable to move or be moved by his desires for Ludwik—affixed by borders, by ties to heterosexuality, and by political aspirations. The novel in whole is narrated from the perspective of Ludwik in New York, looking back on his life, attempting to unravel its unresolved traumas—the injustices of state socialism, his inability to pursue a life of love with Janusz, and his enduring sense of himself as a Polish queer person. He asks, "Did we even believe that we deserved to get away with happiness?"[44] Happiness, or the feeling of suspended freedom, lingers only in that lake in the woods and the time the two men shared in that brief period.

Transnational Readings of Queer Texts

A final core theme of the book involves the role of the transnational flow of queer texts under censorship in Poland. Ludwik's first interaction with James Baldwin's *Giovanni's Room* (1956) appears early in the book when his politically outspoken friend, Karolina, invites him to a covert gay bar and he hears whispered conversation about a book by Baldwin and how "if that won't make you wake up, nothing will."[45] Not long after, while studying in a library, he remembers Baldwin's name and goes in search of the book. He finally gets lucky and finds it at an *antykwariat* used bookstore, where a man who appears as if he "could have been a friend of those men in the bar" brings the book out in a brown-paper package.[46] Importantly, *Giovanni's Room*, like so many books that symbolized a Western ethos of hedonism and excess, was censored during state socialism, even as it was circulated among communities of readers through an underground network.[47] As Ludwik frames it, discussing his postsecondary education, "we couldn't read what we wanted and were meant to see the decadence of capitalism in all Western texts."[48]

Censorship was a key element of population control during state socialism in Poland, with television, film, radio, print sources, and content delivered at universities all undergoing censorship. As Madina Tlostanova writes, "in relation to its colonies the Soviet tactic became more cruel and refined, based on methodical elimination of all alternative thinking and being," part and parcel of which was stringent control of information.[49] At the same time, an underground press was bustling in Poland, especially during the Solidarity era in the 1980s, and many émigré Polish authors wrote books that were then smuggled into Poland. Further, Poland has a rich history of clandestine "Flying Universities" (Uniwersytety Latające), as spaces for independent and anti-totalitarian thinking, and Flying Universities were a key site of revolutionary self-determination in late 1970s Poland.[50] Themes of censorship appear elsewhere in the novel, with Ludzio's mother and grandmother tuning in to the outlawed *Radio Free Europe* (Radio Wolna Europa), the only form of objective news on and about Poland at the time. Further, and ironically, Janusz works at the Office of Press Control, responsible for deciding which books and print materials are censored.

The appearance and transmission of *Giovanni's Room* (1956) throughout *Swimming in the Dark* provides a transnational link to global queer cultures and queer world literatures. Authored by gay African American writer and theorist, it is a story of complex and ambivalent male desire between David, a white bisexual American living in Paris, and Giovanni, an Italian bartender who is sentenced to death for murdering his employer.[51] Reflecting on the importance of this book, Jedrowski writes that while in Brooklyn and shortly after coming out to his parents, he came across Baldwin's book and found that it resonated with his feelings of internalized shame, that it "spoke directly at [him]."[52] Jedrowski's character, Ludwik, similarly finds solace in *Giovanni's Room*, as it "connects him to the wider world."[53] He brings it with him to the youth labor camp after gluing it into the cover of another book, opening it in private after his second meeting with Janusz by the river. He finds that the book "was written for [him] … [that it] united [him] with something."[54] As Ludwik's desire for Janusz builds, he also passes on the book to him—continuing the network of underground state-censored publications.

Importantly, Baldwin's book assists Ludwik in coming to understand his sense of self and it also helps provide a binding force in his relationship with Janusz. Shortly after Janusz borrows the text they spend their formative days by the lake in the pine woods, engulfed by the magic of their love. For Ludwik, these feel like "the first days of [his] life, as if [he'd] been born by that lake and its water."[55] They spend these days "[swimming], fearless and free and invisible in the brilliant dark."[56] Soon after, though, all this begins to fade as Janusz rises in the ranks and Ludwik is left behind with his queer longing. Janusz asks at one point that Ludzio "stop comparing [their relationship] to that book."[57] It is only at the end of the novel when Ludzio is leaving the country and Janusz returns *Giovanni's Room* to him that a note from Janusz confessing that "[he] adored the book more than [Ludwik] knew"[58] slips out.

Giovanni's Room functions as a core element of Jedrowski's novel, gesturing to the worldly travels of queer literature. This intertextual networking partakes in "politicized planetary consciousness."[59] While on the one hand the appearance of Baldwin's novel might be read as flattening LGBTQ+ struggles around the world or even as US literary imperialism, its particular use and circulation in the novel grounds it in the context of Poland, contributing to the texture of Polish queerness. Polish queerness emerges as present and visible in state socialist Poland through the inclusion of a gay bar, the circulation of queer content, and the presence of queer love in the text. The inclusion of Baldwin's book also pushes against an idealization of the West as a place where LGBTQ+ people are free since in Baldwin's text the characters are hiding and lurking in ways similar to the cautions that Ludzio and Janusz practice. Rather than an "enlightened (core)" and backward Central and Eastern Europe, the homophobia navigated by both Baldwin's and Jedrowski's characters suggests links of struggle.[60] Ultimately not suggesting that a move to "the West" is a move to freedom, Jedrowski instead paints a sense of the layers of loss and longing that characterize the lives of both the displaced and those who are forbidden to love, read, and dream on their own terms.

Conclusion

When first reading *Swimming in the Dark*, I was struck by how effortlessly it portrayed queer longing under state socialism while centering a diasporic Polish perspective. *Swimming in the Dark* felt like my own *Giovanni's Room*, diving deep to those currents present yet previously underrepresented in world literature. Tomasz Jedrowski's novel, as I have been arguing, presents us with a series of movements that decentralize heterosexuality and make a case for the centrality of queerness to Polish literature and worldviews. And it is through an analytics of water attuned to flow and movement that we can gain insight into the rigidity of borders and literature understood through those borders. Throughout this chapter I have been drawing out the themes of water from Jedrowski's text in order to make a case for the powerful movements that Polish queer literature presents: offering a movement across borders of Polishness, the flows of sexual desire, and the circulation of censored texts. Readers open to the movements that Polish queer writing presents can find themselves experiencing "a sensation of lightness and power and total inconsequence."[61]

Notes

1   Fernando G. Pagnoni Berns, "Water and Queer Intimacy," in *Space and Subjectivity in Contemporary Brazilian Cinema*, edited by Antônio Márcio da Silva and Mariana Cunha (Cham: Palgrave, 2017), 186 (185–200).

2   Tomasz Jedrowski, *Swimming in the Dark* (New York: HarperCollins, 2020); Magdalena Grabowska, "Bringing the Second World In: Conservative Revolution(s), Socialist Legacies, and Transnational Silences in the Trajectories of Polish Feminism," *Signs*, vol. 37, no. 2 (2012): 385–411.

3   Niviaq Korneliussen, *Last Night in Nuuk*, translated by Anna Halager (New York: Grove Atlantic, [2014] 2019); Pajtim Statovci, *Crossing: A Novel*, translated by David Hackston (New York: Penguin Random House, [2016] 2020); Wanuri Kahiu, *Rafiki*, film, 2018; Qiu Miaojin, *Notes of a Crocodile*, translated by Bonnie Huie (New York: New York Review Books, [1994] 2017).

4   Agnieszka Graff, "Report from the Gender Trenches: War Against 'Genderism' in Poland," *European Journal of Women's Studies*, vol. 21, no. 4 (2014): 431–42; Elizabeth S. Corredor, "Unpacking 'Gender Ideology' and the Global Right's Antigender Countermovement," *Signs*, vol. 44, no. 3 (2019): 613–38.

5   Izabela Filipiak, *Absolutna Amnezja* (Poznań: Obserwator, 1995); Michał Witkowski, *Lovetown* (London: Granta Books, [2004] 2011); Krzysztof Tomasik, *Homobiografie* (Warsaw: Wydawnictwo Krytyki Politycznej, [2008] 2014); Alessandro Amenta, Tomasz Kaliściak, and Błażej Warkocki (eds.), *Dezorientacje: Antologia Polskiej Literatury Queer* (Warsaw: Wydawnictwo Krytyki Politycznej, 2021); Natalia Osińska, *Fanfik* (Warszawa: Krytyka Polityczna, 2016); Natalia Osińska, *Slash* (Warszawa: Agora SA, 2017); Natalia Osińska, *Fluff* (Warszawa: Agora SA, 2019); Lauren Berlant and Michael Warner, "Sex in Public," *Critical Inquiry*, vol. 24, no. 2 (1998): 547–66; José Esteban Muñoz, *Disidentifications: Queers of Color and the Performance of Politics* (Durham, NC: Duke University Press, 1999), 195.

6   Debra Castillo, "Gender and Sexuality in World Literature," in *The Routledge Companion to World Literature*, edited by Theo D'haen, David Damrosch, and Djelal Kadir (London: Routledge, 2012), 394.

7   Edward Said, "The Politics of Knowledge (1991)," in *Reflections on Exile and Other Essays* (Cambridge, MA: Harvard University Press, 2000).

8   James Baldwin, *Giovanni's Room* (New York: Penguin Books, [1956] 2001).

9 Tiffany Lethabo King, *The Black Shoals: Offshore Formations of Black and Native Studies* (Durham, NC: Duke University Press, 2019), 5.

10 Michel Foucault, *The History of Sexuality: An Introduction*, vol. 1 (New York: Vintage Books, [1978] 1990), 43; David Chioni Moore, "Is the Post- in Postcolonial the Post- in Post-Soviet? Toward a Global Postcolonial Critique," *PMLA*, vol. 116, no. 1 (2001): Special Topic: Globalizing Literary Studies 111–28.

11 Maria Konopnicka, *Rota* (*The Oath*), 1908: https://wolnelektury.pl/katalog/lektura/rota.html.

12 Tomasik, *Homobiografie.*

13 Witold Gombrowicz, *Trans-Atlantyk*, translated by Carolyn French and Nina Karsov (New Haven, CT: Yale University Press, [1953] 2008).

14 Jerzy Andrzejewski, *Ashes and Diamonds* (*Popiół i Diament*), translated by D. J. Welsh (Evanston, IL: Northwestern University Press, [1948] 1996); Andrzej Wajda, *Popiół i Diament*, film, 1961.

15 Piotr Sobolczyk, *Polish Queer Modernism* (Warsaw: Peter Lang, 2015), 22, 141–3.

16 Agnieszka Graff, "Lost between the Waves? The Paradoxes of Feminist Chronology and Activism in Contemporary Poland," *Journal of International Women's Studies*, vol. 4, no. 2 (2003): 100–16; Robert Kulpa and Joanna Mizielinska (eds.), *De-Centring Western Sexualities: Central and Eastern European Perspectives* (Farnham: Ashgate, 2011).

17 Kulpa and Mizielinska, *De-Centring Western Sexualities.*

18 Piotr Sobolczyk, "Foucault: Madness and Surveillance in Warsaw," *Foucault Studies*, no. 25 (2018): 187; Krzysztof Tomasik, *Gejerel: Mniejszości Seksualne w PRL-u* (Warszawa: Wydawnictwo Krytyki Politycznej, 2018).

19 Graff, "Report from the Gender Trenches"; Corredor, "Unpacking 'Gender Ideology' and the Global Right's Antigender Countermovement."

20 Kulpa and Mizielinska, *De-Centring Western Sexualities*, 15, 16.

21 Baldwin, *Giovanni's Room*; Said, "The Politics of Knowledge."

22 Tomasz Jedrowski, "On Writing the Story of Polish Queerness: Tomasz Jedrowski Returns to Warsaw," *Literary Hub* (April 30, 2020), https://lithub.com/on-writing-the-story-of-polish-queerness/, n.p.

23 Adi Kuntsman, *Figurations of Violence and Belonging: Queerness, Migranthood and Nationalism in Cyberspace and Beyond* (Frankfurt am Main: Peter Lang, 2009), viii.

24 Jedrowski, "On Writing the Story of Polish Queerness," n.p.

25 Ann Steiner, "World Literature and the Book Market," in *The Routledge Companion to World Literature*, edited by Theo D'haen, David Damrosch, and Djelal Kadir (London: Routledge, 2012), 316 (316–24).

26 Tamara Trojanowska, Joanna Niżyńska, and Przemysław Czapliński, *Being Poland: A New History of Polish Literature and Culture since 1918* (Toronto: University of Toronto Press, 2018), xix.

27 Jedrowski, *Swimming in the Dark*, 1.

28 Jedrowski, "On Writing the Story of Polish Queerness," n.p.

29 Jedrowski, *Swimming in the Dark*, 5.

30 Ewa Płonowska Ziarek, "Melancholic Nationalism and the Pathologies of Commemorating the Holocaust in Poland," in *Imaginary Neighbors: Mediating Polish-Jewish Relations after the Holocaust*, edited by Dorota Glowacka and Joanna Zylinska (Lincoln: University of Nebraska Press, 2007), 310 (301–26).

31 Jedrowski, *Swimming in the Dark*, 71; Sobolczyk, "Foucault: Madness and Surveillance in Warsaw," 186.

32 Jedrowski, *Swimming in the Dark*.

33 In the context of Poland, queer or *kłir*, often signifies differently than in Anglocentric contexts, being perceived as more dirty and less respectable a term as well as sometimes a Western import. I use the term nonetheless in its Polish spelling to hone the Polish queerness of the novel. See Łukasz Szulc, "From Queer to Gay to Queer.pl: The Names we Dare to Speak in Poland," *Lambda Nordica*, vol. 17, no. 4: 65–98. For more on language used for queer people in Poland, see also: Tomasz Basiuk and Jędrzej Burszta, "Introduction: Queers in the People's Republic of Poland: An Uneven Landscape," 5.in *Queers in State Socialism: Cruising 1970s Poland*, edited by Tomasz Basiuk and Jędrzej Burszta (London: Routledge, 2021), 5 (1–8).

34 Jedrowski, *Swimming in the Dark*, 28.

35 Sobolczyk, "Foucault," 187–8; Tomasik, *Gejerel*, 41; Basiuk and Burszta, "Introduction Queers in the People's Republic of Poland: An Uneven Landscape," 2.

36 Remigiusz Ryziński, *Foucault w Warszawie* (Warszawa: Dowody na Istnienie Wydawnictwo, 2017).

37 Jedrowski, *Swimming in the Dark*, 38.

38 Ibid., 62.

39 Ibid., 63.

40 Berns, "Water and Queer Intimacy," 187.

41 Ibid., 188–9.

42 Audre Lorde, "Uses of the Erotic: The Erotic as Power," in *Sister Outsider* (Berkeley, CA: Crossing Press, [1984] 2007), 56–7 (53–9).

43 Jedrowski, *Swimming in the Dark*, 63.

44 Ibid., 190.

45 Baldwin, *Giovanni's Room*; Jedrowski, *Swimming in the Dark*, 21.

46 Jedrowski, *Swimming in the Dark*, 22.

47 This is based on historical facts, as there is testimony of Polish gay men in Poland reading *Giovanni's Room* in translation. See Tomasz Basiuk, "One's Younger Self in Personal Testimony and Literary Translation," in *Queers in*

State Socialism: Cruising 1970s Poland, edited by Tomasz Basiuk and Jędrzej Burszta (London: Routledge, 2021), 23–32.

48 Jedrowski, *Swimming in the Dark*, 37.

49 Madina Tlostanova, "Postsocialist ≠ Postcolonial? On Post-Soviet Imaginary and Global Coloniality," *Journal of Postcolonial Writing*, vol. 48, no. 2 (2012): 135. *The Black Book of Censorship in Poland* provides a partial account of the books censored in Poland. See: Aleksandar Niczow, *Black Book of Polish Censorship* (Warsaw: Główny Urząd Kontroli Prasy, Publikacji i Widowisk w Warszawie, 1982).

50 Hanna Buczynska-Garewicz, "The Flying University in Poland, 1978–1980," *Harvard Educational Review*, vol. 55, no. 1 (1985): 20–33.

51 Baldwin, *Giovanni's Room*.

52 Jedrowski, "On Writing the Story of Polish Queerness," n.p.

53 Ibid.

54 Jedrowski, *Swimming in the Dark*, 45.

55 Ibid., 65.

56 Ibid., 66.

57 Ibid., 177.

58 Ibid., 191.

59 Wendy Knepper and Sharae Deckard, "Towards a Radical World Literature: Experimental Writing in a Globalizing World," *ariel: A Review of International English Literature*, vol. 47, nos. 1–2 (2016): 13.

60 Jon Binnie and Christian Klesse, "Like a Bomb in the Gasoline Station': East–West Migration and Transnational Activism around Lesbian, Gay, Bisexual, Transgender and Queer Politics in Poland," *Journal of Ethnic and Migration Studies*, vol. 39, no. 7 (2013): 1114.

61 Jedrowski, *Swimming in the Dark*, 63.

12

Between the Mythical and the Modern: Polishness in the Work of Olga Tokarczuk and Dorota Masłowska

Marta Koronkiewicz and Paweł Kaczmarski

1

Born over two decades apart—and having published their first books in, respectively, 1993 and 2002—Olga Tokarczuk and Dorota Masłowska started their careers in two distinct historical moments. In the early 1990s, the future Nobel Prize winner entered what must have seemed at the time like an open and relatively level field: a literary scene defined by a vast network of independent publishing houses, journals, and magazines, as well as a newly found sense of artistic freedom (due to the recent dissolution of the state censorship apparatus). For a while, many writers and commentators were eager to associate the free market with emancipation rather than competition.[1] It was in this context that Tokarczuk's work sought to reconcile high- and lowbrow literature, combining an array of modernist themes and techniques with an appeal to more popular tastes; her goal, as described by some of her early readers, was to make modernism accessible to a wider, more mainstream audience.

Dorota Masłowska, on the other hand, published her first novel *Snow White and Russian Red* after this moment of euphoria had arguably passed.[2] Her early books, full of black humor and ostensibly cynical or even nihilistic in nature, are steeped from the get-go in the peculiar mood of working-class Poland of the late 1990s and early 2000s, with its overwhelming sense of hopelessness, social inertia, and the "plastic-like" quality of the world as it is experienced daily by the novel's protagonists. Here, the choice of "lowbrow" language or form is no longer seen as an actual choice; rather, it is accepted as a prerequisite for a novelist who aims to achieve success in a market society. Thus, whereas Tokarczuk actively sought to make modernism more appealing to the mass reader, Masłowska strived to reinvent certain modernist gestures from deep within the postmodern and pop cultural imaginary. One could say that they approached a similar problem—how to resolve the tension between modernism's traditional inaccessibility and the expectations of the market—from two diametrically opposed sides. Hence the pronounced differences in style and tone between the two writers: Tokarczuk's proclivity for the spiritual and the myth-like stands in stark contrast to Masłowska's ironic pseudo-realism, and the former's cautious, moralizing optimism is politically very distant from the overt, scoffing misanthropy that became somewhat of a signature of the latter's early work. For all their differences, Tokarczuk and Masłowska do, however, touch upon a few shared issues or themes. One of these themes is Polishness as such. They both provide a certain set of observations on and intuitions regarding Polish identity, or the experience of being Polish.

In this chapter, we aim to compare some of the ways in which Tokarczuk and Masłowska imagine, describe, or represent Polishness. In addition to being one of the central themes in the work of both authors, the issue of Polishness may be seen as a focal point of sorts, channeling some of the intuitions or assumptions foundational to their work. In the first part of the article, drawing on the work of Krzysztof Uniłowski, we will expound on some of the ways in which Tokarczuk's work constitutes the repurposing of traditional modernist tropes. In the second part, we will explain how this repurposing affects the novelist's account of Polishness as a quasi-metaphysical condition. Finally, in the third part we will contrast this account with a more critical approach offered by Dorota Masłowska.

2

It seems safe to say that in the English-speaking world the response to Tokarczuk's work has been overwhelmingly positive, especially in recent years. Critics have variously praised her for raising questions rather than providing answers,[3] for standing on the side of "meaningful connectedness" and "fluidity, mobility, illusoriness,"[4] for creating "a general account of the subject position and view of history,"[5] or for asking about such fundamental issues as "the nature of human beings, the meaning of suffering, and the existence or non-existence of God";[6] most, however, seem in agreement as to the aesthetic value of—and the general metaphysical wisdom present in— Tokarczuk's novels. Writing in English, various Polish authors have joined in this praise, eager to present the aforementioned wisdom as a uniquely Polish contribution to the canon of world literature.[7]

Considering all that, and the fact that outside of the English-speaking world the Nobel Prize is often seen as a symbol not just of international recognition but also of *national* recognition—confirming the writer's status not only as one of the most influential authors in the world but also the leading author *of their language*—the Western reader may be excused for assuming that the response to Tokarczuk's work has been similarly positive in Poland itself. This, however, has hardly been the case.

Much has been made of the fierce, politically motivated right-wing backlash against Tokarczuk;[8] an avid vegan, self-proclaimed leftist, and a former member of the editorial team of the social–liberal *Krytyka Polityczna*, she certainly embodies a political attitude perceived as dangerous and hostile by most conservatives. Over the years, she has been harassed and even threatened by those who perceived her work as "anti-Polish"—journalists and politicians, as well as anonymous readers. This allowed the mainstream media, both in Poland and abroad, to offer a straightforward narrative about Tokarczuk as a major left-leaning writer forced to defend herself from conservative populists, with those defending her automatically branded as progressive, and everyone else relegated to the nationalist right. And certainly, much praise for Tokarczuk's work, both as a writer and an activist, has indeed come from those associated with the political left.[9] However, such a narrative risks omitting a crucial fact: from the very beginning of Tokarczuk's career, she was criticized by a variety of authors and critics not affiliated with the right; indeed, some of the most prominent critical voices came from the left. Moreover, the initial response to Tokarczuk's work was overwhelmingly negative.[10] And although over the years critics and academics have undoubtedly warmed up to Tokarczuk—with the critical voices reduced to a clear minority—she is still in no way universally admired by those outside of the nationalist right, as some journalistic accounts seem to suggest.

The reasons for this ambiguity vary. In the early 1990s, Tokarczuk's contemporaries criticized her for an insufficiently experimental approach to literary form, and a general aesthetic conformism. Today, young left-leaning critics tend, primarily, to take issue with her generalized or insufficiently concrete moral and political observations;[11] others have criticized her for the allegedly simplistic, naïve, or superficial messages of her novels.[12] However, arguably the most influential, and the most extensive critique of Tokarczuk's general approach to writing and literature was developed from the mid-1990s onward by Krzysztof Uniłowski—an early proponent of postmodernism in Polish prose, and an influential critic and academic broadly associated with the non-Marxist left. It was Uniłowski who famously described Tokarczuk as the embodiment of the new Polish *proza środka*.[13] Loosely translated as *middlebrow prose*, in Uniłowski's account *proza środka* was defined specifically not by its target audience but by its approach to certain "high modernist" strategies and conventions. It was, in other words, a technical term describing the work itself, rather than its place in the canon.

In essence, *proza środka*—embodied, according to Uniłowski, most perfectly by Tokarczuk's novels such as *Primeval and Other Times* or *House of Day, House of Night*—aimed for a certain superficial resemblance to the works of the modernist canon, while at the same time reversing the very role of the specific modernist gestures or techniques that it employed. For, although Tokarczuk's books looked and sounded like typical modernist novels, Uniłowski argued, they did so in order to draw in, rather than challenge or distance themselves from, their intended audience. Uniłowski pointed out that, for instance, while critics derived clear pleasure from the work of decoding the rich intertextual layer of *Primeval and Other Times*, such decoding seemed to hardly impact their overall interpretation and opinion of the novel, as if each intertextual reference was a self-contained, isolated puzzle for the reader to solve. This resulted in what Uniłowski called the "yes, and ..." model of interpretation, or a "conjunction-based" criticism: where the critics' account of the novel took the form of a simple enumeration of elements and intertextual links, rather than a coherent argument.[14] Importantly, such a way of reading did not stem from the critics' failure to connect with the work, or their inability to grasp its intertextual nature—quite the contrary, it was only possible insofar as the readers were able to understand the intended references. Meanwhile, the central message of Tokarczuk's books remained clear—to embrace the fleeting nature of all being, and to approach other living beings with empathy and kindness, in order to alleviate the well-known fundamental ills of the modern world[15]—but, crucially, it was also independent of any singular reference or intertextual connection. As Uniłowski pointed out, one could argue that the various literary, philosophical, or spiritual traditions from which Tokarczuk borrowed were fundamentally incompatible,[16] and that, when incorporated into a single work, they should bring about a tension which the author would then be forced to try and resolve in one way or another; however, having subsumed them all into a straightforward "metaphysical" or "parabolic" message (two words often used in the context of Tokarczuk's early work), the novelist virtually dismissed their potentially contradictory implications. Similarly, the self-referential commentary present in most of Tokarczuk's books, the play of genres and forms in novels such as *House of Day, House of Night* (and later *Flights*), or the pop psychology of *E.E.* were easy enough to comprehend, but their role in shaping the overall meaning of the text was ultimately unclear, as it could be grasped independently of the reader's ability to solve any given "puzzle."

According to Unilowski, this meant that *proza środka* was a perfect fit for a new kind of postsocialist middle-class Polish reader. Born of the transition to capitalism and liberal democracy in the 1990s, this new bourgeois audience was in the market for literature that would be relatively easy (and, perhaps more importantly, *quick*) to read, while also able to double as a status symbol. Formal ambitions would go here hand in hand with thematic ones, but both would be ultimately betrayed by the essentially *undemanding* nature of the work:

> [Tokarczuk's books] were presented in full glory of artistic achievement, as partners in conversation with the greatest works of the global canon— they offered an analysis of the Polish "here and now," whilst speaking of the fundamentals: the meaning and meaninglessness of the human existence, the crumbling values, the various paths and wildernesses of civilization ... All this delivered a unique readerly pleasure, rooted in the sense that we're standing face in face with a work of the highest order, while simultaneously we're being validated as readers—because apparently the work can't hide any secrets from us.[17]

In other words, *proza środka* was targeted not just at those interested in the modern novel but at those who expected a modern novel to look a certain way as well—without, necessarily, requiring a huge amount of effort on the part of the reader. The goal was to provide such an audience first and foremost with *pleasure* rather than any original meanings. Thus, the same forms, techniques, and conventions that, in the original modernist novel, might have seemed demanding for the audience were now transformed in such a way as to seem inviting instead. They no longer expressed an author's expectation of the audience; rather, they were a response to the audience's own expectations. Or, to put it in slightly different terms, rather than constitute a demand, they *supplied* a demand.

Of course, this brought about a potentially deeper problem. To the extent that Tokarczuk's modernism was simply intended to answer the reader's preexisting expectations, it did not—could not—contribute to the meaning of her novels; it was not a vehicle of any particular authorial intention. Unilowski describes this in terms of a distinction between two kinds of "faith" that may emerge in the act of reading: the faith that the work of literature compels by itself, and the reader's own faith that is only reflected back at them by the work. "Good literature certainly compels us to believe in it. What's deceitful about the review, is the reviewer's conflating of what the work compels us to believe and our own beliefs."[18] In its late stage of *proza środka*, the modernist novel is reduced to a passive reflection of the reader's faith, specifically, their faith in the inherent value of the modernist tropes, forms, and conventions. In this sense, *proza środka* was entirely self-referential. As one English-speaking critic put it, "*Flights* seeks itself—it's a cabinet of curiosities that is about cabinets of curiosities, a work of cultural tourism about cultural tourism, a series of movements about movement."[19] Uniłowski called this the *erosion* of modern literature; the more fitting word might be *implosion*:

> *The middlebrow prose* as a distinct phenomenon emerged as the modern culture and artistic consciousness eroded. By adapting certain solutions from the field of poetics, "the middlebrow prose" secures its superficial similarity to the works of "high" modernism—thus even serving to preserve, one could argue, the remnants of the old literary code. This, however, results in that code being fetishized. From now on, it is considered precious not because it allows one to achieve certain artistic values (aesthetic, cognitive, literary-historical etc.), but because it appears as a value in itself.[20]

3

This repurposing of modernist conventions in Tokarczuk's work sheds new light on the oft-emphasized role of *mystery* in her writing. As far back as the early 1990s, "mystery" was a key word in the reception of her novels; critics have always recognized that Tokarczuk's proclivity for the myth, the parable, and the fairytale stemmed from her desire to evoke an air of metaphysical or mystical secrecy.[21] This was of course only reinforced by her frequent usage of Buddhist, gnostic—and later, in *The Books of Jacob*, kabbalistic—tropes. And, just as Tokarczuk's modernism was largely aimed at providing the reader with a certain kind of pleasure, this sense of occult-like knowledge had a very similar purpose:

> The commentary presented alongside the plot suggests that we're in the presence of things mysterious and extraordinary. Meanwhile, its simplicity and lack of ambiguity turn the mystery transparent. Thus the reader is able to move lightning fast, time after time, the whole path from total ignorance to complete knowledge and initiation—without any effort on their part ... Rather than mean anything, the narrator's comments now serve to attribute a certain "depth" to the world, which may then be contemplated.[22]

Clearly, the reduction in distance between the mystery and its solution is partly the result of the way Tokarczuk builds the intertextual layer of her novels: a series of self-contained puzzles, entirely reliant on the reader's prior knowledge and aimed at providing the audience with "readerly pleasure," they allow the reader to traverse the way quickly and repeatedly from the occult to the revealed and back again.

Writing about *Drive Your Plow Over the Bones of the Dead*, one of the otherwise enthusiastic critics seemingly unintentionally admits as much: "This book is not a mere whodunit: It's a philosophical fairy tale about life and death that's been trying to spill its secrets. Secrets that, if you've kept your ear to the ground, you knew in your bones all along."[23] Tokarczuk shares with us secrets that *we already know*. This allegorical transparency of much of Tokarczuk's work results in some unintentionally humorous moments, like in this interview for the online site *Literary Hub*:

JF: There is something in this book about the elements, that water keeps coming up and whales which are swimming through the book. It does feel like a real journey, in a classical sense, ends at or travels across water. Do you think there's something mythic about water? That we long for it in some way?

OT: Of course it is. This is the metaphor of our unconsciousness.[24]

When elaborating on references to William Blake—the poet whose ubiquitous presence in the novel, *Drive Your Plow Over the Bones of the Dead*, is arguably solely responsible not just for its thematic consistency but also its narrative coherence—Tokarczuk reaffirms the importance of Blake's mystical–philosophical thought to her work, while simultaneously reducing the contents of said thought to a simple, unambiguous affective message:

IJB: The protagonist loves animals, wants to save them, believes they have souls, that they are our smaller brothers. She should therefore be the personification of goodness, warmth, gentleness; but, in the meantime, we meet someone full of anger. Isn't that a contradiction?

OT: This book tells the story of a world which, according to the protagonist, is unjust, evil, and built on bad foundations. This is what reading Blake is all about for her; she draws on his philosophy, and it is rather a negative assessment of the world in which we live, the Ulro Earth. Duszejko, as a pure and innocent person, cannot abide in a world that is sinister, aggressive, terrible, cruel, and sometimes macabre. So the only emotion that is born in a holy person is anger. Anger is not a bad energy.[25]

Curiously, some critics praise Tokarczuk for this immediacy of meaning, in a way that feels just a step away from a thinly disguised criticism:

In fact, Tokarczuk's ability to teeter on the edge of out-and-out didacticism—"What sort of a world is this? Someone's body is made into shoes, into meatballs, sausages, a bedside rug, someone's bones are boiled to make broth"; "what about the deluge of meat that falls on our cities day after day like never-ending, apocalyptic rain?"—while only very rarely lapsing into sententiousness ("the human psyche evolved in order to defend us against seeing the truth") is a remarkable achievement in itself.[26]

The difference between such an assessment and a much more unfavorable one—for example, "Tokarczuk's binarism sounds too close to easy campus wisdom, to postmodern piety, even to neoliberal commerce: leaving is good, staying is bad; deracination is expansive, rootedness is dangerous"[27]—seems largely arbitrary, and rooted in the critics' preexisting goodwill.

Considering how foundational the strategy of instant revelation has been to most, if not all, of Tokarczuk's novels, it is hardly surprising that the alleged reverence for the mysterious, the mythical, and the occult was quickly recognized as her signature of sorts. It was not a result of an arbitrary decision; rather, as we have shown, it seems to have stemmed from a series of formal choices, and a very specific approach to the legacy of the modernist novel. It is also not surprising that the same mythical/mystical aura has come to define the novelist's approach to Polishness. Tokarczuk's English-speaking reader may be familiar with her ideas on the epistemic difference between the East and the West, as laid out, for instance, in an interview for the *Guardian*:

> The first thing is that we [Poles] don't trust reality as much as you do. Reading English novels I always adore the ability to write without fear about inner psychological things that are so delicate. In such a form you can develop a story in a very linear way, but we don't have this patience. We feel that in every moment something must be wrong because our own story wasn't linear. Another difference is that you are rooted in psychoanalysis while we're still thinking in a mythical, religious way.[28]

Setting aside the potentially controversial claim about English novels being consistently dismissive of human psychology, this statement ties neatly into Tokarczuk's opinions on the Enlightenment ("when the people started to think about the world as a collection of mechanisms, toys, manners"[29]) and her appreciative account of heterodox fields of knowledge such as astrology ("It's a very old science, or rather art, that foreshadowed psychology, perhaps even some kind of sociological way or thinking ... I think that every modern educated person should be familiar with the basic astrological vocabulary"[30]). Speaking on the literature of Central Europe in general, the writer reiterates the view that it "questions reality more. It's more distrustful of stable, permanent things."[31]

Curiously, this implicit essentialism has, on occasion, led the avowedly antinationalist author to observations that wouldn't seem entirely out of place coming from the mouth of a right-wing intellectual: "I suddenly realized that being Polish meant belonging to a cultural community that posed a real challenge. It's not easy to be Polish. You can easily lose your Polishness by disappearing into the big world."[32] Again, Tokarczuk's account of the unique nature of Polish experience and history seems rooted in the idea of Polishness as something unstable, ever-changing, "non-linear"—which, in this particular case, means that to be Polish is to always verge on nonexistence. But the idea of Polishness as a precarious or liminal condition is a returning theme in most of Tokarczuk's novels. In *E.E.*, the nature of Breslau as a historical no-man's-land—that ultimately ended up in Polish hands—seems to reflect and even influence the mental state of the protagonist. In *House of Day, House of Night*, the entire region of Lower Silesia is portrayed in similar terms: "Like the region in which the story takes place, with its ever-shifting national borders, both characters [Paschalis and Wilgefortis] inhabit a liminal state, which seems to enhance their capacity for empathy."[33] These ideas, in early novels largely limited to a particular region of the country, come to be extrapolated in *The Books of Jacob*— where Poland itself becomes the land of the sacred messianic promise—and before that, to a smaller extent, in *Flights*. Interestingly, in *Drive Your Plow Over the Bones of the Dead*, the only novel where Tokarczuk openly and explicitly confronts contemporary Polish identity as a potentially harmful political construct, the place of the mystical melting pot of cultures is taken instead by Czechia: "The Czech Republic is fetishized [here] as a low-key Shangri-La where people are 'capable of discussing things calmly and nobody quarrels with anyone else'."[34]

Of course, Tokarczuk's mysticism of Polishness may be seen as a marketing strategy; such a reading would be in line with Uniłowski's observations. Undoubtedly, the novelist's insistence on the unique nature of Polish identity and history has led some Western readers to judge favorably elements of her novels that would otherwise probably go unnoticed. The fragmented narrative of *Flights*, for instance, hardly formally innovative on its own, was praised for its connection to the ever-changing nature of the Polish borders.[35] Some critics who otherwise remained relatively skeptical about Tokarczuk's work, have nonetheless appreciated the parts of her books where she explicitly touches on the issue of Polish identity.[36] And it was the account of Polishness as a unique metaphysical condition that allowed Per Wästberg—in his Nobel Prize presentation speech—to present *The Books of Jacob* as an important commentary on not just local but global politics: on the alleged dangers of populism, and the value of open borders.[37] Of course, Tokarczuk would not be the first Polish writer to rely on the idea of a historical–epistemic difference between Poland and the Western world in order to amplify her voice: among modern authors, such a strategy is probably associated first and foremost with Czesław Miłosz.[38]

However, even if this is true—that is, even if Tokarczuk's account of Polishness stems from essentially extratextual reasons—it is, as we have aimed to show, equally strongly rooted in a particular approach to literary form; specifically, a repurposing of tropes and conventions traditionally associated (at least in the Polish context) with the modernist novel. Tokarczuk's idea of an *accessible* modernism, of reconciling the modernist legacy with the imperative of instant readerly gratification—as described by Uniłowski in his account of *proza środka*—lays the foundation for a general aura of secrecy, mysteriousness, and metaphysical enigma that has over time become the signature mood of Tokarczuk's work. This aura, when projected back onto the author's own culture and language, results in something that may only be described as a mysticism of Polishness.

4

Polishness is an explicit theme in virtually all of Dorota Masłowska's books, and a central one—ostensibly, at least—in most of them. It is therefore of little surprise that many reviewers of her breakthrough debut novel *Snow White and Russian Red* from 2002 saw it first and foremost as an account of life in Poland at the turn of the century, as seen through the eyes of the young generation (to which the author herself belonged). Such interpretation was shared by Polish-, as well as English-speaking readers—although among the former, the focus on alleged realism in *Snow White and Russian Red* was particularly strong in the more mainstream media.[39] Meanwhile, the latter frequently saw Masłowska as a "voice of a generation," an author who speaks on behalf of the young Poles confused and frustrated by the less-than-perfect postsocialist reality. Occasionally, this could lead to some harsh criticism:

> Perhaps a portrait of what might be termed Poland's Generation No can hardly look any different. With the pieties of the Communist years discredited and the dividends of European integration still years away, the country's youth idles in a no man's land. That will change as Poland gains a surer sense of itself, but until then characters like Maslowska's are lost, and so are her American readers.[40]

This is not to say that Masłowska's account of Polishness was seen as a realistic one, at least not in any straightforward sense. English-speaking critics noted her "postmodernist" ambitions and experimental proclivities, comparing her—not always favorably—to authors such as Ginsberg, Burroughs, or Bret Easton Ellis. However, even Masłowska's potential anti-realism was seen first and foremost as a means to an essentially realistic end: a more persuasive, more insightful depiction of everyday life in modern Poland. Similarly, even when discussing the more linguistic aspects of Masłowska's novel—as her American translator, Benjamin Paloff, rightly pointed out, Masłowska's work often relies more on the language of her characters than the plot as such[41]—many critics were quick to assume that the speech patterns of characters such as Nails (*Snow White and Russian Red*'s protagonist) were meant to mimic the actually existing language of the Polish lower class, especially its young and urban members.[42] (Curiously, this led at least one reviewer to ignore the fact that the novel is clearly written using free indirect speech and to condemn it as a piece of nationalist propaganda.[43])

All of this, however, was nothing less than an act of intentional deception on Masłowska's part. Nails's odd, meandering monologue, which constitutes the entirety of *Snow White and Russian Red*'s narrative, in no way resembles the everyday speech of any identifiable demographic living in Poland today. Which is not to say that the novel's language is entirely made up, invented by the author from scratch—rather, it was designed as an amalgam of various existing languages, discourses, and speech habits; a tightly knit patchwork of words and phrases taken from intentionally—and sometimes radically—distant realms of contemporary Polish language. To quote once more her American translator, Masłowska has a "preternatural gift for hearing all kinds of language and then making them glue together ... We giggle because there's a mash-up, gray-album quality to hearing political sloganeering and street lingo in the same utterance."[44] Far from being a straightforward rendition of the way young Poles talked and acted on an everyday basis at the turn of the century, Nails's language borrowed as much from the media, political discourse, business, and even literature, as it did from the lower-class "street lingo."

The recognition of the ultimate unrealism of *Snow White and Russian Red* poses the question about the purpose of such approach. On a superficial level, it allows for an ad hoc commentary on the nature of various "assimilated" discourses, and the unexpected, hidden, or even shameful links between them. The argument about whether there is anything *beyond* that in the novel—whether Masłowska's linguistic panache serves anything besides simple satire—dominated much of the Polish discussion of *Snow White and Russian Red*, and Masłowska's work in general, at least outside of the mainstream media.[45] Today, two responses seem to stand out in particular: Przemysław Czapliński's and Krzysztof Uniłowski's.

Czapliński was quick to emphasize that Nails did not represent any coherent identity, any single class or demographic, and that to assume otherwise would constitute a clear "interpretive error" on the part of the reader:

> The protagonist of *Snow White and Russian Red*—who exactly is he?
> I think it's a serious interpretive error to see him as a chav, a thug, or a

lumpen … To put it briefly, Nails' head is full of the same mess, the same mistaking of wishes for analyses, that we might find in the heads of many members of society and its representatives … Nails is simultaneously progressive and regressive, revolutionary and reactionary, left-wing and right-wing, anti-European and pro-European. His consciousness is ruled by frustrations, and it's them that tell him to snort in—alongside a large dose of fet—all the possible contemporary languages, all the doctrines and theories. Nails combines them in an incoherent manner because he's after words that are effective, rather than any coherence. This is why he acts like a garbage processing plant, not sorting anything, but rather transforming it all into a uniform pulp: once totalizing concepts— the welfare state, the individual liberation, liberalism, free market— are unceremoniously cut up and glued back together. We could call it: remnantisation.[46]

According to Czapliński, at the end of the day, Masłowska's linguistic patchwork *is* indeed intended as a commentary on the history of Polishness. It is not, however, a straightforward depiction of the experience of any particular person, or a group of people; rather, Masłowska offers a social commentary by way of linguistic discontinuity: a practical rejection of the idea of a common language, or a common identity. Hence what the critic calls the "ambiguous realism" of Masłowska's work: at the end of the day, the book offers a *certain kind* of an indirectly realist account, but its nature—the *object* of the account—is very different from what the reader could expect. Specifically, what Masłowska strives to depict is not the language or behavior of any specific demographic but, first, the very impossibility of common language, and, second, the "affective" layer beneath, the "glue" that holds together the wildly different habits and discourses, and which consists chiefly of fears, phobias, and impotent anger that implicitly organize Polish society. This, according to Czapliński, is the main message of *Snow White and Russian Red*, and perhaps Masłowska's work more generally: the history of modern Poland has been ruled by affects, and not just any affects but primarily the regressive, defensive, and ultimately futile ones. "The protagonists are humiliated: factually or phantasmatically, in reality or according to their own delusions; either way they experience the world as a source of humiliation. And this point of view, this humiliation, is the only point of view shared across all of the author's work."[47] Polishness as fear and humiliation, a purely negative vision: seen in such light, Masłowska emerges as almost an antithesis of Tokarczuk's mythologizing attitude.

Uniłowski remains as radical in his reading of *Snow White and Russian Red* as Czapliński, although his interpretation points in a significantly different direction—at least initially. He, too, agrees that Nails does not represent any existing demographic:

Undoubtedly, [the recent popularity of] the idea of "getting back to representation" helped the book a lot. Here, the representation could even just mean the discovery of a new part of the world, where no other novelist has been before. This was supposed to be achieved by the force of the linguistic sensitivity of the teenage author, who had allegedly torn whole pieces of the language-flesh out of the fabric of reality, and now dished them out in the form of Nails' somewhat gibberish monologues. But the youth slang, as far as it is used in the book, is not used here as a reference, a quote. It has become a tool of author's creation. What she did, is describe the world as it emerges from that language. For the reality created in the work is not a representation of something prior, but a simulation, a linguistic (and not drug-fuelled) projection.

...

Ultimately, the protagonist—as the author's deputy and partner—becomes her victim. Masłowska takes away his voice, in order to emphasize her own authorship.[48]

What's crucial for Uniłowski is the seemingly inverted relationship between "the world" and "the language" in Masłowska's novel. The language comes first: it is made up, entirely invented, and subsumed unto authorial intent in what is arguably a very modernist gesture. The world appears here at all only insofar as it may organically emerge out of that initial forceful act of its creator, as its implicit conclusion. In this sense, Polish history or identity is seen here as incidental; Masłowska's deception does not divert our attention away from one account of Polish identity and onto another, rather, it tricks us into thinking that Poland as such is at all important in the novel. Meanwhile, nothing could be further from the truth; Polishness was never intended as an object of full-fledged authorial commentary, and served, instead, as merely a stepping stone on Masłowska's path toward dramatically different themes and issues, such as the nature of fiction and the possibility of true control over language.

But this, in itself, is obviously a commentary on Polishness. Just like in Czapliński's interpretation Masłowska deceived the reader in order to question the idea of a coherent Polish identity, of Polishness as anything more than a loose set of fears and humiliations, Uniłowski's Masłowska ultimately rejects Polishness as a theme, a potential foundation for a compelling narrative. Czapliński sees Masłowska as actively subversive, Uniłowski as indifferent—although intentionally and conspicuously so. In both cases, the critics seem to suggest that Masłowska ultimately sees Polishness as something profoundly *insufficient*, an identity that remains unable to stand up to readerly (and, possibly, writerly) expectations. This indifference to expectations, the refusal to provide the reader with a coherent (and practical) account of Polishness, clearly differentiates Masłowska from Tokarczuk.

It also explains the confusion professed by some English-speaking critics in relation to Masłowska's later work, specifically two of her plays that were translated into English: *A Couple of Poor, Polish-Speaking Romanians* and *No Matter How Hard We Try*. At least some reviewers felt that Masłowska's text proved elusive, difficult to understand without prior knowledge of its original cultural context. "It's easy to imagine symbolic resonances in Poland that elude the viewer here,"[49] said one critic of *A Couple of Poor, Polish-Speaking Romanians*; another, approaching Masłowska less favorably, speculated, "Dorota Masłowska has been lauded in her native Poland, but something appears to have been lost in translation because this road movie for the stage often loses its way."[50] Yet another advised,

> Those not as well-informed about contemporary Poland or the style of post-modernism will feel more challenged by *No Matter How Hard We Try*, but I think they'll still get a lot out of it if they approach it with curiosity and don't demand that everything make sense to them in the moment ... Masłowska's determination to cut through nationalist mythology and uncover what truly ails people is more prescient than ever.[51]

This non-immediacy of meaning, the recovering of modernism from within postmodernism, and an account of Polishness that intentionally eludes any straightforward identity-building narrative allow Masłowska to attempt a genuine work of demystification and demythologization.

Notes

1 See Przemysław Czapliński, *Powrót centrali: literatura w nowej rzeczywistości* (Kraków: Wydawnictwo Literackie, 2009).

2 All translations belong to the authors unless noted elsewhere.

3 Eileen Battersby, "Complex Harmonies," *Los Angeles Review of Books* (April 11, 2018).

4 Kapka Kasabova, "Flights by Olga Tokarczuk review—the ways of wanderers," *The Guardian* (June 3, 2017).

5 Marta Figlerowicz, "Rewriting Poland," *Boston Review* (September 17, 2018).

6 Ania Ready, "Word without God," *Times Literary Supplement*, [n.d.], https://www.the-tls.co.uk/articles/olga-tokarczuk-fiction/.

7 See especially contents of *The Polish Review: The Literary Landscape of Olga Tokarczuk*, vol. 66, no. 2 (2021).

8 See, that is, Ruth Franklin, "Olga Tokarczuk's Novel against Nationalism," *New Yorker* (July 29, 2019), https://www.newyorker.com/magazine/2019/08/05/olga-tokarczuks-novels-against-nationalism.

9   Monika Świerkosz, "Strategie ocalania," *Dwutygodnik* (2020), nr 11.

10 Krzysztof Uniłowski, *Granice nowoczesności: Proza polska i wyczerpanie modernizmu* (Katowice: Wydawnictwo Uniwersytetu Śląskiego, 2006), 165–6.

11 See, for example, Patryk Kosenda, "Golem z gatunkowej gliny, czyli noblistka na manowcach fantastyki," *Nowy Napis Co Tydzień*, 49 (May 14, 2020), https://nowynapis.eu/tygodnik/nr-49/artykul/golem-z-gatunkowej-gliny-czyli-noblistka-na-manowcach-fantastyki; also see Zuzanna Sala, "Zainteresowania obserwatora," *Nowy Napis Co Tydzień* 43 (April 4, 2020), https://nowynapis.eu/tygodnik/nr-43/artykul/zainteresowania-obserwatora.

12 Maciej Jakubowiak, "Opowieści zwyczajne," *Dwutygodnik*, nr 9 (2019).

13 Krzysztof Uniłowski, *Granice nowoczesności: Proza polska i wyczerpanie modernizmu* (Katowice: Wydawnictwo Uniwersytetu Śląskiego, 2006).

14 Uniłowski, *Granice*, 178–9.

15 Krzysztof, Uniłowski, "Cała prawda o "prozie środka," cz. 2," *FA-art*, nr 4 (2002): 39.

16 Uniłowski, *Granice*, 178–80.

17 Uniłowski, *Granice*, 164.

18 Krzysztof Uniłowski, "Cała prawda o 'prozie środka', cz. 3," *FA-art*, nr ½ (2003): 74. Uniłowski's comments seem to tie interestingly into certain wider observations on the nature of modernism, made recently by Walter Benn Michaels and Nicholas Brown; for more on this, see Paweł Kaczmarski, "Cała prawda o 'czułym narratorze'," *Nowa Dekada* (Spring 2021): https://nowadekada-online.pl/pawel-kaczmarski-cala-prawda-o-czulym-narratorze/.

19 James Wood, "'Flights': A Novel That Never Settles Down," *New Yorker* (October 1, 2018).

20 Uniłowski, "Cała prawda ... cz. 3," 74.

21 Uniłowski, *Granice*, 174–6.

22 Ibid., 184.

23 Sloane Crosley, "One by One, Her Neighbors Are Dying: An Elderly Polish Woman Is on the Case," *New York Times* (August 12, 2019).

24 Olga Tokarczuk, "Nobel Prize-Winner Olga Tokarczuk in Conversation with John Freeman," *Literary Hub* (October 10, 2019).

25 Olga Tokarczuk, "Anger Is Not a Bad Energy": Interview by Izabela Joanna Barry, *Brooklyn Public Library* (January 12, 2020).

26 Evelyn Toynton, "Written in the Stars," *Times Literary Supplement* (November 16, 2018).

27 Wood, "'Flights': A Novel That Never Settles Down."

28 Olga Tokarczuk, "I was very naive. I thought Poland would be able to discuss the dark areas of our history." Interview by Claire Armistead, *The Guardian* (April 20, 2018).

29 Tokarczuk, "Nobel Prize-Winner Olga Tokarczuk in Conversation with John Freeman."

30   Tokarczuk, "Anger Is Not a Bad Energy."

31   Franklin, "Olga Tokarczuk's Novel against Nationalism."

32   Olga Tokarczuk, "On Poland." Interview by Marie Tetzlaff. Dezign Ark, September 13, 2018.

33   Franklin, "Olga Tokarczuk's Novel against Nationalism."

34   Crosley, "One by One, Her Neighbors Are Dying."

35   Franklin "Olga Tokarczuk's Novel against Nationalism."

36   Wood, "'Flights': A Novel That Never Settles Down."

37   Per Wästberg, Award ceremony speech, December 10, 2019, https://www.nob elprize.org/prizes/literature/2018/ceremony-speech/.

38   See, for example, Stanley S. Bill, "Miłosz w dialogu z literackim centrum świata," *Poznańskie Studia Polonistyczne Seria Literacka*, 20, no. 40 (2012): 137–50.

39   See, for example, Elżbieta Bajcar, "Silny myśli," *Charaktery*, nr 3 (2003); Marcel Andino Velez, "Lekcja języka dresiarskiego," *Przekrój*, nr 37 (2002).

40   Boris Fishman, "Bloc Party," *New York Times* (May 1, 2005).

41   Alan Lockwood, "Laugh til you don't: Dorota Maslowska's *A Couple of Poor, Polish-Speaking Romanians*," *Brooklyn Rail* (February 2011).

42   See, for example, Steve Horotwitz, "*Snow White and Russian Red* by Dorota Masłowska," *Pop Matters* (June 17, 2005); Tania Barnes, "Review of *Snow White and Russian Red*," *Library Journal* (January 1, 2005).

43   Elena Seymenliyska, "Rotten Russkies," *The Guardian* (May 7, 2005).

44   Lockwood, "Laugh til you don't."

45   See, for example, Marek Zaleski, "Bajka raczej smutna," *Res Publica Nowa*, nr 11 (2002); Jerzy Pilch, "Monolog Silnego," *Polityka*, nr 37 (2002); Jarosław Klejnocki, "Oda do dresu. Debiut Doroty Masłowskiej: rewelacja czy banał," *Tygodnik Powszechny*, nr 42 (2002).

46   Przemysław Czapliński, "Niepoprawna Masłowska," *Tygodnik Powszechny* (October 14, 2012).

47   Czapliński, "Niepoprawna."

48   Krzysztof Uniłowski, *Kup pan książkę!* (Katowice: FA-art, 2008), 26–7.

49   Eric Grode, "In Poland, at Mercy of Weirdos," *New York Times* (February 20, 2011).

50   Lyn Gardner, "A Couple of Poor, Polish-Speaking Romanians," *The Guardian* (March 7, 2008).

51   Tom Williams, "No Matter How Hard We Try," *Chicago Critic*, https://chicag ocritic.com/no-matter-how-hard-we-try/.

13

Liberature as World Literature

Katarzyna Bazarnik

Introduction

Liberature, a neologism coined by Polish poet Zenon Fajfer, refers to a literary genre in which the text and the material body of the book are fused into a meaningful whole.[1] Described as a book-bound, multimodal genre by the present author,[2] it embraces the kind of creative writing characterized by a linguistic, typographical, and architectural unity designed so by the writer or poet, and "published within an enhancing physical structure."[3] Instances of liberatic works can be found in the past, but it was only at the turn of the millennium that such a category could be properly conceptualized, not least because increasingly more authors have been exploiting such "liberatic," or bookish, poetics. This artistic tendency has been paralleled by an increased critical interest in the multimodality and materiality of writing, evidenced by terms and concepts intended to capture its specificity. In highlighting the combination of semiotic modes within the writing space, liberature is akin to, if not a type of, multimodal literature described by Alison Gibbons.[4] Due to exposing the book as a writing technology and using material metaphors, liberature is related to N. Katherine Hayle's technotexts.[5] Moreover, its poetics is akin to Jessica Pressman's "aesthetics of bookishness," "a trend in novels published since 2000" across the world that "exploit the power of the print page in ways that draw attention to the book as a multimedia format, one informed and connected to digital technologies."[6] Coinciding with or preceding them, liberature emerged at that cultural moment in the region that the Western world perceives as its periphery, to propose a way of reading world literature that would enable us to identify a specific constellation of "material textuality"[7] in the Gutenberg galaxy.

Historicizing the Moment, or a Brief History of Liberature

In 1999 Polish avant-garde poet Zenon Fajfer published an article entitled "Liberature. An Appendix to a Dictionary of Literary Terms," which accompanied "Booksday," an exhibition held as part of Kraków Bloomsday celebrations. The exhibition featured books dubbed "unconventional" by the curators: Fajfer, his artistic collaborator Katarzyna Bazarnik, and Radosław Nowakowski, a writer, translator, and musician. The exhibition included bookworks inspired by Joyce's *ouvre*, experimental poetry and fiction, as well as artists' books from Wexford Arts Centre and those by selected Polish book artists. Reflecting on the exhibits and his own work-in-progress, Fajfer sketched a specific vision of a "World Republic of Letters." Setting the author of *Ulysses* as an example, he distinguished a category of writers "characterized by a rich imagination, unusual courage, and intense desire for totality, complemented by the ability to look at old and well-known matters from unexpected angles"; most importantly, however, they shared a strong belief "that the whole world can be contained in one Book."[8] Pondering the questions of medium, form, space, and time of literature, Fajfer argued that writers could use visual features of writing such as the kind of typeface, layout, types of paper, and the structure of the physical book in a deliberate and self-conscious way, as legitimate means of expression. In the conclusion he suggested that this type of spatialized writing could constitute a theretofore unrecognized literary genre. He labeled it "liberature," deriving its name from Latin *liber*, that is, "book."

In the ensuing volume of essays *Od Joyce'a do liberatury* [From Joyce to Liberature], the present author pointed to other connotations of the term: "*Liber, libra, libera, literature*," expounding that it hints at creative freedom or liberties with regard to dominant literary conventions, as well as the scales or balance, suggestive of aesthetic harmony of textual, visual, and material components.[9] Fajfer and Bazarnik perceived James Joyce as a writer displaying such sensibility,[10] and stressed that instances of liberatic writing could be found in the past. In "A Brief History of Liberature," sketched a few years later, they trace "liberary thinking" to the origins of writing, sacred books of various cultures, shaped poems of antiquity, magic squares, and permutational texts. Their attention focuses on works "driven by the ambition to imitate cosmic or architectonic order" in the "structure of the whole volume," such as Hrabanus Maurus's *Liber de laudibus sanctae crucis*, Dante's "mathematically precise *Divine Comedy*," George Herbert's *The Temple*, Laurence Sterne's *Tristram Shandy*, William Blake's illuminated books, and Stephane Mallarmé's *Un Coup de Des*.[11] More examples of similar sensibility include modernist, postmodernist, and contemporary authors:

Guillaume Apollinaire's *Calligrammes* (1918), e.e. cumming's typographic poetry, the works of Franciszka and Stefan Themersons, Antoine de Saint-Exupéry's *Le Petit Prince* (1943), some works of Michel Butor and Oulipo writers, Tove Jansson's Moomin cycle, W. H. Gass's *Willie Masters' Lonesome Wife* (1968) built out of text and photos, Madeline Gins's *Word Rain* (1969), Raymond Federman's graphic novels, John Cage's mesostichs, anthologies of one-page-long pieces collected by Richard Kostelanetz, Ronald Suckenick's *Out* (1973), Milorad Pavic's *Dictionary of the Khazars* (1984) consisting of two volumes: a male and a female one, and Tadeusz Różewicz's *Płaskorzeźba* (1991), where reproduced autographs of the poems play as important a part as their typeset versions.[12]

They also see liberatic approach in Lawrence Durrell's "spatialized" *Alexandria Quartet*, Julio Cortazar's *Hopscotch*, Mark Z. Danielewski's *House of Leaves*, U. Eco's *La misteriosa fiamma della regina Loana*, and Günter Grass's *Letzte Tänze*, while B. S. Johnson's novels receive a slightly more prominent mention. The British novelist is described as having a "consistently liberary character," and subsequently, has received more in-depth attention in further research stimulated by the concept.[13] His explorations of the architecture of the book (he rejected the word "experiment" as a synonym of an artistic failure) reach its most radical in *The Unfortunates*, a strongly autobiographical narrative printed on unbound signatures placed in a box.

Among Polish writers Fajfer and Bazarnik reference playwright and painter Stanisław Wyspiański, who gave his dramas a refreshingly austere design and supervised their printing, Bruno Schulz whose fiction is complemented by his own illustrations, collaborative poetry volumes of poet Julian Przyboś and designer Władysław Strzemiński, as well as Radosław Nowakowski, who "imagines–writes–draws–designs–edits–prints–binds–calligraphs" his works. The would-be architect, who constructs books instead of houses, used to describe himself as a "book-maker," but with time adopted "liberature" to refer to his work. In 2009 he transformed the informal *książkarnia* "*Ogon słonia*," that is, the Elephant's Tail Book-makery, into a small press called Liberatorium.[14] Along with Bazarnik and Fajfer, he is considered the third key figure in the contemporary liberature movement in Poland.[15]

"Not a Set Canon of Texts but a Mode of Reading"

For the advocates of the proposed genre, these authors and works mapped an emergent "constellation" grouped on the basis of the liberatic (or bookish) poetics. Thus, one important spur to formulate the idea of liberature came from extensive reading motivated by a specific comparatist drive: to spot experiments that entail materiality and spatiality of writing. Such an investigation calls for a historicist enquiry, combined with textual scholarship, genetic criticism, and sociology of texts as developed by Donald F. McKenzie and by Jerome McGann. The liberatic reading requires that the circumstances of a book's creation and production be investigated because it is assumed that the bibliographical code carries authorially shaped meaning on par with the text; thus it is considered a piece of genetic evidence, or a "witness," as textual scholars call it. The expertise of these specialist is essential to identify nodes of such a constellation, whereas the comparative approach is necessary to enable such a grouping at all. The joint pursuit is focused on looking for what has been considered experimental, eccentric, at the margins of the literary, in order to recognize "odd-one-outs" in different cultures and periods.

Admittedly, the above list features quite a few presently canonical names. But one must remember that these works were usually considered highly unconventional when they first appeared. Horace Engdahl reminds us that

> it is easy to become anachronistic when discussing literary values. An intellectual effort is called for to realize that writers such as Proust, Joyce, Kafka and Musil were initially marginal in the literary life of their respective countries, that their works only gradually, and posthumously, found their way to the centre, thanks to new critical methods and thanks to discoverers and followers among writers of subsequent generations.[16]

Interestingly, this is often the case with works that feature in various "world literature" canons. Of Dante David Damrosch remarks that he, "so daunting to Joyce and central in most twentieth-century accounts of the Western tradition, had been virtually ignored for centuries until he was finally rediscovered in the Romantic era."[17] Suffice it to mention *Tristram Shandy*, the model antinovel, subverting the newly established conventions of the genre, of which Samuel Johnson famously declared that "nothing odd will do long."[18] Likewise, Joyce's *Ulysses* puzzled the early readers, not least because of its unconventional typography,[19] while *Finnegans Wake* has been considered an even greater oddity.[20]

The motivation behind drawing such a genealogy of liberature is in line with David Damrosch's observation that "different readers will be obsessed by very different constellations of texts."[21] For liberature, the above-mentioned authors function as both "a common patrimony" and "rich nodes of overlap among many different and highly individual groupings,"[22] transcending national or linguistic traditions. It is evident that those theorizing and analyzing liberature have worked tacitly within the framework of world literature. As we have seen, for Fajfer the primary points of reference are Joyce, Sterne, and Mallarmé, as well as Tadeusz Kantor, an avant-gardist who created autonomous, authorial theater, and Jerzy Grotowski, who drew on ritual practices of India, Mexico, and Haiti.[23] Bazarnik brings in British, American, and French novelists of the 1960s to the discussion.[24] Emiliano Ranocchi perceives liberature as a Polish contemporary movement, "an aesthetically strong issue [sic] in the world," a late offshoot of European modernism that, however, responds to the posthuman world in a non-reactionary way.[25] Although focused on theoretical questions, in her discussion of liberature Agnieszka Przybyszewska refers to a geographically and chronologically broad range of examples of Polish, French, Anglo-American, Italian, Mexican, Brazilian, Russian cultures, including baroque visual poems, early-twentieth-century avant-gardes, and contemporary electronic literature.[26] So does Wojciech Kalaga, who defines liberature as a trans-genre hybridizing different semiotic media.[27] Also Kris Van Heuckelom, offering a formal analysis of Jonathan Safran Foer's *Tree of Codes*, a die-cut novel appropriating Bruno Schulz's *The Street of Crocodiles* in a liberatic manner, locates Foer's book in a transnational context of similarly experimenting writers. Referring to Schulz as "the most world-literary of Polish writers," he concludes that "what seems to link both Foer's and Schulz's artistic projects is their correspondence with a 'transgenre' of literature that the Polish writer Zenon Fajfer has called 'liberature.'"[28]

This array of works appears rather Western-centric, but the inclusion of poetic volumes *Pink Noise* and *60 poems* by Taiwanese poet and lyricist Hsia Yu's in Bazarnik's recent discussion of typology of liberatic book forms[29] opens it up to other cultural zones. Teju Cole's *Blind Spot* analyzed by Sakine Weikert in *Refresh the Book* along Bazarnik's chapter could qualify as liberature by an African writer. Simultaneously, both Hsia Yu and Teju Cole are positioned by commentators as "world authors" thanks to their broad range of cultural references, and living between Taipei, New York, and Paris, or Lagos and New York respectively.[30]

The kind of formalist approach that initially helped formulate the concept suggests that liberature falls within the first of Damrosch's threefold definition of world literature, described "not [as] a set of canon of texts but a mode of reading: a form of detached engagement with worlds beyond our own place and time."[31] Yet, it is also evident that, as Damrosch observes,

> different groups within a society, and different individuals within any group, will create distinctive congeries of works, blending canonical and noncanonical works into effective microcanons. As Bruce Robbins says of a locally inflected cosmopolitanism, it involves not an ideal detachment but "a reality of (re)attachment, multiple attachment, or attachment at a distance" (*Cosmopolitics* 3).[32]

I will illustrate this complex reality using Fajfer and Bazarnik's *Oka-leczenie*, the work whose writing informed the formulation of the concept.

Then, I will present "Liberature" publishing line and the Liberature Reading Room as embodiments of such "effective microcanons."

Oka-leczenie (*I Saw Eyes-Ore*, or *Mute-I-Late*): An Elliptical Refractor

Another, perhaps more significant spur to propose liberature came from Fajfer's own creative work. *Oka-leczenie*, written jointly with the present author in the 1990s, was first issued in the private edition of nine prototype copies in 2000 (the trade edition appeared only in 2009).[33] It is a story about a farewell to the dying father and welcoming a newborn son. Two of its three parts feature a family gathered round the deathbed of the patient in coma, and a couple in labor in the maternity ward of a foreign hospital.[34] The third part seems to be set in an in-between sphere: either stretching between the birth and death, focusing on the moment "when the two bodies participate in the creation of another one, being the very Beginning of the World,"[35] or in *bardo*,[36] according to Buddhist beliefs a kind of transitional state between death and rebirth. The physical structure of the book reflects this ambiguity. The three parts are printed in three separate volumes[37] joined by the shared covers in a concertina-like manner, forming what the German bookbinders call *das Mehrlingsbuch*.

The two narratives set in hospital are written in the so-called emanational technique. As Fajfer explains, he invented it in order to create invisible texts through which he wished to express the impossible: "to render the very moment of death, the moment when the man is exactly In Between—when he has not fully died yet but is no longer alive, when both worlds overlap in the mind of the dying person, accompanied by his relatives unaware of what's going on," and the parallel moment when the baby isn't born yet, "when It is still There, but It will be Here in a little while, emerging from the Invisible into the Visible."[38] The title, an oxymoronic play on words, provides a veiled instruction on how to read the invisible text. *Okaleczenie* means "mutilation," but when cut into two words, the phrase means "healing of the eye." The pun indicates that one should "cut off" (and put together) the initials of every visible word to see the invisible layers. In Fajfer's multileveled acrostic, the procedure should be repeated to uncover three further textual strata until the reader reaches a single word underlying the textual edifice, the word from whose letters the whole text has as if "emanated." Thus decoded text can be interpreted as the gradually extinguishing stream of consciousness of the dying person, and the gradually evolving consciousness of the growing fetus. The readers involved in the delivery of the hidden texts act as guides in the underworld or as midwives, respectively.[39]

The eye featured in the title also hints at the strong visual dimension of the work. A variety of fonts is used to distinguish among different characters taking part in the conversations. The various typefaces are iconically suggestive of the speakers' ages and appearance. For example, an elderly, presumably obese uncle "speaks" in the voice rendered in bold, square font, while a slender, italicized typeface is used for a sickly aunt. This resembles differentiating narrators with various typefaces by Danielewski in *House of Leaves*. The middle volume is inscribed in two types of handwriting. They are used to form sixty-four hexastichs made of broken and continuous lines; they correspond to the complete set of *I Cing: The Book of Changes* (易經) hexagrams. The outer codices contain so-called sign-poems, that is, words whose letters are arranged as a kind of pictogram, one of which Agnieszka Przybyszewska interpreted as the Chinese word kūn (坤),[40] meaning "field," "earth," or "the receptive." Indeed, two sign-poems, made of the letters A, D, E, N, T, form two images: as if a human body stretched on a bed (suggestive of DENAT, i.e., "the deceased"), and a fetus in a womb (anagrammatically changed into DANTE, presumably the name of the baby to be born).[41] Thus, the pages of the book appear as a field of play, where elements of writing (letters, punctuation marks) constantly move to form new words and communicate new meanings.

A few other sign-poems are portraits of the above-mentioned liberatic forefathers: Joyce, Beckett, (T. S.) Eliot, and Dante.[42] They appear at the (visually represented) moments of death and of conception, as if "patron-spirits" of the (textual) being to be born. The Western apparitions are complemented by a reference to a corresponding Eastern deity. What sounds like an apparent spoonerism, "Kurma wać" (a transposition of the common swear word *kurwa mać*),[43] may be in fact an inadvertent invocation to Vāc (also spelled Vach, pronounced as Polish *wać*), a Vedic goddess, a personification of speech, the wife of Vision, the mother of emotions, who gives birth to the uncreated potentialities.[44] The presence of sacred Hindu myths as important intertexts is reinforced in the parallel dialogue in the maternity ward when the couple jokingly allude to the unborn baby as an avatar, and Maitreya.[45] So through the dense network of references to Western and Eastern texts, *Oka-leczenie* aptly exemplifies how a (national) literature transcends its local perspective, absorbing and refracting works of chronologically and spatially distant cultures. This can also serve as an illustration of Damrosch's observations, that "world literature is fully in play once several foreign works begin to resonate together in our mind."[46]

Gained in Translation

Another way in which liberature emerges as a variant of "world literature" is exemplified in the eponymous reading room and publishing series, established soon after the publication of Fajfer's seminal article. They corroborate the third part of Damrosch's definition: that "world literature is writing that gains in translation."[47] In 2002 Fajfer and Bazarnik's long-term loan of their collection of books featuring some of the above-listed titles inaugurated the Liberature Reading Room, initially established in Małopolski Instytut Kultury [Małopolska Institute of Culture] in Kraków. The motivation to found it was to offer both the reading public and prospective scholars access to some unavailable or hardly available works of liberatic character in order to demonstrate a "liberatic constellation" in practice. After a decade it was transferred to the Regional Public Library. For twenty years it has grown to over five hundred items,[48] and in June 2021 was donated to the Jagiellonian Library, one of the two national libraries in Poland, where it is going to form a distinct subcollection in the Rare Books department.[49]

A year after the opening of the Reading Room, *Ha!art Magazine*, a transdisciplinary journal on literature and culture, devoted an issue to Fajfer and Bazarnik's artistic activities. That became an occasion to put the theory into practice by launching a book series in Ha!art publishing house. Bazarnik and Fajfer's *(O)patrzenie* (2003), a slim poetry book, an offshoot of *Oka-leczenie*, became the first title in the series.[50] The aim of the series is to introduce Polish readers to liberatic works so far unknown to them, or to offer more accurate versions of liberatic works already present in Polish translations. The rationale is that, if evidenced, the author's involvement with the extratextual features of the text should be respected. The editorial policy is to respect the specificity of a source work by attempting to reproduce its material features as closely as possible. That's why Raymond Queneau's *Cent mille milliards de poèmes* (*Sto tysięcy miliardów wierszy*, 2008), adapted into Polish by Jan Gondowicz, was published as a book containing the sonnets printed on movable strips. Jerzy Kutnik's translation of Raymond Federman's *Double or Nothing* (*Podwójna wygrana jak nic*, 2010) meticulously reproduces the typescript format of the first edition,[51] the decision that was corroborated by the author. Herta Müller's *Der Wächter nimmt seinen Kamm* (*Strażnik bierze swój grzebień*, 2010), her first collection of collage poems published on postcard-size, loose pages in a box, appeared in the same form, reproducing the original poems with their translations on the reverse. The Polish text does not contain the pictorial components but renders varied typography of newspaper clippings using similar fonts, which was also consulted with the author. Artur Kożuch's translation was the first rendering of Müller's collage poetry into any foreign language, and paved the way for later translations of her collage poems. Of B. S. Johnson's two novels, which have appeared in the series, *The Unfortunates* (*Nieszczęśni*, 2008)[52] is the second foreign translation, and the first one published in a box, as Johnson's original. Though the square format of the first edition was changed into a rectangle, the image of cancer tissue on the cover was preserved. Another highlight of the series is *Finneganów tren* (i.e., James Joyce's *Finnegans Wake* polonized by Krzysztof Bartnicki) whose typographical features and the 628-page length follow the layout of the first edition, prepared in collaboration with the author.

So far twenty-four titles have appeared in the series, including works of contemporary Polish writers who have declared affinity with the idea. Beside Fajfer's works, these are Paweł Dunajko's *an epigraph* (2010), Krzysztof Bartnicki's *Prospekt emisyjny* (Prospectus, 2010), Dariusz Orszulewski's *Jezus nigdy nie był aż tak blady* (Jesus has never been so pale before, 2013) and Robert Szczerbowski's *Antologia* (Anthology, 2013). It also features *Arw* (2007) by Stanisław Czycz. Originated as a screenplay for Andrzej Wajda's unrealized film, this prose poem reconstructed from extant fragments bears many similarities to *The Throw of the Dice*, which it followed in the series. "Rediscovered" in the early 2000s, Czycz's work proved to be as inspirational for then-emergent Polish electronic literature as his French counterpart for modern poetry a hundred years earlier. As Mallarmé's poem, it is also an attempt at representing simultaneity through typographical arrangement of several streams of text. Though not quite qualifying as liberatic, it was perceived as an important element of a wider, international tradition of the works exploiting the material poetics. In the editorial note it was juxtaposed with simultaneous poems of Cabaret Voltaire, Federman's typewritten novel *Double or Nothing*, and Mallarmé's masterpiece.[53]

A Message in the Bottle

Indeed, Mallarmé's *Un coup de des jamais n'abolira de hazard* became the foundational title for the publishing line. Preceding *Arw* in the series, it appeared as *Rzut kośćmi nigdy nie zniesie przypadku* in 2005 in a new translation commissioned specially from Tomasz Różycki, then emerging poet, who received the prestigious Kościelski Prize just before the publication. The bilingual edition contains two versions of the poem: the one published in *Cosmopolis* in 1898, as well as the booklet version prepared by the poet before his death and printed posthumously by his son-in-law in 1914. The editors' note gives a brief editorial history of the French versions with an overview of three prior Polish translations, unfortunately misrepresenting Mallarmé's typographical *espacement*, and justification of editorial choices. It is complemented with the poet's preface from *Cosmopolis*, the translator's commentary, and the foreword and afterword. These paratexts remind the readers how the French poet influenced his English contemporaries by introducing them to free verse,[54] and how the Frenchman himself was deeply impressed by the American Allan Edgar Poe, possibly alluding to his short story "MS. Found in a Bottle" in the poem and compare *Un coup de des* to the Einsteinian breakthrough in literature.[55]

So Mallarmé's work functions in the series as an important node of world literature. However, it appeared only as volume 3 of the series. Since it took some time to raise sufficient funding,[56] in the meantime, when an opportunity arose, Fajfer prepared *Spoglądając Przez Ozonową Dziurę* (*SPOD*, 2004) as volume 2 for the Liberatura series.[57] It is another of Fajfer's emanational poems, and the most unconventional of liberatic publications: the text is printed on a transparent sheet placed in a recycled vodka bottle. *SPOD* met with mixed responses: initially, Przybyszewska dismissed it offhandedly,[58] but a journal for Polish literature teachers *Polonistyka* suggested it for an inclusion in a refreshed canon of contemporary Polish poetry.[59] Yet, Fajfer's gesture was not a trivial one if we consider that Vilém Flusser proposes to consider bottles as revelatory of the "human condition":[60] "Why bottles, of all things? Why, because they are containers, and may therefore reveal something about content and form, the what and the how, matter and method."[61] The philosopher persuasively argues that culture consists in production of forms; the more forms we keep, the richer our culture is. The rejected ones are garbage; disposed of, ignored, yet continually accommodating and causing problems to both natural and cultural ecosystems. Fajfer's work raises the question if the form of a text matters, or whether it is disposable as garbage. As we have seen, for him it is not a transparent container; that's why in the provocative gesture he makes us see this by choosing the paradoxical form. Just like the Czech-Brazilian thinker, the poet believes that "empty bottles kept to be changed (into ash trays or chandeliers [or we might add 'book covers']) are proof of human freedom."[62] As if to corroborate this, the bottled text finishes with the question or appeal: "Podchodzisz i trącasz atelierową flaszę. I uwalniasz mnie?" [You come up and push the atelier bottle. And [do you] set me free?].[63]

Moreover, since the bottle is likely to become a piece of garbage, Fajfer's gesture gives us also an object lesson to Flusser's conclusion that our society

> must learn how to consume or perish in garbage—material garbage, an even more, mental garbage. Philosophy has often been said to be garbage disposal. Philosophy must not die, if we are to live. This is not the least of the hints which a consideration of bottles may suggest, that is, if bottles are considered as revelations of human condition.[64]

Thus, *SPOD* (*DOWN*), through its content and form, speaks alarmingly about the crises of communication, the condition of our planet, and the individual under ubiquitous surveillance.

Conclusions

Sketching his vision of world literature Slovak scholar Dionýz Ďurišin explains,

A perception of world literature can be gained through an understanding of literary-historical units such as national literatures and other analogous historical entities that existed and still exist today. This allows us to see world literature in action, to define its beginning and its final anchorage. ... With this aim in mind, an investigation of world literature proceeds towards an understanding of literary-historical concepts and categories such as literary tradition, convention, style, genre, genre form, artistic translation, periodization of literature and so on. It is becoming apparent that the concept of world literature need not be abstract, but can be quite concrete, compelling us to formulate new literary-historical, but mainly theoretical categories.[65]

Arguably, liberature was formulated as a result of such an approach to world literature. It is a phenomenon that has emerged as a local movement but has posited itself with reference to writers and poets writing in a similar style, and practicing a similar, material poetics. Understood as a genre form, it can be used as a literary-historical and theoretical category that could enable us to reread and reexamine the literary past with the view to uncover a specific strand in the history of world literature. Liberature can facilitate an enquiry into world literature by providing its working model because it demonstrates how to respect local variations while fostering a transnational mode of reading, as well as showing translation that highlights gain over loss.

Notes

1   Zenon Fajfer, "Liberatura. Aneks do słownika terminów literackich," *Dekada Literacka* (June 30, 1999): 8–9. Further cited from the English translation "Liberature. Appendix to a Dictionary of Literary Terms," in *Liberature or Total Literature. Collected Essays 1999–2009*, edited and translated by Katarzyna Bazarnik (Kraków: Ha!art, 2010), 22–8.

2   Katarzyna Bazarnik, *Liberature. A Book-bound Genre* (Kraków: Jagiellonian University Press, 2016).

3   Richard Kostelanetz, "Liberature," in *A Dictionary of the Avant-Gardes*, 3rd ed. (New York: Routledge, 2019), 258.

4   Alison Gibbons, *Multimodality, Cognition and Experimental Literature* (New York: Routledge, 2012).

5   N. Katherine Hayles, *Writing Machines* (Cambridge, MA: MIT Press, 2002).

6   Jessica Pressman, "The Aesthetics of Bookishness in the Twentieth-Century Literature," *Michigan Quarterly Review* (Fall 2009): 48, 4; ProQuest Research Library, 465.

7   Cf. Katarzyna Bazarnik and Izabela Curyłło-Klag (eds.), *Incarnations of Material Textuality: From Modernism to Liberature* (Newcastle-upon-Tyne: Cambridge Scholars, 2014).

8   Fajfer, "Liberature," 22.

9   Katarzyna Bazarnik, "Dlaczego od Joyce'a do liberatury," in *Od Joyce'a do liberatury*, edited by Katarzyna Bazarnik (Kraków: Universitas, 2002), v.

10 Ibid., 22. On Joyce utilizing the space of the material book, and the bibliographical code, see Donald Francis McKenzie, *Bibliography and the Sociology of Texts* (Cambridge: Cambridge University Press, 1999); Jerome McGann, *The Textual Condition* (Princeton, NJ: Princeton University Press, 1991); and Bazarnik, *Joyce and Liberature* (Prague: Univerzita Karlova v Praze, 2011, Litteraria Pragensia series).

11 Katarzyna Bazarnik and Zenon Fajfer, "A Brief History of Liberature," in Fajfer, *Liberature or Total Literature*, 86–7. First published in *Liberature* (Kraków: Artpartner, 2005), a booklet prepared for the 5th Symposium on Iconicity in Language and Literature held in Kraków.

12 Ibid., 89.

13 Bazarnik discusses him in several articles and in her monograph *Liberature. A Book-bound Genre*. Katarzyna Biela, which has published on him, too, is currently working on a comparative study on B. S. Johnson and liberature (see https://orcid.org/0000-0002-7392-2546).

14 Radosław Nowakowski, "The Author," Liberatorium website, accessed August 10, 2021, https://www.liberatorium.com/autor/author.html.

15 Cf. Agnieszka Przybyszewska, *Liberackość dzieła literackiego* (Łódź: Wydawnictwo Uniwersytetu Łódzkiego, 2015), 35–44.

16 Horace Engdahl, "Canonization and World Literature: The Nobel Experience," in *World Literature. A Reader*, edited by Theo D'haen, Cesar Dominguez, and Mads Rosendahl Thomsen (New York: Routledge, 2013), 316–28, esp. 325.

17 David Damrosch, *What Is World Literature?* (Princeton, NJ: Princeton University Press, 2003), 133.

18 Quoted in Ian Campbell Ross, "Laurence Sterne's Life, Milieu, and Literary Career," in *The Cambridge Companion to Laurence Sterne*, edited by Thomas Keymer (Cambridge: Cambridge University Press, 2009), 12.

19 Cf. Bazarnik, *Joyce and Liberature*, 97.

20 Cf. for example, Richard Ellmann, *James Joyce* (Oxford: Oxford University Press, 1982), 722; Charles Carroll Bombaugh, *Oddities and Curiosities of Words and Literature: Gleanings for the Curious*, edited by Martin Gardner (New York: Dover, 1961), vi, and Vladimir Nabokov's essay on *Ulysses* in which he calls *Finnegans Wake* "one of the greatest failures in literature" (in *Lectures on Literature*, edited by Fredson Bowers, San Diego: Harvest Book, Harcourt, 1982), 349. Similarly, many titles published in Liberatura series of Ha!art Publishing House have earned a similar label.

21 Damrosch, *What Is World Literature?*, 281.

22 Ibid.

23 Fajfer, *Liberature*, 26.

24 Bazarnik, *Joyce and Liberature*, 19–26; and Bazarnik, *Liberature: A Book-bound Genre*, 62–4.

25 Emiliano Ranocchi, "Literature and Person: An Anthropological Question," in *Incarnations of Material Textuality*, 110, 116.

26 Przybyszewska, *Liberackość*, passim.

27 Wojciech Kalaga, "Tekst hybrydyczny: Polifonie i aporie doświadczenia hybrydycznego," in *Kulturowe wizualizacje doświadczenia,* edited by Włodzimierz Bolecki and Adam Dziadek (Warszawa: IBL PAN, 2010), 76.

28 Kris Van Heuckelom, "(S)Tree(t) of (Cro)Cod(il)es: Jonathan Safran Foer 'okalecza' Brunona Schulza," in *Literatura polska w świecie. Tom IV Oblicza światowości*, edited by Romuald Cudak (Katowice: Wydawnictwo Gnome and Uniwersytet Śląski, 2012), 15 and 29.

29 Katarzyna Bazarnik, "Affordances of the Book: A Tentative Typology of Liberature," in *Refresh the Book*. On the Hybrid Nature of the Book in the Age of Electronic Publishing, edited by Viola Hildebrand-Schat, Katarzyna Bazarnik, and Christoph Benjamin Schulz (Leiden: Brill, Rodopi, 2021), 56.

30 See Cosima Bruno, "Translation Poetry: The Poetics of Noise in Hsia Yü's *Pink Noise*," in *Prismatic Translation*, edited by Matthew Reynolds (Cambridge: Legenda, 2019), 175; and Sakine Weikert, "Teju Cole's Blind Spot/#blindspot, between Analogue and Digital Narrative Devices," in *Refresh the Book*, 391.

31 Damrosch, *What Is World Literature?*, 281.

32 Ibid., 298.

33 Zenon Fajfer and Katarzyna Bazarnik, *Oka-leczenie* (Kraków: Ha!art, [2000] 2009, Liberatura series vol. 8).

34 The medical staff speak English to them.

35 Zenon Fajfer, "Liberature or Total Literature. (Appendix to the 'Appendix to the Dictionary of Literary Terms')," in Fajfer, *Liberature or Total Literature*, 38.

36 The word appears twice in the text: see Zenon Fajfer and Katarzyna Bazarnik, *Oka-leczenie* (Kraków: Ha!art, 2009), 8, 12.

37 The pagination of *Oka-leczenie* also requires a comment. The part featuring the dying man is paginated with negative numbers: from minus 64 to minus 1; the one set in the maternity ward is numbered from 1 to 64, while the middle part uses roman numerals from I to LXIV.

38 Fajfer, "Liberature or Total Literature," 37–8.

39 Incidentally, Fajfer's programmatic emanational poem "Ars Poetica," demonstrating the animated, electronic version of the poetic structure, is included in *Electronic Literature Collection 3*, an anthology of electronic world literature: https://collection.eliterature.org/3/work.html?work=ars-poetica.

40 Agnieszka Przybyszewska, "Close Reading of the Liberatic Canon: On *Oka-leczenie*," in *Incarnations of Material Textuality*, 100.

41 Zenon Fajfer, and Katarzyna Bazarnik. *Oka-leczenie* (Kraków: Ha!art, [2000] 2009); Cf. Przybyszewska, "Close Reading of the Liberatic Canon," 95.

42 Ibid.

43 Ibid., 60.

44 See Alain Daniélou, *The Myths and Gods of India: The Classic Work on Hindu Polytheism* (Rochester: Inner Traditions International, 1991), 260–1. Kurma is an avatar of Vishnu, taking the form of a turtle, or tortoise, that supports the world (ibid., 167).

45 Fajfer and Bazarnik, *Oka-leczenie*, 60. *Bardo* is another Buddhist term appearing in this part.

46 Damrosch, *What Is World literature*, 298.

47 Ibid., 281.

48 Some of them were donated by writers who were sympathetic to the concept; they include Michael Joyce and Carolyn Guyer, Raymond Federman, Radosław Nowakowski, and Marek Gajewski.

49 One of the highlights of the collection, Andrzej Bednarczyk's *The Temple of Stone* features on the Rare Book section webpage: https://bj.uj.edu.pl/en_GB/about-library/collections/rare-books (accessed August 10, 2021).

50 *Oka-leczenie*, which was discussed in the magazine, too, had still to wait six years before it could be published in a trade edition in 2009.

51 In 1990 the University of Alabama Press brought out the 2nd edition using DTP technology.

52 The other one is *House Mother Normal* (*Przełożona w normie*, 2011).

53 Katarzyna Bazarnik and Zenon Fajfer, "Arw z perspektywy liberatury," in Stanisław Czycz, *Arw*, edited by Dorota Niedziałkowska and Dariusz Pachocki (Kraków: Ha!art, 2007), 68–9.

54 Michał Paweł Markowski, "Nicość i czcionka: Wprowadzenie do lektury *Rzutu kośćmi* Stephane'a Mallarmego," in Stephané Mallarmé, *Rzut kośćmi nigdy nie zniesie przypadku*, translated by Tomasz Różycki (Kraków: Ha!art, 2005), 18.

55 Katarzyna Bazarnik and Zenon Fajfer, "Dwa *Rzuty kośćmi* czyli szczególna i ogólna teoria liberatury," in Mallarmé, *Rzut kośćmi*, 123.

56 The publication was finally facilitated by a small grant from the Faculty of Philology of the Jagiellonian University.

57 Zenon Fajfer, *Spoglądając Przez Ozonową Dziurę* (Kraków: Ha!art, 2004). Its English translation, entitled *Detect Ozone Whole Nearby* (*DOWN*), was made by Katarzyna Bazarnik, Finn Fordham, and Zenon Fajfer. Fajfer has privately made several single English copies on individual requests.

58 Agnieszka Przybyszewska, "Liberacka analiza tekstu (o czytaniu *Oka-leczenia* Zenona Fajfera i Katarzyny Bazarnik)," in *Polska literatura najnowsza—poza kanonem*, edited by Paulina Kierzek (Łódź: University of Łódź Press, 2008), 218.

59 Jerzy Borowczyk and Krzysztof Hoffman, "Wymarzona przygoda," *Polonistyka*, 2 (2009): 5–6.

60 Vilém Flusser, "Bottles," *ETC: A Review of General Semantics*, vol. 45, no. 2 (Summer 1988): 154.

61 Ibid., 148.

62 Ibid., 150.

63 In the above-mentioned English translation this appeal is even stronger: "Everywhere. Prisoners initiate liberation. Out!"

64 Flusser, "Bottles," 154.

65 Dionýz Ďurišin, "World Literature as Target Category," in *World Literature: A Reader*, edited by Theo D'haen, César Domníguez, and Mads Rosendahl Thomsen (London: Routledge, 2016), 152.

BIBLIOGRAPHY

Abraham, Karl. *Selected Papers of Karl Abraham*. London: Hogarth Press and the Institute of Psychoanalysis, 1954.

Abraham, Nicolaus, and Maria Török. *The Shell and the Kernel: Renewals of Psychoanalysis*. Chicago: University of Chicago Press, 1972.

Adams, Carol. *The Pornography of Meat*. New York: Lantern Books, 2019.

Agence France-Presse. "Binyavanga Wainaina, Gay Kenyan Author, Hopes to Boost LGBT Rights with Coming Out." *HuffPost*, January 28, 2014, https://www.huffpost.com/entry/binyavanga-wainaina-lgbt-rights-n_4677847?guccounter=1. Accessed June 15, 2021.

Allen, Esther, and Susan Bernofsky (eds.). *In Translation: Translators on Their Work and What It Means*. New York: Columbia University Press, 2013.

Altieri, Charles. "Polish Envy: American Poetry's Polonising in the 1970s and 80s." *Metre* 15 (Spring 2004): 80–96.

Alvarez, Al. *Under Pressure: The Writer in Society: Eastern Europe and the U.S.A.* New York: Penguin Books, 1965.

Alvarez, Al. "Witness." *New York Review of Books*, vol. 35, no. 9 (July 2, 1988): 21–2.

Amenta, Alessandro, Tomasz Kaliściak, and Błażej Warkocki (eds.). *Dezorientacje: Antologia Polskiej Literatury Queer*. Warsaw: Wydawnictwo Krytyki Politycznej, 2021.

Ammons, Elizabeth. "Cool Diana and the Blood-Red Muse: Edith Wharton on Innocence and Art." In *American Novelists Revisited: Essays in Feminist Criticism*, edited by Fritz Fleischman, 209–24. Boston, MA: G. K. Hall, 1982.

Andino Velez, Marcel. "Lekcja języka dresiarskiego." *Przekrój*, 37 (2002): n.pag.

Andrzejewski, Jerzy. *Ashes and Diamonds (Popiół i Diament)*. Translated by D. J. Welsh. Evanston, IL: Northwestern University Press, [1948] 1996.

Arkin, Marian, and Barbara Shollar. *Longman Anthology of World Literature by Women, 1875–1975*. New York: Longman, 1989.

Armstrong, Nancy. *How Novels Think: The Limits of Individualism from 1719–1900*. New York: Columbia University Press, 2005.

Ashbery, John. *Collected Poems*. New York: Library of America, 2008.

Ashbery, John. *Houseboat Days*. New York: Farrar, Straus, and Giroux, 1977.

Ashbery, John. *No i wiesz*. Translated by Piotr Sommer, Andrzej Sosnowski, and Bohdan Zadura. Warszawa: Duszniki Zdrój, 1993.

Ashbery, John. "The System." In *Three Poems*, 53. New York: Ecco, 1972.

Aslam, Nadeem. "*The Street of Crocodiles* by Bruno Schulz." *The Independent* (February 23, 2013): 28–9.

Avramescu, Cătălin. *An Intellectual History of Cannibalism*. Princeton, NJ: Princeton University Press, 2009.

Axer, Jerzy. "Rola kryptocytatów z literatury łacińskiej w polskojęzycznej twórczości Jana Kochanowskiego." In *Jan Kochanowski i kultura Odrodzenia*, edited by Zdzisław Libera and Maciej Żurowski, 107–20. Warszawa: PWN, 1985.

Badkhen, Anna. "The View from 35,000 Feet." Review of Flights by Olga Tokarczuk. *New York Review of Books*, December 4, 2018.

Baldwin, James. *Giovanni's Room*. New York: Penguin Books, [1956] 2001.

Banach, Jerzy. *Hercules Polonus: Studium z ikonografii sztuki nowożytnej* [Hercules Polonus: A Study of Modern Iconography]. Warszawa: PWN, 1984.

Barcz, Anna. *Realizm ekologiczny: od ekokrytyki do zookrytyki w literaturze polskiej*. Katowice: Wydawnictwo Naukowe Śląsk, 2016.

Barker, Francis, Peter Hulme, and Margaret Iversen (eds.). *Cannibalism and the Colonial World (Cultural Margins)*. Cambridge: Cambridge University Press, 1998.

Barnes, Tania. "Review of Snow White and Russian Red." *Library Journal* (January 1, 2005): 94.

Bartczak, Kacper. "Autokreacja wielościowa w poetyce Johna Ashbery'ego." In *Poeci Szkoły Nowojorskiej*, edited by Kacper Bartczak, 170–97. Warszawa: Wydawnictwo UW, 2018.

Bartczak, Kacper. "Końce kodowania: Andrzej Sosnowski i John Ashbery." In *Dialog międzykulturowy w (o) literaturze polskiej*, edited by Marta Skwara, Katarzyna Krasoń, and Jerzy Kazimierski, 105–22. Szczecin: Wydawnictwo Uniwersytetu Szczecińskiego, 2008.

Basiuk, Tomasz. "One's Younger Self in Personal Testimony and Literary Translation." In *Queers in State Socialism Cruising 1970s Poland*, edited by Tomasz Basiuk and Jędrzej Burszta, 23–32. London: Routledge, 2021.

Basiuk, Tomasz, and Jędrzej Burszta. "Introduction Queers in the People's Republic of Poland: An Uneven Landscape." In *Queers in State Socialism Cruising 1970s Poland*, edited by Tomasz Basiuk and Jędrzej Burszta, 1–8. London: Routledge, 2021.

Bataille, Georges. *The Accursed Share*. Volume 1. Consumption. New York: Zone Books, 1991.

Battersby, Eileen. "Complex Harmonies." Review of Flights by Olga Tokarczuk. *Los Angeles Review of Books* (April 11, 2018).

Bazarnik, Katarzyna. "Affordances of the Book. A Tentative Typology of Liberature." In *Refresh the Book. On the Hybrid Nature of the Book in the Age of Electronic Publishing*, edited by Viola Hildebrand-Schat, Katarzyna Bazarnik, and Christoph Benjamin Schulz, 41–70. Leiden: Brill, 2021.

Bazarnik, Katarzyna. "Dlaczego od Joyce'a do liberatury." In *Od Joyce'a do liberatury*, edited by Katarzyna Bazarnik, v–xvi. Kraków: Universitas, 2002.

Bazarnik, Katarzyna. *Joyce and Liberature*. Litteraria Pragensia series. Prague: Univerzita Karlova v Praze, 2011.

Bazarnik, Katarzyna. *Liberature: A Book-bound Genre*. Krakow: Jagiellonian University Press, 2016.

Bazarnik, Katarzyna. "Liberature or on the Origin of (Literary) Species." In Zenon Fajfer, *Liberature or Total Literature: Collected Essays 1999–2009*, edited and translated by Katarzyna Bazarnik, 151–63. Kraków: Korporacja Ha!art, 2010.

Bazarnik, Katarzyna, and Curyłło-Klag Izabela (eds.). *Incarnations of Material Textuality: From Modernism to Liberature*. Newcastle-upon-Tyne: Cambridge Scholars, 2014.

Bazarnik, Katarzyna, and Zenon Fajfer. "Arw z perspektywy liberatury." In Stanisław Czycz, *Arw*, edited by Dorota Niedziałkowska and Dariusz Pachocki, 67–9. Kraków: Ha!art, 2007.

Bazarnik, Katarzyna, and Zenon Fajfer. "A Brief History of Liberature." In Zenon Fajfer, *Liberature or Total Literature: Collected Essays 1999–2009*, edited and translated by Katarzyna Bazarnik, 85–92. Kraków: Korporacja Ha!art, [2005] 2010.

Beardsley, Monroe, and W. K. Wimsatt. "The Intentional Fallacy." *Sewanee Review* 57, no. 1 (Winter 1949): 468–88.

Beauvois, Daniel. "Entre l'analyse et l'action politiques. Jean Potocki voyageur 'éclairé.'" In *Modèles et moyens de la réflexion politique au XVIIIᵉ siècle*, 39–63. Villeneuve-d'Ascq: Publications de l'université de Lille III, 1973.

Beauvois, Daniel. "Un proche encombrant de Stanislas Auguste: Jean Potocki et ses papillonnements politico-diplomatiques entre la Grande Diète et le voyage au Maroc (avec une lettre inédite)." *Wiek Oświecenia* 15 (1999): 229–46.

Beecroft, Alexander. *An Ecology of World Literature: From Antiquity to the Present Day*. New York: Verso, 2015.

Belknap, Robert. "Ten Contemporary Polish Short Stories by Edmund Ordon." *Polish Review* 4, nos. 1/2 (1959): 148–50.

Bennett, Jane. *Vibrant Matter: A Political Ecology of Things*. Durham, NC: Duke University Press, 2010.

Benstock, Shari. *No gifts from Chance: A biography of Edith Wharton*. New York: Charles Scribner's Sons, 1994.

Berlant, Lauren, and Michael Warner. "Sex in Public." *Critical Inquiry* 24, no. 2 (1998): 547–66.

Berns, Fernando G. Pagnoni. "Water and Queer Intimacy." In *Space and Subjectivity in Contemporary Brazilian Cinema*, edited by Antônio Márcio da Silva and Mariana Cunha, 185–200. Cham: Palgrave, 2017.

Białas, Tadeusz. *Liga Morska i Kolonialna, 1930–1939*. Gdańsk: Wydawnictwo Morskie, 1983.

Bieńkowska, Danuta. "Anthologies of Contemporary Polish Prose in English Translation." *Canadian Slavonic Papers* 8 (1966): 243–9.

Bill, Stanley S. "Miłosz w dialogu z literackim centrum świata." *Poznańskie Studia Polonistyczne Seria Literacka* 20, no. 40 (2012): 137–48.

Bill, Stanley S. "W poszukiwaniu autentyczności. Kultura polska i natura teorii postkolonialnej." *Praktyka Teoretyczna* 11, no. 1 (2014): 107–27. https://pressto.amu.edu.pl/index.php/prt/article/view/436/349.

Binnie, Jon, and Christian Klesse. "'Like a Bomb in the Gasoline Station': East—West Migration and Transnational Activism around Lesbian, Gay, Bisexual, Transgender and Queer Politics in Poland." *Journal of Ethnic and Migration Studies* 39, no. 7 (2013): 1107–24.

Black, Scott. *Without the Novel: Romance and the History of Prose Fiction.*
Charlottesville: University of Virginia Press, 2019.

Bois, Yves-Alain, and Rosalind E. Krauss. *Formless: A User's Guide.*
New York: Zone Books, 1997.

Bolecki, Włodzimierz. "Od potworów do znaków pustych. Z dziejów groteski:
Młoda Polska i dwudziestolecie międzywojenne." *Pamiętnik Literacki*, nos. 80/1
(1989): 73–121.

Boltanski, Luc, and Laurent Thévenot. *On Justification: Economies of Worth.*
Translated by Catherine Porter. Princeton, NJ: Princeton University Press, 2006.

Bombaugh, Charles Carroll. *Oddities and Curiosities of Words and
Literature: Gleanings for the Curious*, edited by Martin Gardner.
New York: Dover, 1961.

Borchardt, Danuta. "Translator's Note." In Witold Gombrowicz, *Trans-
Atlantyk: An Alternate Translation*, translated by Danuta Borchardt, vii–xi. New
Haven, CT: Yale University Press, 2014.

Borkowska, Grażyna. *Alienated Women: A Study on Polish Women's Fiction 1845–
1918.* Translated by Ursula Phillips. Budapest: Central European University
Press, 2001.

Borowczyk, Jerzy, and Hoffman, Krzysztof. "Wymarzona przygoda." *Polonistyka*, 2
(2009): 5–6.

Bourdieu, Pierre. "Rules of Art: Genesis and Structure of the Literary Field." In
The Norton Anthology of Theory and Criticism, 2nd ed., edited by Vincent B.
Leitch, 1670–80. New York: W. W. Norton, 2010.

Bromiley, G. W. *The International Standard Bible Encyclopedia.* Grand Rapids,
MI: Eerdmans, 1979.

Brouillette, Sarah. *Postcolonial Writers in the Global Literary Marketplace.*
London: Palgrave Macmillan, 2007.

Bruno, Cosima. "Translation Poetry: The Poetics of Noise in Hsia Yü's Pink
Noise." In *Prismatic Translation*, edited by Matthew Reynolds, 173–88.
Cambridge: Legenda, 2019.

Brzozowski, Stanisław. *Legenda Młodej Polski. Studia o strukturze duszy
kulturalnej.* Lwów: Księgarnia Połonieckiego, 1908.

Burney, Fatima, and Sara Hakeen Grewal (eds.). "'West-East' Lyric: A Comparative
Approach to Lyric History." *Comparative Critical Studies* 17, no. 2 (June
2020): 173–80.

Buszewicz, Elwira. "Forma gatunkowa ody w łacińskiej poezji Jana
Kochanowskiego (*Lyricorum libellus*)" [Ode as an genre in latin poetry of Jan
Kochanowski (*Lyricorum libellus*)]. *Terminus* 30, no. 1 (2014): 21–38.

Casanova, Pascale. *The World Republic of Letters.* Translated by M. B. DeBevoise.
Cambridge, MA: Harvard University Press, 2004.

Castillo, Debra. "Gender and Sexuality in World Literature." In *The Routledge
Companion to World Literature*, edited by Theo D'haen, David Damrosch, and
Djelal Kadir, 393–403. London: Routledge, 2012.

Cavanagh, Clare. *Lyric Poetry and Modern Politics: Russia, Poland, and the West.*
New Haven, CT: Yale University Press, 2009.

Cetera-Włodarczyk, Anna. "'It Takes a Genius to Set the Tune, and a Poet to Play
Variations on It': Some Remarks on the Irksome (Im)Possibility of Editing

Shakespeare in Translation." Translated by Zofia Ziemann. *Przekładaniec*, special issue "Translation History in the Polish Context" (2019): 46–62.

Chambers, Dianne L. *Feminist Readings of Edith Wharton: From Silence to Speech*. New York: Palgrave Macmillan, 2009.

Chmielewska, Katarzyna. *Strategie podmiotu*. Dziennik *Witolda Gombrowicza*. Warszawa: IBL PAN, 2010.

Ciekliński, Piotr. *Potrójny z Plauta* [*Plaut's Trinummus*]. Edited by Julian Krzyżanowski and Stanisław Rospond. Wrocław: IBL PAN, 1966.

Cornis-Pope, Marcel, and John Neubauer. "Towards a History of the Literary Cultures in East-Central Europe: Theoretical Reflections." *ACLS Occasional Paper*, no. 52 (2002): 1–50. https://www.acls.org/uploadedFiles/Publications/OP/52_Literary_Cultures_in_East_Central_Europe.pdf.

Corredor, Elizabeth S. "Unpacking 'Gender Ideology' and the Global Right's Antigender Countermovement." *Signs* 44, no. 3 (2019): 613–38.

Costanzo William V. *World Cinema through Global Genres*. Chichester: Wiley-Blackwell, 2014, 47.

Crosley, Sloane. "One by One, Her Neighbors Are Dying: An Elderly Polish Woman Is on the Case." *New York Times* (August 12, 2019).

Czapliński, Przemysław. "Mapa, córka nostalgii." In *Wzniosłe tęsknoty: nostalgie w prozie lat dziewięćdziesiątych*, 105–28. Kraków: Wydawnictwo Literackie, 2001.

Czapliński, Przemysław. "Niepoprawna Masłowska." *Tygodnik Powszechny* (October 14, 2012).

Czapliński, Przemysław. *Poruszona mapa: wyobraźnia geograficzno-kulturowa polskiej literatury przełomu XX i XXI wieku*. Kraków: Wydawnictwo Literackie, 2017.

Czapliński, Przemysław. *Powrót centrali: literatura w nowej rzeczywistości*. Kraków: Wydawnictwo Literackie, 2009.

Dąbkowska-Kujko, Justyna. *Justus Lipsjusz i dawne przekłady jego dzieł na język polski* [*Justus Lipsius and Translations of His Works in Old Polish Literature*]. Lublin: TN KUL, 2010.

Damrosch, David. *How to Read World Literature*. Chichester: Wiley-Blackwell, 2008.

Damrosch, David. *What Is World Literature?* Princeton, NJ: Princeton University Press, 2003.

Daniélou, Alain. *The Myths and Gods of India: The Classic Work on Hindu Polytheism*. Rochester: Inner Traditions International, 1991.

Dębowski, Marek. "Parades: le début de l'idée subversive dans l'œuvre de Potocki." In *Jean Potocki à nouveau*, edited by Emilie Klene, 65–74. Amsterdam: Rodopi, 2010.

Dębowski, Marek. *Jean Potocki et le théâtre polonaise: Entre Lumières et premier romantisme*. Paris: Garnier 2014.

Deleuze, Gilles, and Félix Guattari. *Anti-Oedipus: Capitalism and Schizophrenia*. New York: Continuum, 1984.

Deleuze, Gilles, and Felix Guattari. "What Is Minor Literature." In *Kafka: Toward Minor Literature*, translated by Dana Pollan. Minneapolis: University of Minnesota Press, 1986.

D'hulst, Lieven. "Translation History." In *Handbook of Translation Studies*, edited by Yves Gambier and Luc van Doorslaer, 397–405. Amsterdam: John Benjamins, 2010.

DiAntonio, Robert. "A Fresh, Distinctive Voice from Israel." *St. Louis Post-Dispatch* (June 14, 1992): 5C.

Dimock, Wai-Chee. "Debasing Exchange. Edith Wharton's *The House of Mirth*." *PMLA* 100, no. 5 (1985): 783–92.

Dowse, Sara. "Memory and Regret in a Cold Climate." *Canberra Times* (July 25, 2009): 12.

Dunin, Kinga. "Literatura polska czy literatura w Polsce." *Ex Libris*, no. 48 (1994): 1–2.

Dunin-Wąsowicz, Piotr, and Krzysztof Varga. *Parnas bis*. Warszawa: Lampa i Iskra Boża, 1995.

Ďurišin, Dionýz. "World Literature as Target Category." In *World Literature. A Reader*, edited by Theo D'haen, César Domníguez, and Mads Rosendahl Thomsen, 150–9. London: Routledge, 2016.

Eisner, Robert. "Euripides' Use Of Myth." *Arethusa* 12, no. 2 (1979): 153–74.

Ellmann, Richard. *James Joyce*. Oxford: Oxford University Press, 1982.

Engdahl, Horace. "Canonization and World Literature: the Nobel Experience." In *World Literature. A Reader*, edited by Theo D'haen, Cesar Dominguez, and Mads Rosendahl Thomsen, 316–28. New York: Routledge, 2013.

English, James, F. *The Economy of Prestige: Prizes, Awards, and the Circulation of Cultural Value*. Cambridge, MA: Harvard University Press, 2005.

Erlich, Gloria C. *The Sexual Education of Edith Wharton*. Berkeley: University of California Press, 1992.

Eyerman Ron and Löfgren Orvar, "Romancing the Road: Road Movies and Images of Mobility." *Theory, Culture & Society* 12 (1995): 53–79.

Fajfer, Zenon. "Ars Poetica." In *Electronic Literature Collection 3*, edited by Stephanie Boluk, Leonardo Flores, Jacob Garbe, and Anastasia Salter. Cambridge, MA: Electronic Literature Organization, 2016. Accessed August 10, 2021. https://collection.eliterature.org/3/work.html?work=ars-poetica.

Fajfer, Zenon. "Liberatura: Aneks do słownika terminów literackich." *Dekada Literacka*, 5/6, no. (153/154) (June 30, 1999): 8–9.

Fajfer, Zenon. "Liberature or Total Literature. (Appendix to the 'Appendix to the Dictionary of Literary Terms')." In Zenon Fajfer, *Liberature or Total Literature: Collected Essays 1999–2009*, edited and translated by Katarzyna Bazarnik, 29–41. Kraków: Korporacja Ha!art, 2010.

Fajfer, Zenon. *Spoglądając Przez Ozonową Dziurę*. Kraków: Ha!art, 2004.

Fajfer, Zenon, and Katarzyna Bazarnik. *Oka-leczenie*. Kraków: Ha!art, [2000] 2009.

Famulska-Ciesielska, Karolina, and Sławomir JacekŻurek. *Literatura Polska W Izraelu*. Kraków [u.a.]: Wydawn. Austeria, 2012.

Fauvel-Gouraud, Francis. *Phreno-Mnemotechny; or the Art of Memory: The Series of Lectures, Explanatory of the Principles of the System, Delivered in New York and Philadelphia, in the Beginning of 1844*. New York: Wiley and Putnam, 1845.

Feldman, Yael S. "'Not as Sheep Led to Slaughter?' on Trauma, Selective Memory, and the Making of Historical Consciousness." *Jewish social studies* 19, no. 3 (2013): 139–69.

Ferguson, Jamie Harmon. "Whose Turn Is It Anyway?" *Chicago Review* 46, nos. 3/4 (2000): 219–21.

Figlerowicz, Marta. "Rewriting Poland." *Boston Review* (September 17, 2018).

Fijoł, Elżbieta. "Masłowskiej wojna przegrana." *Czas Kultury*, 6 (2002): 127–9.

Filipiak, Izabela. *Absolutna Amnezja*. Poznań: Obserwator, 1995.

Filipowicz, Halina. "Is There a World beyond Krasicki and Gombrowicz?" *Polish Review* 49, no. 2 (2004): 839–46.

Finnin, Rory. "Attendants to the Duel: Classical Intertexts in Philipe Desportes's 'Adieu à Pologne' and Jan Kochanowski's 'Gallo Crocitanti'." *Comparative Literary Studies* 44, no. 4 (2007): 458–83.

Fishman, Boris. "Bloc Party." Review of *Snow White and Russian Red* by Dorota Masłowska. *New York Times* (May 1, 2005).

Fisk, Gloria. *Orhan Pamuk and the Good of World Literature.* New York: Columbia University Press, 2018.

Flinn, Caryl. *The New German Cinema: Music, History, and the Matters of Style.* Berkeley: University of California Press, 2004.

Flood, Alison. "Olga Tokarczuk's 'Magnum Opus' Finally Gets English Release—after Seven Years of Translation." *The Guardian* (February 26, 2021).

Flusser, Vilém. "Bottles." *ETC: A Review of General Semantics* 45, no. 2 (1988): 148–54.

Foucault, Michel. *The History of Sexuality: An Introduction* (vol. 1). New York: Vintage, [1978] 1990.

Fraisse, Luc, *Potocki et l'imaginaire de la creation*. Paris: PUPS, 2006.

Franch, Carolyn, and Nina Karsov. "Translators' Note." In Witold Gombrowicz,*Trans-Atlantyk*, translated by Carolyn French and Nina Karsov, xxii–xxvii. New Haven, CT: Yale University Press, 1994.

Frank, Marcie. *The Novel Stage: Narrative Form from the Restoration to Jane Austen*. Lewisburg, PA: Bucknell University Press, 2020.

Franklin, Ruth. "Olga Tokarczuk's Novel against Nationalism." *New Yorker* (August 5 and 12, 2019).

Freedgood, Elaine. *Worlds Enough: The Invention of Realism in the Victorian Novel*. Princeton, NJ: Princeton University Press, 2019.

Freud, Sigmund. *Neurosis and Psychosis.* Translated by Joan Riviere, *Standard Edition of the Complete Psychological Works of Sigmund Freud*, volume XIX (1923–1925): *The Ego and the Id and Other Works*. London: Hoghart Press, 1971.

Freud, Sigmund. *The Standard Edition of the Complete Psychological Works. Vol. XIII, Totem and Taboo.* London: Hogarth Press, 1955.

Freud, Sigmund. "Three Essays on the Theory of Sexuality." In *The Freud Reader*, edited by Peter Gay, 239–93. New York: W.W. Norton, 1989.

Fulińska, Agnieszka. *Naśladowanie i twórczość: renesansowe teorie imitacji, emulacji i przekładu* [Imitation and creation: Renaissance theories of *imitatio*, *emulatio* and *translatio*]. Wrocław: Fundacja Nauki Polskiej, 2000.

Gardner, Lyn. "A Couple of Poor, Polish-Speaking Romanians." Review of *A Couple of Poor, Polish-Speaking Romanians* at Soho Theater, London. *The Guardian* (March 7, 2008).

Gasyna, George Z. *Polish, Hybrid, and Otherwise: Exilic Discourse in Joseph Conrad and Witold Gombrowicz.* New York: Bloomsbury, 2013.

Gibbons, Alison. *Multimodality, Cognition and Experimental Literature.* New York: Routledge, 2012.

Gilbert, Roger. *Walks in the World: Representation and Experience in Modern American Poetry.* Princeton, NJ: Princeton University Press, 1991.

Gillon, Adam, and Ludwik Krzyzanowski (eds.). *Introduction to Modern Polish Literature: An Anthology of Fiction and Poetry.* New York: Twayne Publishers, 1964.

Gladsky, Thomas S. *Princes, Peasants, and Other Polish Selves: Ethnicity in American Literature.* Amherst: University of Massachusetts Press, 2009.

Glomski, Jacqueline. "Historiography as Art: Jan Kochanowski's *Lyricorum libellous* (1580)." In *Renaissance Culture in Context. Theory and Practice,* edited by J. R. Brink and W. F. Gentrup, 145–54. Aldershot: Scolar Press, 1993.

Gombrowicz, Witold. *Diary.* Translated by Lillian Vallee. New Haven, CT: Yale University Press, 2012.

Gombrowicz, Witold. *A Kind of Testament,* edited by Dominique de Roux, translated by Alastair Hamilton and with an introduction by Maurice Nadeau. London: Calder and Boyars, 1973.

Gombrowicz, Witold. "Preface to the 1957 Edition." In Witold Gombrowicz, *Trans-Atlantyk: An Alternate Translation,* translated by Danuta Borchardt, xv–xix. New Haven, CT: Yale University Press, 2014.

Gombrowicz, Witold. "Przedmowa do *Trans-Atlantyku* (1953)." In Witold Gombrowicz, *Trans-Atlantyk,* 135–40. Kraków: Wydawnictwo Literackie, 1993

Gombrowicz, Witold. *Trans-Atlantyk: An Alternate Translation,* translated by Danuta Borchardt. New Haven, CT: Yale University Press, 2014.

Gombrowicz, Witold. *Trans-Atlantyk,* translated by Carolyn French and Nina Karsov. New Haven, CT: Yale University Press, [1952] 2008.

Gömöri, George. "*Cochanoviana* in foreign libraries," *Polish Review* 47, no. 4 (2002): 407–10.

Górnicki, Łukasz. *Dworzanin polski* [The Polish Courtier]. Edited by Roman Pollak. Warszawa: Państwowy Instytut Wydawniczy, 1961.

Gosk, Hanna. "Pożytki z zastosowania instrumentarium *postcolonial studies.* Perspektywa lokalności." In *(Nie)obecność. Pominięcia i przemilczenia w narracjach XX wieku,* edited by Karwowska Bożena and Gosk Hanna, 75–9. Warszawa: Elipsa, 2008.

Gott, Michael. "Borderless Possibilities, Hesitant Voyagers: Mapping Identity in Three post-1989 Czech Road Movies." *Studies in Eastern European Cinema* 3, no. 1 (2012): 7–22.

Gournay, Marie de. "Préface sur Les Essais de Michel seigneur de Montaigne par sa fille d'alliance." In *Les Essais de Michel seigneur de Montaigne.* Paris: MDCLII, b-ciiij.

Graff, Agnieszka. "Lost between the Waves? The Paradoxes of Feminist Chronology and Activism in Contemporary Poland." *Journal of International Women's Studies* 4, no. 2 (2003): 100–16.

Graff, Agnieszka. "Report from the Gender Trenches: War against 'Genderism' in Poland." *European Journal of Women's Studies* 21, no. 4 (2014): 431–42.

Grode, Eric. "In Poland, at Mercy of Weirdos." Review of *A Couple of Poor, Polish-Speaking Romanians* at Henry Street Settlement—Abrons Arts Center. *New York Times*, February 20, 2011.

Gürçağlar, Şehnaz Tahir. "What Texts Don't Tell: The Uses of Paratexts in Translation Research. " In *Crosscultural Transgressions: Research Models in Translation Studies II: Historical and Ideological Issues*, edited by Theo Hermans, 46–60. Manchester: St. Jerome, 2002.

Gutorow, Jacek. *Urwany ślad*. Wrocław: Biuro Literackie, 2007.

Hamel, Paul. "Realities in Illusion." *New York Times* (March 29, 1964): 26.

Hanczakowski, Michał. "*Odprawa posłów greckich*." In *Lektury polonistyczne: Jan Kochanowski*, edited by A. Gorzkowski, 150–78. Kraków: Księgarnia Akademicka, 2001.

Hayles, N. Katherine. *Writing Machines*. Cambridge, MA: MIT Press, 2002.

Hershinow, Stephanie Insley. *Born Yesterday: Inexperience and the Early Realist Novel*. Baltimore, MD: Johns Hopkins University Press, 2019.

Hertz, Paweł. *Świat i dom. Szkice i uwagi wybrane*. Warszawa: PIW, 1977.

Heuckelom, Kris Van. "(S)Tree(t) of (Cro)Cod(il)es: Jonathan Safran Foer 'okalecza' Brunona Schulza." In *Literatura polska w świecie: Tom IV Oblicza światowości*, edited by Romuald Cudak, 16–29. Katowice: Wydawnictwo Gnome and Uniwersytet Śląski, 2012.

Heydel, Magda, and Zofia Ziemann (eds.). *Retracing the History of Literary Translation in Poland: People—Politics—Poetics*. New York: Routledge, 2022.

Hofmann, Michael. "Young Man from Drohobycz." *New York Times* (March 9, 2003).

Holohan, Conn, "Wrong Turns: Radical Spaces in the Road Movies of Tony Gatlif." *Transnational Cinemas* 2, no. 1 (2011): 21–35.

Hopkin, James. "Drinking to the Fall of Communism," *The Guardian*, February 3, 2001, https://www.theguardian.com/books/2001/feb/03/fiction.

Horotwitz, Steve. "Snow White and Russian Red by Dorota Masłowska." *Pop Matters* (June 17, 2005).

Hunter, J. Paul. *Before Novels: The Cultural Contexts of Eighteenth-Century English Fiction*. New York: W.W. Norton, 1990.

Hunter, Walt. "For a Global Poetics." *ASAP/Journal* 1, no. 3 (September 2016), 365–77.

Irzykowski, Karol. "O plagiatowym charakterze przełomów literackich." In *Słoń wśród porcelany: Studia nad nowszą myślą literacką w Polsce*. Warszawa: Rój, 1934.

Irzykowski, Karol. "Plagiatowy charakter przełomów literackich w Polsce." In *Słoń w składzie porcelany (studia nad nowszą myślą literacką w Polsce)*, 27–60. Warszawa: Towarzystwo Wydawnicze "Rój."

Jakubowiak, Maciej. "Opowieści zwyczajne." *Dwutygodnik*, 9 (2019). https://www.dwutygodnik.com/artykul/7783-opowiesci-zwyczajne.html. Accessed May 17, 2021.

Janion, Maria. *Do Europy tak, ale razem z naszymi umarłymi*. Warszawa: Sic!, 2000.

Janion, Maria. *Kobiety i duch inności*. Warszawa: Sic!, 1996.

Jankowicz, Grzegorz. "Otwarcie: Hasos." In *Lekcja żywego języka: o poezji Andrzeja Sosnowskiego*, edited by Grzegorz Jankowicz, 5–11. Kraków: biblioteka Studium, 2003.

Jankowicz, Grzegorz. "Sosnowski i nowoczesność." In *Lekcja żywego języka: o poezji Andrzeja Sosnowskiego*, edited by Grzegorz Jankowicz, 13–37. Kraków: biblioteka Studium, 2003.

Jankowski, Edmund. *Eliza Orzeszkowa*. Warszawa: Państwowy Instytut Wydawniczy, 1966.

Jankowski, Jerzy. *Człowiek-serce*. Warszawa: Wydawnictwo Futuryzm Polski, 1920.

Jarczyk, Gwendoline. "Penser la Mort." *Le Cahier*, no. 7 (April 1989): 133–48.

Jarniewicz, Jerzy. *Gościnność słowa. Szkice o przekładzie literackim*. Kraków, Poland: Znak, 2014.

Jasieński, Bruno. "Mięso kobiet." *Nuż w bżuhu. 2 Jednodńuwka futurytuw*, Warszawa: n.p., 1921.

Jaworski, Krzysztof. *Dandys. Słowo o Brunonie Jasieńskim*. Warszawa: Wydawnictwo Iskry, 2009.

Jedrowski, Tomasz. *Swimming in the Dark*. New York: HarperCollins, 2020.

Jedrowski, Tomasz. "On Writing the Story of Polish Queerness: Tomasz Jedrowski Returns to Warsaw." *Literary Hub*, April 30, 2020. https://lithub.com/on-writ ing-the-story-of-polish-queerness/.

Jędrzejewicz, Wacław. "Affirmations of Freedom." *Saturday Review* (August 9, 1958): 26–7.

Johnson, B. S. "Short Stories from Four Countries." *The Spectator* (March 29, 1963): 30.

Johnston, Bill. "Translated from the Polish: The Fates, Feats, and Foibles of Polish Literature in English." In *Being Poland: A New History of Polish Literature and Culture since 1918*, edited by Tamara Trojanowska, Joanna Niżyńska, and Przemyslaw Czapliński, 308–25. Toronto: Toronto University Press, 2018.

Kaczmarski, Paweł. "Cała prawda o 'czułym narratorze'." *Nowa Dekada* (Spring 2021). https://nowadekada-online.pl/pawel-kaczmarski-cala-prawda-o-czulym-narratorze/. Accessed June 1, 2022.

Kahiu, Wanuri. *Rafiki*. Film, 2018.

Kalaga, Wojciech. "Tekst hybrydyczny. Polifonie i aporie doświadczenia hybrydycznego." In *Kulturowe wizualizacje doświadczenia*, edited by Włodzimierz Bolecki and Adam Dziadek, 7–104. Warszawa: IBL PAN, 2010.

Kałążny, Jerzy. "Kiedy właściwie skończył się romantyzm? O (nie)trwałości paradygmatu romantycznego w kulturze polskiej i niemieckiej." September 30, 2021. http://www.polska-niemcy-interakcje.pl/articles/show/31.

Kasabova, Kapka. "Flights by Olga Tokarczuk review—the ways of wanderers." *The Guardian* (June 3, 2017).

Kielak, Anna M. *Zielnik Elizy Orzeszkowej: Nieznany zabytek botaniczny przechowywany z zbiorach PTPN*. Poznań: Kontekst, 2004.

Kijowski, Andrzej. *Dziennik 1970–1977*. Edited by J. Błoński and K. Kijowska. Kraków: Wydawnictwo Literackie, 1998.

Kijowski, Andrzej. *Dziennik 1978–1984*. Edited by J. Błoński, K. Kijowska. Kraków: Wydawnictwo Literackie 1998.

Kijowski, Andrzej. *Szósta dekada*. Warszawa: PIW, 1972.

Kiślak, Elżbieta. *Walka Jakuba z aniołem: Czesław Miłosz wobec romantyczności*. Warszawa: IBL PAN, 2000.

Klejnocki, Jarosław. "Oda do dresu. Debiut Doroty Masłowskiej: rewelacja czy banał." *Tygodnik Powszechny*, no. 42 (2002): 13.

Klene, Émilie (ed.). *Jean Potocki à nouveau*. Amsterdam: Rodopi, 2010.

Klene, Émilie. *Jean Potocki: L'Homme à l'épreuve du relative*. Montpellier: Presses universitaires de la Méditerranée, 2016.

Kłosińska, Krystyna. "Kobieta autorka." *Teksty Drugie*, nos. 3/4 (1995): 87–112.

Knepper, Wendy, and Sharae Deckard. "Towards a Radical World Literature: Experimental Writing in a Globalizing World." *ariel: A Review of International English Literature* 47, nos. 1–2 (2016): 1–25.

Kochanowski, Jan. *Dzieła polskie*. Edited by Julian Krzyżanowski. Warszawa: Świat Książki, 2002.

Kochanowski, Jan. *Odprawa posłów greckich. The Envoys*. Translated by Bill Johnston. Introduction by Krzysztof Koehler. Kraków: Księgarnia Akademicka, 2007.

Koehler, Krzysztof. "O'Harism." *Chicago Review* 46, nos. 3/4 (2000): 280–1.

Kolesnikoff, Nina. *Bruno Jasieński: His Evolution from Futurism to Socialist Realism*. Waterloo: Wilfrid Laurier University Press, 1982.

Konopnicka, Maria. *Rota (The Oath)*. 1908. https://wolnelektury.pl/katalog/lekt ura/rota.html.

Korneliussen, Niviaq. *Last Night in Nuuk*. Translated by Anna Halager. New York: Grove Atlantic, [2014] 2019.

Kornhauser, Jakub. *Premie górskie najwyższej kategorii*. Wrocław: Książkowe Klimaty, 2020.

Koronkiewicz, Marta. *I jest moc odległego życia w tej elegii: uwagi o wierszach Andrzeja Sosnowskiego*. Wrocław: Fundacja im. Karpowicza, 2019.

Koropeckyj, Roman. *Adam Mickiewicz: The Life of a Romantic*. Ithaca, NY: Cornell University Press, 2008.

Koropeckyj, Roman. *The Poetics of Revitalization: Adam Mickiewicz Between "Forefathers' Eve, Part 3" and "Pan Tadeusz."* New York: Columbia University Press, 2001.

Koschalka, Ben. "The Challenges of Bringing Polish Literature to the World: An Interview with Translator Antonia Lloyd-Jones." *Notes from Poland*. May 10, 2021. https://notesfrompoland.com/2021/05/10/the-challenges-of-bringing-pol ish-literature-to-the-world-an-interview-with-translator-antonia-lloyd-jones/ (accessed July 22, 2021).

Kosenda, Patryk. "Golem z gatunkowej gliny, czyli noblistka na manowcach fantastyki." *Nowy Napis Co Tydzień*, no. 49 (May 14, 2020).

Kostelanetz, Richard. "Liberature." In *A Dictionary of the Avant-Gardes: Third Edition*, 258. New York: Routledge, 2019.

Kowzan, Tadeusz. "La parodie, le grotesque et l'absurde dans les *Parades* de Jean Potocki." *Les Cahiers de Varsovie, Centre de civilisation française de l'Université de Varsovie* 3 (1974): 231–44.

Kozicka, Dorota. "Podróżny horyzont rozumienia." *Teksty Drugie*, nos. 1–2 (2006): 270–85.

Kozicka, Dorota. *Wędrowcy światów prawdziwych. Dwudziestowieczne relacje z podróży*, Kraków: Universitas, 2003.

Kozłowska, Marta. *Stopa od nogi* (Warszawa: W.A.B., 2018).

Krasick, Ignacy. *Mikołaja Doświadczyńskiego przypadki*. Wrocław: Wydawnictwo Siedmioróg, 1998.

Krasiński, Zygmunt. *Listy do ojca*. Edited by S. Pigoń. Warszawa: PIW, 1963.

Kristal, Efrain. "'Considering Coldly ...'" *New Left Review* 15 (May–June 2002): 61–74.

Kristeva, Julia. *Black Sun: Depression and Melancholia*. New York: Columbia University Press 1992.

Król Admet [Admetus rex]." In *Dramat staropolski. Antologia*, edited by Julian Lewański, vol. IV. Warszawa: PIW, 1961.

Krzychylkiewicz, Agata. *The Grotesque in the Works of Bruno Jasieński*. Bern: Peter Lang, 2006.

Krzyżanowski, Julian. *The History of Polish Literature*. Translated by Doris Ronowicz. Warsaw: Polish Scientific, 1978.

Kubiak, Ewa. "Anthropophagy as a Concept of the Brazilian Avant-garde at the End of the 1920s: Between History, Myth and Artistic Conception." *Art Inquiry: Avant-garde and Avant-gardes* 19 (2017): 187–204.

Kuenzli, Rudolf E. "Surrealism and Misogyny." In *Surrealism and Women*, Mary Ann Caws, Rudolf Kuenzli, and Gwen Raaberg, 17–36. Cambridge, MA: MIT Press, 1990.

Kulpa, Robert, and Joanna Mizielinska (eds.). *De-Centring Western Sexualities: Central and Eastern European Perspectives*. Farnham: Ashgate, 2011.

Kundera, Milan. *The Curtain: An Essay in Seven Parts*. Translated by Linda Asher. New York: Harper Perennial, 2008.

Kuntsman, Adi. *Figurations of Violence and Belonging: Queerness, Migranthood and Nationalism in Cyberspace and Beyond*. Frankfurt am Main: Peter Lang, 2009.

Kuziak, Michał. *Inny Mickiewicz*. Gdańsk: Słowo/Obraz terytoria, 2013.

Laderman, David. *Driving Visions. Exploring the Road Movie*. Austin: University of Texas Press, 2002.

Lechoń, Jan. "Literatura polska i literatura w Polsce." *Wiadomości*, nos. 36–7 (September 14, 1952): 1.

Leder, Andrzej. *Prześniona Rewolucja*. Warszawa: Wydawnictwo Krytyki Politycznej, 2014.

Lednicki, Wacław (ed.). *Adam Mickiewicz in World Literature*. Berkeley: University of California Press, 1956.

Lee, Wendy Anne. *Failures of Feeling: Insensibility and the Novel*. Stanford, CA: Stanford University Press, 2018.

Leitao, D. D. *The Pregnant Male as Myth and Metaphor*. Cambridge: Cambridge University Press, 2012.

Lem, Stanisław, "O polskiej drodze do motoryzacji." *Przekrój*, no. 645 (1957). https://przekroj.pl/kultura/o-polskiej-drodze-do-motoryzacji-stanislaw-lem.

Leociak, Jacek. "Na Obu Brzegach." *Nowe Książki* 3 (1994): 70–1.

Leszczyński, Adam. *No dno po prostu jest Polska: Dlaczego Polacy tak bardzo nie lubią swojego kraju i innych Polaków.* Warszawa: WAB, 2017.

Levin, Hanoch. "Krum." In *Selected Plays One*, 1–67. Translated by Jessica Cohen, Evan Fallenberg, and Naaman Tammuz. London: Oberon Books, 2020.

Lewański, Julian. *Studia nad dramatem polskiego odrodzenia* [Studies on Polish Renaissance Drama]. Wrocław: Zakład im. Ossolińskich, 1956.

Lewis, R. W. B. *Edith Wharton. A Biography.* New York: Harper & Row, 1975.

"Liberia might be gobbled up by Poland's Greed." *The Pittsburgh Courier* (July 17, 1937): 5.

Lipski, Leo. "Jak Powstawał Piotruś." *Kultura* 9 (1998): 143–6.

Lipski, Leo. "Piotruś." In *Powrót*, edited by Agnieszka Maciejowska, 199–257. Paryż: Instytut Literacki Kultura, 2015.

Lockwood, Alan. "Laugh til you don't: Dorota Maslowska's A Couple of Poor, Polish-Speaking Romanians." Review of *A Couple of Poor, Polish-Speaking Romanians* at Henry Street Settlement—Abrons Arts Center. The Brooklyn Rail, February 2011.

Longinović, Tomislav Z. "I, Witold Gombrowicz: Formal Abjection and the Power of Writing in *A Kind of Testament*." In *Gombrowicz's Grimaces. Modernism, Gender, Nationality*, edited by Ewa Płonowska Ziarek, 33–50. Albany: State University of Albany Press, 1998.

Lorde, Audre. "Uses of the Erotic: The Erotic as Power." In *Sister Outsider*, 53–9. Berkeley, CA: Crossing Press, [1984] 2007.

Lubbock, Piercy. *A portrait of Edith Wharton.* London: Jonathan Cape, 1947.

Ma, Ning. *The Age of Silver: The Rise of the Novel, West and East.* Oxford: Oxford University Press, 2017.

Madeleine, Hurd, Donnan Hastings, and Carolin Leutloff-Grandits (eds.). *Migrating Borders and Moving Times: Temporality and the Crossing of Borders in Europe.* Manchester: Manchester University Press, 2017.

Majeran, Tomasz. "Umysł nierozpoznany." *Czas Kultury*, no. 1 (1994): 61.

Majerski, Paweł. "O języku (w) poezji Anatola Sterna." In *Odmiany awangardy*. Katowice: EGO, 2001.

Malinowski, Bronisław. "Kultura jako wyznacznik zachowania się." *Ruch Prawniczy, Ekonomiczny i Socjologiczny* 17, no. 1 (1937): 101–27.

Maliszewski, Karol. *Nasi klasycy, nasi barbarzyńcy: szkice o nowej poezji.* Bydgoszcz: Instytut Wydawniczy Świadectwo, 1999.

Mańkowski, Jerzy. "Nowa Alcestis—kobieta sportretowana we fraszkach (II, 67 i 68)" [New Alcestis—Alcestis as presented in epigrams (II, 67 and 68)]. In: *Jan Kochanowski 1584–1984. Epoka—twórczość – recepcja.* [Jan Kochanowski 1584–1984. His times—his literary works—its reception], edited by Jerzy Pelc, Paulina Buchwald-Pelcowa and Barbara Otwinowska, vol. I, 245–72. Lublin: Wydawnictwo Lubelskie, 1989.

Marecki, Piotr. *Polska przydrożna.* Wołowiec: Czarne, 2020.

Margalit, Avishai. *The Ethics of Memory.* Cambridge, MA: Harvard University Press, 2004.

Markowski, Michał Paweł. *Czarny nurt. Gombrowicz, świat, literatura.* Kraków: Wydawnictwo Literackie, 2004.

Markowski, Michał Paweł. *Czarny Nurt*. Wyd. 1., dodruk ed. Kraków: Wydawn. Literackie, 2005.

Markowski, Michał Paweł. "Du vomi ou au-déla de l'économie: Gombrowicz contre Sartre." In *Witold Gombrowicz entre l'Europe et l'Amérique*, edited by M. Tomaszewski. Lille: Presses Universitaires de Septentrion, 2007, 171–80.

Markowski, Michał Paweł. "Między nerwicą i psychozą. Rzeczywistości Rolanda Barthesa." *Teksty Drugie*, no. 3 (2012): 127–42.

Markowski, Michał Paweł. "Nicość i czcionka: Wprowadzenie do lektury *Rzutu kośćmi* Stephané'a Mallarmégo." In Stephané Mallarmé, *Rzut kośćmi nigdy nie zniesie przypadku*, translated by Tomasz Różycki, edited by Katarzyna Bazarnik and Zenon Fajfer, 7–24. Kraków: Ha!art, 2005.

Markowski, Michał Paweł. "Ręka kelnera, czyli o obsesji w literaturze." In *Kultura afektu – afekty w kulturze: Humanistyka po zwrocie afektywnym*, edited by Ryszard Nycz, Anna Łebkowska, and Agnieszka Dauksza. Warszawa: IBL, 2015.

Masing-Delic, Irene. "The Transfiguration of Cannibals: Fedorov and the Avant-Garde." In *Laboratory of Dreams: The Russian Avant-garde and Cultural Experiment*, edited by John Bowlt and Olga Matich, 17–36. Stanford, CA: Stanford University Press 1996.

Masłowska, Dorota. *A Couple of Poor, Polish-Speaking Romanians*. Translated by Lisa Goldman and Paul Sirett. London: Oberon Books, 2008.

Masłowska, Dorota. *Snow White and Russian Red*. Translated by Benjamin Paloff. New York: Grove Atlantic, 2005.

Mastronarde, Donald J. *The Art of Euripides*. Cambridge: Cambridge University Press, 2010.

Nieznanowski, Stefan. *O poezji Kaspra Miaskowskiego: Studium o kształtowaniu się baroku w poezji polskiej* [*On Kasper Miaskowski's poety: A study on the birth of Polish baroque poety*]. Lublin: Towarzystwo Naukowe KUL, 1965.

Marta, Cuber. *Trofea Wyobraźni: O Prozie Leo Lipskiego*. 1st ed. Katowice: Uniwersytet Śląski, 2014.

Marzec, Grzegorz. *Ekonomia pamięci*. Warszawa: IBL PAN, 2016.

Marzec, Grzegorz. "Logika spóźnionego postkolonializmu: Przypadek Jarosława Marka Rymkiewicza." In *Romantyzm środkowoeuropejski w kontekście postkolonialnym, cz. 2*, edited by Michał Kuziak, 351–73. Kraków: Universitas, 2016.

Mazierska, Ewa, and Rascaroli Laura. *Crossing New Europe: Postmodern Travel and the European Road Movie*. London: Wallflower Press, 2006.

McGann, Jerome. *The Textual Condition*. Princeton, NJ: Princeton University Press, 1991.

McGlothlin, Erin Heather. *Second-Generation Holocaust Literature Legacies of Survival and Perpetration*. Rochester, NY: Camden House, 2006.

McInturff, Kate. "The Uses and Abuses of World Literature." *Journal of American Culture* 16, no. 2 (2003): 224–36.

McKenzie, Donald Francis. *Bibliography and the Sociology of Texts*. Cambridge: Cambridge University Press, 1999.

Mengham, Rod. "Introduction." In *Altered State: The New Polish Poetry*, edited by Rod Mengham, Tadeusz Pióro, and Piotr Szymor, 11–15. Todmorden, Lancs: Arc Publications, 2003.

Miaojin, Qiu. *Notes of a Crocodile*. Translated by Bonnie Huie. New York: New York Review Books, [1994] 2017.

Mickiewicz, Adam. *Dzieła: wydanie rocznicowe 1798–1998*. Edited by Julian Maślanka. Warszawa: Czytelnik, 1997.

Mickiewicz, Adam. *Pan Tadeusz: The Last Foray in Lithuania*. Translated by Bill Johnston. New York: Archipelago Books, 2018.

Miłosz, Czesław. *The History of Polish Literature*. Berkeley: University of California Press, 1969.

Miłosz, Czesław. *Native Realm: A Search for Self-definition*. Translated by Catherine S. Leach Berkeley: University of California Press, 1981.

Miłosz, Czesław. *New and Collected Poems 1931–2001*. New York: Ecco, 2003.

Miłosz, Czesław. "A Poet's Reply." *New York Review of Books* (July 21, 1988): 42.

Miłosz, Czesław (ed.). *Postwar Polish Poetry*. Berkeley: University of California Press, 1983.

Miłosz, Czesław. *Road-Side Dog*. Translated by the author and Robert Hass. New York: Farrar, Strauss, and Giroux, 1998.

Miłosz, Czesław. *The Witness of Poetry*. Cambridge, MA: Harvard University Press, 1983.

Mitosek, Zofia (ed.). *Adam Mickiewicz w oczach Francuzów*. Translated by Remigiusz Forycki. Warszawa: PWN, 1999.

Moore, David Chioni. "Is the Post- in Postcolonial the Post- in Post-Soviet? Toward a Global Postcolonial Critique." *PMLA* 116, no. 1 (2001): Special Topic: Globalizing Literary Studies: 111–28.

Moore, Steven. *The Novel: An Alternative History, Beginnings to 1600*. London: Bloomsbury, 2011.

Moretti, Franco. "Conjectures on World Literature." *New Left Review* 1 (January–February 2000): 54–68.

Moretti, Franco (ed.). *The Novel*. Princeton, NJ: Princeton University Press, 2007.

Mostowska, Anna. *Powieści, Listy*. Edited and with an introduction by Monika Urbańska. Łódź: Wydawnictwo Uniwersytetu Łódzkiego, 2014.

Munday, Jeremy. "Using Primary Sources to Produce a Microhistory of Translation and Translators: Theoretical and Methodological Concerns." *The Translator* 20, no. 1 (2014): 64–80.

Muñoz, José Esteban. *Disidentifications: Queers of Color and the Performance of Politics*. Durham, NC: Duke University Press, 1999.

Mytych-Forajter, Beata. *Zwierzęta na zakręcie*. Warszawa: IBL PAN, 2017.

Nabokov, Vladimir. "James Joyce. *Ulysses*." In *Lectures on Literature*, edited by Fredson Bowers, 285–370. San Diego: Harcourt, Harvest Book, 1982.

Najder, Zdzisław. "The Development of the Polish Novel: Functions and Structure." *Slavic Review* 29, no. 4 (December 1970): 651–62.

Nandrea, Lorri. *Misfit Forms: Paths Not Taken by the British Novel*. New York: Fordham University Press, 2015.

Nawarecki, Aleksander. *Mały Mickiewicz: studia mikrologiczne*. Katowice: Uniwersytet Śląski, 2003.

Niczow, Aleksandar. *Black Book of Polish Censorship*. Warsaw: Główny Urząd Kontroli Prasy, Publikacji i Widowisk w Warszawie, 1982.

(Nie)opowiedziane. Polskie doświadczenie wstydu i upokorzenia od czasu rozbiorow do dzisiaj, edited by Gosk Hanna, Kuziak Michał, and Paczoska Ewa. Kraków: Universitas, 2019.

Nieukerken van, Arent. "Czesław Miłosz wobec tradycji europejskiego romantyzmu." *Teksty Drugie*, nos. 3–4 (2001): 39–56. https://rcin.org.pl/Cont ent/57837/WA248_71461_P-I-2524_nieukerken-czeslaw_o.pdf.

Niranjana, Tejaswini. *Siting Translation: History, Post-Structrualism, and the Colonial Context*. Berkeley: University of California Press, 1992. Print.

Niziolek, Grzegorz. *Warlikowski: Extra Ecclesiam*. Krakow: Homini, 2008.

Niżyńska, Joanna. "The Impossibility of Shrugging One's Shoulders: O'Harists, O'Hara, and Post-1989 Polish Poetry." *Slavic Review* 66, no. 3 (Fall 2007): 463–83.

Niżyńska, Joanna. *The Kingdom of Insignificance: Miron Bialoszewski and the Quotidian, the Queer, and the Traumatic*. Chicago: Northwestern University Press, 2013.

Niżyńska, Joanna. *Królestwo Małoznaczącości: Miron Białoszewski a Trauma, Codzienność iQueer*. Kraków: Universitas, 2018.

Nowacki, Dariusz. "Dziurawa siatka na motyle: Wokół prozy autorów urodzonych po roku 1960." *Fraza* nr 11–12 (1996): 128.

Nowacki, Dariusz. "Satysfakcja i satys-fuck-cja." *FA-art* no. 3 (1996): 74

Nowakowski, Radosław. "The Author." Liberatorium website. Accessed August 10, 2021. https://www.liberatorium.com/autor/author.html.

Nyman, Jopi. *Displacement, Memory, and Travel in Contemporary Migrant Writing*. Leiden: Brill, 2017.

O'Keeffe, Terrence. "Flight into Light and Darkness-Andrzej Stasiuk's Travel Essays." *Polish Review* 57, no. 3 (2012): 83–99.

Okoń, Jan. "Barokowy dramat i teatr szkolny w Polsce wśród zadań publicznych i religijnych." In *Popularny dramat i teatr religijny w Polsce*, edited by Irena Sławińska i Maria Barbara Stykowa, 7–26. Lublin: Towarzystwo Naukowe KUL, 1990.

Okulska, Inez. "Miłość i fetysz a spotkanie języków." In *Wiersze na Głos: szkice o twórczości Andrzeja Sosnowskiego*, edited by Piotr Śliwiński, 168–77. Poznań: WBP, 2010.

Opacki, Ireneusz. *Poezja romantycznych przełomów: szkice*. Wrocław: Zakład Narodowy im. Ossolińskich, 1972.

Ordon, Edmund (ed.). *Ten Contemporary Polish Short Stories*. Detroit: Wayne State University Press, 1958.

Orliński, Wojciech. *Ameryka nie istnieje*. Bielsko-Biała: Pascal, 2010.

Orska, Joanna. "Co to jest o'haryzm—próba krytycznej rewizji pojęcia." *Kresy*, nr. 3 (1998): 44–56.

Orska, Joanna. "Podróż poematu (tłumaczenie jako tranzyt)." In *Poeci Szkoły Nowojorskiej*, edited by Kacper Bartczak, 304–28. Warszawa: Wydawnictwo UW, 2018.

Orska, Joanna. "Polska i świat: Nowojorskie historie i nowa poezja polska." *Teksty Drugie* no. 5 (1999): 53–70.

Orzeszkowa, Eliza. *Dwa bieguny*. Warszawa: Książka i wiedza, 1950.

Orzeszkowa, Eliza. *Marta: A Novel*. Translated by Anna Gąsienica Byrcyn and Stephanie Kraft. Athens: Ohio University Press, 2018.

Orzeszkowa, Eliza. *O sobie*. Edited by Julian Krzyżanowski. Warszawa: Czytelnik, 1974.

Osińska, Natalia. *Fanfik*. Warszawa: Krytyka Polityczna, 2016.

Osińska, Natalia. *Slash*. Warszawa: Agora SA, 2017.

Osińska, Natalia. *Fluff*. Warszawa: Agora SA, 2019.

Ozick, Cynthia. "*The Streets of Crocodiles*." *New York Times Book Review* (February 13, 1977): 2.

Paige, Nicholas. *Before Fiction: The Ancien Regime of the Novel*. Philadelphia: University of Pennsylvania Press, 2011.

Paloff, Benjamin. "Czy fraza 'Polish literature' oznacza 'literaturę polską'? (Problem teorii recepcji i nie tylko...)." *Wielogłos* 2, no. 4 (2008): 53–64.

Paloposki, Outi, and Kaisa Koskinen. "A Thousand and One Translations: Revisiting Retranslation." In *Claims Changes and Challenges in Translation Studies*, edited by Gyde Hansen, Kirsten Malmkjær, and Daniel Gile, 27–38. Amsterdam: John Benjamins, 2004.

Pavel, Thomas. *The Lives of the Novel: A History*. Princeton, NJ: Princeton University Press, 2013.

Pawluśkiewicz, Joanna. *Pani na domkach*. Kraków: Korporacja Ha!art, 2006.

Paziński, Piotr, Jagoda Budzik, and Bartłomiej Krupa. "Tam Jest Życie, a Tu Już Jakby Nie-życie." Z Piotrem Pazińskim O Hebrajskiej Literaturze Zagłady Rozmawiają Jagoda Budzik i Bartłomiej Krupa." *Narracje o Zagładzie* no. 4 (2019): 15–40.

Pelc, Janusz. *Jan Kochanowski w tradycjach literatury polskiej (od XVI do połowy XVIII wieku)* [The reception of Jan Kochanowski in Polish literature (from 16th till the middle of 18th century]. Warszawa: Państwowy Instytut Wydawniczy, 1965.

Piątek, Tomasz. *Kartoflada*. Warszawa: W.A.B., 2016.

Pijanowski, Paweł. "Jadąc do Mordoru," *Popmoderna*, July 8, 2013. https://pop moderna.pl/jadac-do-mordoru-%e2%80%9eprzyjdzie-mordaor-i-nas-zje-ziemowita-szczerka/.

Pilch, Jerzy. "Monolog Silnego." *Polityka* nr 37 (2002): 103.

Pióro, Tadeusz. "The Influence of the New York School on Contemporary Polish Poetry." In *Exorcising Modernism*, edited by Mikołaj Wiśniewski, 186–203. Wrocław: SWPS, 2014.

Pleijel, Agneta. *Zapach mężczyzny*. Translated by Justyna Czechowska. Kraków: Karakter, 2017.

Płonowska Ziarek, Ewa. "Introduction." In *Gombrowicz's Grimaces: Modernism, Gender, Nationality*, edited by Ewa Plonowska Ziarek, 1–30. Albany: State University of Albany, 1998.

Płonowska Ziarek, Ewa. "The Scar of the Foreigner and the Fold of the Baroque: National Affiliations and Homosexuality in Gombrowicz's *Trans-Atlantyk*." In *Gombrowicz's Grimaces: Modernism, Gender, Nationality*, edited by Ewa Plonowska Ziarek, 213–44. Albany: State University of Albany Press, 1998.

Popiel, M., T. Bilczewski, and S. Bill *Światowa historia literatury polskiej. Interpretacje*. Kraków: WUJ, 2020.

Potocki, Jean. *Œuvres*, 5 vol. Louvain: Peeters, 2004–6.

Pouzet-Duzer, Virginie. "Dada, Surrealism, Antropofagia: The Consuming Process of the Avant-garde." *L'Esprit Créateur* 53, no. 3, *Old and New, Avant-garde and 'Arrière-garde' in Modernist Literature* (Fall 2013): 79–90.

Prendergast, Christopher (ed.). *Debating World Literature*. New York: Verso, 2004.

Presner, Todd Samuel. *Muscular Judaism: The Jewish Body and the Politics of Regeneration*. London: Routledge, 2007.

Pressman, Jessica. "The Aesthetic of Bookishness in Twenty-First Century Literature." *Michigan Quarterly Review* 48, no. 4 (2009): 465–82.

Prokop-Janiec, Eugenia. "Literatura Polska W Izraelu: Pomiędzy Pamięcią Europy a Nowym Życiem." *Roczniki humanistyczne* 64, no. 1 (2016): 63–74.

Przybyszewska, Agnieszka. "Close Reading of the Liberatic Canon: On *Oka-leczenie*." In *Incarnations of Material Textuality. From Modernism to Liberature*, edited by Katarzyna Bazarnik and Izabela Curyłło-Klag, 73–106. Newcastle-upon-Tyne: Cambridge Scholars, 2014.

Przybyszewska, Agnieszka. "Liberacka analiza tekstu (o czytaniu *Oka-leczenia* Zenona Fajfera i Katarzyny Bazarnik)." In *Polska literatura najnowsza—poza kanonem*, edited by Paulina Kierzek, 190–218. Łódź: University of Łódź Press, 2008.

Przybyszewska, Agnieszka. *Liberackość dzieła literackiego*. Łódź: Wydawnictwo Uniwersytetu Łódzkiego, 2015.

Pym, Anthony. *Method in Translation History*. Manchester: St. Jerome Publishing, 1998.

Quinn, Justin. *Between Two Fires: Transnationalism and Cold War Poetry*. Oxford: Oxford University Press, 2015.

Rączka-Jeziorska, Teresa. "*Przez fale rozeznać myśl wód*": *o romantycznych przedstawieniach rzeki w twórczości Adama Mickiewicza i Tarasa Szewczenki*. Katowice: Uniwersytet Śląski, 2011.

Ranocchi, Emiliano. "Liberature and Person: an Anthropological Question." In *Incarnations of Material Textuality: From Modernism to Liberature*, edited by Katarzyna Bazarnik and Izabela Curyłło-Klag, 107–18. Newcastle-upon-Tyne: Cambridge Scholars, 2014.

Ready, Ania. "Word without God." *Times Literary Supplement*, https://www.the-tls.co.uk/articles/olga-tokarczuk-fiction/.

Reid, Kerry. "'No Matter How Hard We Try' Set in a World of Hardships and despair." *Chicago Tribune* (May 26, 2016).

Richter, Johann Paul. *Jean Paul's sämmtliche Werke, vol. 32*. Berlin: G. Reimer, 1842.

Roberston, Jenny. "Two Threnodies after Jan Kochanowski." *Poetry Ireland Review*, no. 29 (Summer 1990): 142–3.

Ross, Ian Campbell. "Laurence Sterne's Life, Milieu, and Literary Career." In *The Cambridge Companion to Laurence Sterne*, edited by Thomas Keymer, 5–20. Cambridge: Cambridge University Press, 2009.

Rosset, François. "Manuscrit trouvé à Saragosse et protocole intertextuel." In *Le Manuscrit trouvé à Saragosse et ses intertextes*, 15–31. Louvain: Peeters, 2001.

Rosset, François. *Le Théâtre du romanesque: Manuscrit trouvé à Saragosse entre construction et maçonnerie*. Lausanne: L'Âge d'Homme, 1991.

Rosset, François, and Dominique Triaire. *De Varsovie à Saragosse. Jean Potocki et son œuvre*. Louvain: Peeters, 2000.

Rosset, François, and Dominique Triaire. *Jean Potocki. Biographie.* Paris: Flammarion, 2004.

Rosset, François, and Dominique Triaire (ed.). *Jean Potocki où le dédale des Lumières.* Montpellier: Presses universitaires de la Méditerranée, 2010.

Rosslyn, Felicity. "Kochanowski's Humanist Laments." *Cambridge Quarterly* 26, no. 4 (1997): 369–75.

Rubin, Isaak Illich. *Essays on Marx's Theory of Value.* Detroit: Black and Red, 1972.

Rudaś-Grodzka, Monika. *Sfinks słowiański i mumia polska.* Warszawa: IBL PAN, 2013.

Ryziński, Remigiusz. *Foucault w Warszawie.* Warszawa: Dowody na Istnienie, 2017.

Sadzik, Piotr. "Zdrobniałe Jąkanie. Teologia Afatyczna W "Piotrusiu" Leo Lipskiego." *Wielogłos* 40, no. 2 (2019): 57–84.

Said, Edward. "The Politics of Knowledge (1991)." In *Reflections on Exile and Other Essays.*Cambridge, MA: Harvard University Press, 2000.

Saint-Amour, Paul. "Weak Theory, Weak Modernism." *Modernism/Modernity* 25, no. 3 (2018).

Sala, Zuzanna. "Zainteresowania obserwatora." *Nowy Napis Co Tydzień*, no. 43 (April 4, 2020). https://nowynapis.eu/tygodnik/nr-43/artykul/zainteresowania-obserwatora. Accessed May 1, 2021.

Sallis, James. "Irreverent and Spiteful, Arenas' *Assault* Attacks Senses." *The Orlando Sentinel* (July 20, 1994): E3.

Schmidt, Michael. *The Novel: A Biography.* Cambridge, MA: Harvard University Press, 2014.

Schollenberger, Justyna. "*Wejść między sforę*—projekt duchowości zwierząt: Mickiewicz-Emerson." *Wiek XIX. Rocznik Towarzystwa Literackiego im. Adama Mickiewicza* 45, no. 1 (2010): 36–49.

Schulz, Bruno. *Cinnamon Shops and Other Stories.* Translated by Celina Wieniewska. London: McGibbon&Kee, 1963.

Schulz, Bruno. "Cinnamon Shops." *Poland* 50 (October 1958): 25–8.

Schulz, Bruno. "Cinnamon Shops," "Sanatorium under Water Clock." Translated by Christina Cenkalska, Poland 134 (October 1965): 29–31.

Schulz, Bruno. "Father's Last Escape." Translated by Celina Wieniewska. *New Yorker* (January 2, 1978): 24–6.

Schulz, Bruno. *Księga listów.* In *Dzieła zebrane*, t. 5, edited by J. Ficowski and S. Danecki. Gdańsk: słowo/obraz terytoria, 2012.

Schulz, Bruno. "Loneliness." Translated by Celina Wieniewska. *The New Yorker* (November 14, 1977): 43.

Schulz, Bruno. "Sanatorium Under the Sign of the Hourglass." Translated by Celina Wieniewska. *New Yorker* (December 12, 1977): 44–54.

Schulz, Bruno. "Solitude." In *Collected Stories.* Translated by Madelcinc G. Levine. Evanston, IL: Northwestern University Press, 2018.

Schulz, Bruno. *The Street of Crocodiles.* Translated by. Celina Wieniewska, New York: Walker, 1963.

Schulz, Bruno. *Szkice krytyczne.* In Dzieła zebrine, t. 7, edited by Włodzimierz Bolecki, Mirosław Wójcik, and Piotr Sitkiewicz. Gdańsk: słowo/obraz terytoria, 2017.

Scullion, Scott. "Tradition and Invention in Euripidean Aitiology." *Illinois Classical Studies* 24, no. 5 (1999–2000): 217–233.

Segev, Tom. *The Seventh Million: The Israelis and the Holocaust.* 1st ed. New York: Hill and Wang, 1993.

Seymenliyska, Elena. "Rotten Russkies." Review of *Snow White and Russian Red* by Dorota Masłowska. *The Guardian* (May 7, 2005).

Shakespeare, William. *The Tragedy of Hamlet, Prince of Denmark.* Fully annotated, with an Introduction by Burton Raffel, with an essay by Harold Bloom. New Haven, CT: Yale University Press, 2003.

Showalter, Elaine. "The Death of the Lady (Novelist): Wharton's *House of Mirth.*" *Representations* 9 (1985): 133–49.

Showalter, Elaine. *A Jury of Her Peers. American Women Writers from Anne Bradstreet to Annie Proulx.* London: Virago, 2010.

Singer, Isaac B. "Burlesquing Life with Father," *Herald Tribune* (December 22, 1963).

Singer, Isaac B. "A Polish Franz Kafka." *New York Times Book Review* (July 9, 1978): 1, 34.

Siwicka, Dorota. *Mapy romantyków.* Warszawa: IBL PAN, 2018.

Siwicka, Dorota, and Marek Bieńczyk (ed.). *Nasze pojedynki o romantyzm.* Warszawa: IBL PAN, 1995.

Skórczewski, Dariusz. *Aby rozpoznać siebie. Rzecz o Andrzeju Kijowskim-krytyku literackim i publicyście.* Lublin: Towarzystwo Naukowe Katolickiego Uniwersytetu Lubelskiego, 1996.

Skórczewski, Dariusz. *Teoria—literatura—dyskurs: pejzaż postkolonialny.* Lublin: Wydawnictwo KUL, 2013.

Śliwiński, Piotr. "Fermentacja kanonów." *Teksty Drugie*, no. 5 (2020): 138–55.

Śliwiński, Piotr. *Przygody z wolnością. Uwagi o poezji współczesnej.* Kraków: Znak, 2002.

Sływynski, Ostap. "Źródła i metamofrozy poetyki personizmu: szkoła nowojorska—polski o'haryzm—poezja ukraińska XXI wieku." *Postscriptum Polonistyczne*, no. 1 (2009): 19–30. https://www.ceeol.com/search/article-det ail?id=203837.

Sobolczyk, Piotr. *Polish Queer Modernism.* Warsaw: Peter Lang, 2015.

Sobolczyk, Piotr. "Foucault: Madness and Surveillance in Warsaw." *Foucault Studies*, 25 (2018): 174–90.

Sokolski, Jacek. *Bogini, pojęcie, demon: Fortuna w dziełach autorów staropolskich* [The Goddess, the Idea, the Daemon: Fortune in Old Polish Literature]. Wrocław: Wydawnictwo Uniwersytetu Wrocławskiego, 1996.

Sommer, Piotr. "'O krok od nich': szkic do portretu wierszy Franka O'Hary." *Literatura na Świecie*, 7 (1986): 195–208.

Sommer, Piotr. "An Interview with Piotr Sommer." By W. Martin. *Chicago Review* 46, nos. 3/4 (2000): 191–212.

Sośnicki, Dariusz. "Fortuna i fatum." *Czas Kultury*, no. 3 (2008): 98–107.

Sosnowski, Andrzej. "Big Bang, jak to się czasem mówi." Interview by Grzegorz Jankowicz. In *Trop w trop: rozmowy z Andrzejem Sosnowskim*, edited by Grzegorz Jankowicz, 113–23. Wrocław: Biuro Literackie, 2010.

Sosnowski, Andrzej. *Konwój Opera.* Wrocław: Pomona, 1999.

Sosnowski, Andrzej. "50 lat po Oświęcimiu i inne sezony." Interview by Mariusz Maciejewski and Tomasz Majeran. In Trop w trop: rozmowy z Andrzejem Sosnowskim, edited by Grzegorz Jankowicz, 25–35. Wrocław: Biuro Literackie, 2010.

Sosnowski, Andrzej. Nouvelles impressions d'Amerique. Wrocław: Biuro Literackie, 2004.

Sosnowski, Andrzej. "Trop w trop." Interview by Jacek Gutorow. In Trop w trop: rozmowy z Andrzejem Sosnowskim, edited by Grzegorz Jankowicz, 49–56. Wrocław: Biuro Literackie, 2010.

Spacks, Patricia Meyer. Novel Beginnings: Experiments in Eighteenth-Century English Fiction. New Haven, CT: Yale University Press, 2006.

Stanford Friedman, Susan. "Creativity and the Childbirth Metaphor: Gender Difference in Literary Discourse." Feminist Studies, 13, no. 1 (1987): 49–82.

Stasiuk, Andrzej. On the Road to Babadag: Travels in Other Europe. Translated by Kandel Michael. London: Vintage Books, 2012.

Stasiuk, Andrzej. White Raven. Translated by Powaga Wiesiek. London: Serpent's Tail, 2001.

Statovci, Pajtim. Crossing: A Novel. Translated by David Hackston. New York: Penguin/ Random House, [2016] 2020.

Steiner, Ann. "World Literature and the Book Market." In The Routledge Companion to World Literature, edited by Theo D'haen, David Damrosch, and Djelal Kadir, 316–24. London: Routledge, 2012.

Stern, Anatol. "Barbarzyński dzień." Wiersze zebrane. Kraków: Wydawnictwo Literackie, 1985, 94.

Stern, Anatol. "Emeryt merytoryzmu. Z powodu ostatniego artykułu Irzykowskiego pt. "Plagiatowy charakter przełomów literackich w Polsce" czyli jeszcze o wiatrologii. Głód jednoznaczności i inne szkice. Warszawa: Czytelnik 1972.

Stern, Anatol. "Romans. Peru." In Wiersze zebrine, edited by Andrzej K. Waśkiewicz, 67–74. Kraków: Wydawnictwo Literackie, 1985.

Stilwell, Robert L. "Suffering and Sea Change." Saturday Review (October 26, 1963): 40, 45.

Świerkosz, Monika. "Strategie ocalania." Dwutygodnik, no. 11 (2020). https://www.dwutygodnik.com/artykul/9231-strategie-ocalania.html. Accessed May 1, 2021.

Świetlicki, Marcin. "Koehlerism." Chicago Review 46, nos. 3/4 (2000): 282–4.

Szczeblewska, Anna. "Słabe pokolenie Silnego." Topos, no. 6 (2002).

Szczerek, Ziemowit. Mordor's Coming to Eat Us: A Secret History of the Slavs [excerpt], Translated by Gilroy Scotia, Asymptote Journal. https://www.asymptotejournal.com/nonfiction/ziemowit-szczerek-mordors-coming-to-eat-us-a-secret-history-of-the-slavs/.

Szczerek, Ziemowit. Siódemka. Kraków: Ha!art, 2015.

Szcześniak, Magda. Normy widzialności. Tożsamość w czasach transformacji. Warszawa: Fundacja Bęc Zmiana, 2016.

Szulc, Łukasz. "From Queer to Gay to Queer.pl: The Names we Dare to Speak in Poland." Lambda Nordica 17, no. 4 (2012): 65–98.

Thompson, Ewa M. "It Is Colonialism after All: Some Epistemological Remarks." *Teksty Drugie. English Edition*, no. 1 (2014): 67–81.

Thompson, Ewa M. *Witold Gombrowicz*. Woodbridge: Twayne, 1979.

Thomsen, Mads Rosenthal. *Mapping World literature: International Canonization and Transnational Literature*. London: Continuum, 2010.

Three Percent: A Resource for International Literature at the University of Rochester. University of Rochester, 2007. Web. October 7, 2015.

Tillyard, H. J. W. (Henry Julius Wetenhall). "Suggestions for an Adult Begginer's Latin Reader." *Greece & Rome* 9, no. 1 (March 1962): 67–71.

Tischner, Łukasz. *Gombrowicza milczenie o Bogu*. Kraków: Wydawnictwo Uniwersytetu Jagiellońskiego, 2013.

Tischner, Łukasz. *Miłosz and the Problem of Evil*. Translated by S. Bill. Evanston, IL: Northwestern University Press, 2015.

Tlostanova, Madina. "Postsocialist ≠ Postcolonial? On Post-Soviet Imaginary and Global Coloniality." *Journal of Postcolonial Writing* 48, no. 2 (2012): 130–42.

Tokarczuk, Olga. "Anger Is Not a Bad Energy." Interview by Izabela Joanna Barry. Brooklyn Public Library, January 12, 2020.

Tokarczuk, Olga. *The Books of Jacob*. Translated by Jennifer Croft. London: Fitzcarraldo Editions, 2021.

Tokarczuk, Olga. *Drive Your Plow Over the Bones of the Dead*. Translated by Antonia Lloyd-Jones. London: Fitzcarraldo Editions, 2018.

Tokarczuk, Olga. *Flights*. Translated by Jennifer Croft. London: Fitzcarraldo Editions, 2017.

Tokarczuk, Olga. *House of Day, House of Night*. Translated by Antonia Lloyd-Jones. London: Granta, 2002.

Tokarczuk, Olga. "I was very naive. I thought Poland would be able to discuss the dark areas of our history." Interview by Claire Armistead. *The Guardian* (April 20, 2018).

Tokarczuk, Olga. "Nobel Prize-Winner Olga Tokarczuk in Conversation with John Freeman." *Literary Hub* (October 10, 2019).

Tokarczuk, Olga. "On Poland." Interview by Marie Tetzlaff. *Dezign Ark* (September 13, 2018).

Tokarczuk, Olga. *Primeval and Other Times*. Translated by Antonia Lloyd-Jones. Prague: Twisted Spoon Press, 2010.

Tomasik, Krzysztof. *Gejerel: Mniejszości Seksualne w PRL-u*. Warszawa: Wydawnictwo Krytyki Politycznej, 2018.

Tomasik, Krzysztof. *Homobiografie*. Warsaw: Wydawnictwo Krytyki Politycznej, [2008] 2014.

Toynton, Evelyn. "Written in the Stars." Review of *Drive Your Plow Over the Bones of the Dead* by Olga Tokarczuk. *Times Literary Supplement*, November 16, 2018."Translation Database." *Publishers Weekly*. https://admin.publisher sweekly.com/pw/translation/search/index.html Accessed January 30, 2019.

Triaire, Dominique. "Les contes orientaux de Jean Potocki." *Féeries* 10 (2013): 169–79.

Triaire, Dominique. "Le théâtre de Jean Potocki." *Cahiers de l'Association Internationale des Études Françaises* 51 (1999): 155–67.

Trojanowska, Tamara, Joanna Niżyńska, and Przemysław Czapliński. *Being Poland: A New History of Polish Literature and Culture since 1918*. Toronto: University of Toronto Press, 2018.

Trojanowska, Tamara, Niżyńska Joanna, and Czapliński Przemysław, " 'Ex Pluribus Plures': Cultural Histories in the Twenty-First Century." In *Being Poland: A New History of Polish Literature and Culture since 1918*, xxi. Toronto: University of Toronto Press, 2018.

Trybuś, Krzysztof. *Pamięć romantyzmu: studia nie tylko z przeszłości*. Poznań: UAM, 2011.

Trześniewska, Agnieszka. "*Dziady cz. IV* w zwierciadle ekosystemu romantycznego." *Polonistyka. Innowacje*, no. 5 (2017): 53–62.

Tsikhanouskaya, Sviatlana. "Bądź jak Poczobut i Mickiewicz." September 30, 2021. https://wyborcza.pl/7,75399,27613926,cichanouska-dla-wyborczej-badz-jak-poczobut-i-jak-mickiewicz.html#S.DT-K.C-B.2-L.3.maly.

Tymoczko, Maria, and Edwin Gentzler (eds.). *Translation and Power*. Amherst: University of Massachusetts Press, 2002.

Ulewicz, Tadeusz. *Oddziaływanie europejskie Jana Kochanowskiego* [Jan Kochanowski's European impact]. Kraków: Polska Akademia Nauk, 1976.

Uniłowski, Krzysztof. "Cała prawda o 'prozie środka,' cz. 1." *FA-art*, nr 3 (2002).

Uniłowski, Krzysztof. "Cała prawda o 'prozie środka,' cz. 2." *FA-art*, nr 4 (2002).

Uniłowski, Krzysztof. "Cała prawda o 'prozie środka,' cz. 3." *FA-art*, nr ½ (2003).

Uniłowski, Krzysztof. *Granice nowoczesności: Proza polska i wyczerpanie modernizmu*. Katowice: Wydawnictwo Uniwersytetu Śląskiego, 2006.

Uniłowski, Krzysztof. *Kup pan książkę!* Katowice: FA-art, 2008.

Updike, John. "Bruno Schulz, Hidden Genius." *New York Times Book Review* (September 9, 1979): 1.

Varga Krzysztof. *Masakra*. Warszawa: Wielka Litera, 2015.

Varga Krzysztof. *Trociny*. Wołowiec: Czarne, 2012.

Wachtel, Andrew Baruch. *Remaining Relevant After Communism: The Role of the Writer in Eastern Europe*. Chicago, IL: University of Chicago Press, 2006.

Waid, Candace. *Edith Wharton's Letters from the Underworld: Fictions of Women and Writing*. Chapel Hill: University of North Carolina Press, 1991.

Wajda, Andrzej. *Popiół i Diament*. Film. 1961.

Walkowitz, Rebecca. *Born Translated: The Contemporary Novel in the Age of World Literature*. New York: Columbia University Press, 2015.

Warlikowski Krzysztof. *Krum*. Warszawa: Teatr Rozmaitości w Warszawie w koprodukcji ze Starym Teatrem w Krakowie, 2005.

Warwick Research Collective. *Combined and Uneven Development: Towards a New Theory of World-Literature*. Liverpool: Liverpool University Press: 2015.

Waśkiewicz, Andrzej K. "Irrealna gwiazda": o poezji Anatola Sterna. *Pamiętnik Literacki: czasopismo kwartalne poświęcone historii i krytyce literatury polskie.j* 74 (1979): 163–90.

Wästberg, Per. Award ceremony speech. December 10, 2019, https://www.nobelprize.org/prizes/literature/2018/ceremony-speech/.

Weikert, Sakine. "Teju Cole's Blind Spot/#blindspot, between Analogue and Digital Narrative Devices." In *Refresh the Book*: *On the Hybrid Nature of the Book in the Age of Electronic Publishing*, edited by Viola Hildebrand-Schat, Katarzyna Bazarnik, and Christoph Benjamin Schulz, 41–70. Leiden: Brill, 2021.

Weizman Eyal. "Introduction to the Politics of Verticality." April 23 [cited 2021]. Available from https://www.opendemocracy.net/en/article_801jsp/.

Wharton, Edith. *The Age of Innocence*. Harmondsworth: Penguin Books, 1984.

Wharton, Edith. *The House of Mirth*. Edited by Shari Benstock. Boston: Bedford Books, 1994.

Wharton, Edith. *Novellas and Other Writings*. New York: Literary Classics of the United States, 1990.

Wierzejska, Jagoda. *Retoryczna Interpretacja Autobiograficzna*. Warszawa: Wydawn. Elipsa, 2012.

Williams, David. *Writing Postcommunism: Towards a Literature of the East European Ruins*. Basingstoke: Palgrave Macmilan, 2013.

Williams, Tom. "No Matter How Hard We Try." Review of *No Matter How Hard We Try* at Trap Door Theatre, Chicago. Chicago Critic, https://chicagocritic. com/no-matter-how-we-try/.

Windakiewicz, Stanisław. "*Admetus rex*, tragedia polska z końca XVI wieku lub początku wieku XVII [*Admetus rex*, Polish tragedy from the end of the 16th century or begining of the 17th century]." *Sprawozdania z posiedzeń Polskiej Akademii Umiejętności* [Proceedings of Polish Academy of Arts and Sciences] 1891: 40–1.

Winiarski, Bolesław. *Polityka gospodarcza*. Warszawa: Wydawnictwo Naukowe PWN, 2021.

Wirtemberska, Maria. *Malwina, czyli domyślność serca*. Kraków: Universitas, 2002.

Wirtemberska, Maria. *Malvina, or the Heart's Intuition*. Translated and with an introduction by Ursula Phillips. DeKalb, IL: Northern Illinois University Press, 2012.

Witkowski, Michał. *Lovetown*. London: Granta Books, [2004] 2011.

Witkowski, Michał. *Margot*. Warszawa: Świat Książki, 2009.

Włodarski, Maciej. *Ars moriendi w literaturze polskiej XV i XVI wieku* [Ars moriendi in Polish Literature of 15th and 16th century]. Kraków: Społeczny Instytut Wydawniczy Znak, 1987.

Włodarski, Maciej. *Motyw "psychomachia" w literaturze polskiej XV i XVI wieku* [*Psychomachia* in Polish Literature of 15th and 16th century]. Warszawa: […], 1983.

Wolff, Cynthia Griffin. *A Feast of Words: The Triumph of Edith Wharton*. New York: Oxford University Press, 1977.

Wood, James. "'Flights': A Novel That Never Settles Down." *New Yorker* (October 1, 2018): n.p. https://www.newyorker.com/magazine/2018/10/01/flig hts-a-novel-that-never-settles-down. Accessed May 20, 2021.

Wordsworth, Christopher. "A Private Individual." *The Guardian* (April 11, 1963): 7.

Wróblewski, Łukasz. "Rozrachunki ze wstrętem w Trocinach Krzysztofa Vargi. Od wstrętu do inwencyjnego poznania." *Teksty Drugie*, 4 (2016): 324–39.

Wyka, Kazimierz, and Stefan Napierski. "Dwugłos o Schulzu." *Ateneum*, no. 1 (1939): 3.

Yarbrough, Steve. "Short-Story Improv: Murakami's Masterful Riffs." *The Oregonian* (October 15, 2006): O15.

Yau, John. "The Poet as Art Critic." *American Poetry Review* 34, no. 3 (May/June 2005): 45–50.

Zadura, Bohdan. "John Ashbery i ja. Poezja spójników?" *Literatura na Świecie*, no. 3 (1992): 105–12.

Zadura, Bohdan. "Otwarcie." *Twórczość*, no. 10 (1994): 112–15.

Zadura, Bohdan. "Overexposed photographs." Translated by Piotr Sommer and M. Kasper. *Chicago Review* 46, nos. 3/4 (2000): 185.

Zadura, Bohdan. *Wiersze Zebrane*, vols. 1 and 2. Wrocław: Biuro Literackie, 2005.

Zagórska, Anna. *ANTYbohater polskiej prozy (po roku 1989)*. Nowy Sącz: Wydawnictwo Pasaże, 2017.

Zajac, Antoni. "Maksimum Wyganania. Marginalne Parodie i Marańskie Rozszczepienia Leo Lipskiego." In *Marani Literatury Polskiej*, edited by Piotr Bogalewski and Adam Lipszyc, 417–63. Kraków: Austeria, 2020.

Zaleski, Marek. "Bajka raczej smutna." *Res Publica Nowa*, no. 11 (2002): 94-95.

Żeromski, Stefan. *Snobizm i postęp oraz inne utwory publicystyczne*, edited by Antonina Lubaszewska. Kraków: Universitas, 2003.

Ziarek, Ewa Płonowska. "Melancholic Nationalism and the Pathologies of Commemorating the Holocaust in Poland." In *Imaginary Neighbors: Mediating Polish-Jewish Relations after the Holocaust*, edited by Dorota Glowacka and Joanna Zylinska, 301–26. Lincoln: University of Nebraska Press, 2007.

Ziemann, Zofia. "The Good Bad Translator: Celina Wieniewska and Her Bruno Schulz." *Asymptote*, September 20, 2017, https://www.asymptotejournal.com/blog/2017/09/20/the-good-bad-translator-celina-wieniewska-and-her-bruno-schulz/.

Ziemann, Zofia. "Extratextual Factors Shaping Preconceptions about Retranslation: Bruno Schulz in English." In *Perspectives on Retranslation: Ideology, Paratexts, Methods*, edited by Özlem Berk Albachten and Şehnaz Tahir Gürçağlar, 87–104. New York: Routledge, 2019.

Ziemann, Zofia. "Translating Polish Jewishness: Bruno Schulz in English." *Translatologica* 1 (2017): 209–29.

Żmigrodzka, Maria. *Orzeszkowa. Młodość pozytywizmu*. Warszawa: PIW, 1965.

Zmroczek, Janet. "The History of the Book in Poland." In *The Book: A Global History*, edited by F. Michael, S. J. Suarez, and H. R. Woudhuysen, 470–9. Oxford: Oxford University Press, 2013.

Żulczyk, Jakub. *Zrób mi jakąś krzywdę*. Warszawa: Lampa i Iskra Boża, 2006.

Zwinger, Thomas. *Theatrum Vitae Humanae*. Basil, 1586. https://reader.digitale-sammlungen.de/de/fs1/object/display/bsb10143614_00077.html.

CONTRIBUTORS

Kacper Bartczak is Associate Professor of American Literature at the University of Łódź. He is the author of *In Search of Communication and Community: I Poetry of John Ashbery* (2006), *Świat nie scalony* (2010), and *Materia i autokreacja* (2019). As a poet, he is the author of several volumes, one of which, *Wiersze organiczne* (2015), was finalist in two major Polish literary awards, Silesius and Gdynia. He also published collections of selected poems by Rae Armantrout, Charles Bernstein, and Peter Gizzi. He lives in Łódź.

Katarzyna Bartoszyńska is Assistant Professor of English and Women's and Gender Studies at Ithaca College. Her research focuses on the novel form and the ways it is theorized. Her work has appeared in *Genre, Comparative Literature, Nineteenth-Century Contexts, New Hibernia Review*, and *Comparative Literature Studies*. Her book, *Estranging the Novel: Poland, Ireland, and Theories of World Literature*, uses a comparison between Polish and Irish literature as a case study to argue for a reconceptualization of the history of the novel. She is also a translator, most recently, of Zygmunt Bauman's *Culture and Art* (2021) and *Sketches in the Theory of Culture* (2017).

Katarzyna Bazarnik teaches English literature and literary theory at Jagiellonian University in Krakow, Poland. She has published on James Joyce, B. S. Johnson, liberature, and literary translation. She coauthored, with Zenon Fajfer, *Oka-leczenie* and *(O)patrzenie*. Together they founded the Liberature Reading Room in Kraków and coedit "Liberatura" series in Ha!art Publishing House.

Andrzej Brylak is a postdoctoral scholar at the University of Southern California, Los Angeles. His primary field of research is Polish and Eastern European modernity, especially in the post–Second World War context. He is currently working on a book titled *Leo Lipski: Expression, Excrement, Existence* in which he examines the prose of the Polish/Israeli writer whose postwar subject turns the main mode of existence from the disintegrated carnality to reconstructed textuality. Andrzej Brylak's research focuses on Interwar Poland, Stalinist Gulag, and Modern Israel and employs discourses such as biopolitics, Jewish and Christian theology, disability studies, and psychoanalysis. He is also interested in Polish and Eastern European modernizations projects and their representations in film, theater, and architecture, as well as the impact the recent migration waves to Poland have on the Polish language.

Piotr Florczyk is Assistant Professor of Global Literary Studies at the University of Washington, Seattle, and an award-winning poet and translator. His recent books include the poetry collection *From the Annals of Krakow*, which is based on the testimonies of Holocaust survivors, as well as several volumes of translations. For more information, please visit www.piotrflorczyk.com.

Jacek Gutorow is a poet, essayist, literary critic, and translator. He teaches literature and theory at the University of Opole in the southwest of Poland. His academic interests concern American and British modernism but he has also written extensively on contemporary Polish literature. He is the author of eight critical books (most recently *Pęknięty kryształ. Szkice o modernistach* [*The Flawed Crystal. Essays on Modernist Writers*], 2019) and seven volumes of poetry. He has translated American and British poets (Wallace Stevens, John Ashbery, Charles Tomlinson, Simon Armitage, Mark Ford, and others).

Agnieszka Jeżyk is Assistant Professor of Polish Language, Literature, and Culture at the University of Toronto, Canada, where she is also an acting director of the Polish Program. At UofT, she teaches an array of undergraduate and graduate courses in different topics related to the twentieth and twenty-first-century cultures of Poland and Central Europe. Agnieszka Jeżyk earned her PhD from the University of Illinois at Chicago in 2019 for her thesis on the excessive matter in Bruno Jasieński's poems, and she is currently working on a manuscript discussing marginal subjectivities in the 1920s Polish avant-garde poetry. Her interests include critical theory with an emphasis on psychoanalysis; animal studies; horror and crime fiction; everyday life and material culture in the Cold War Central Europe; and European avant-gardes.

Paweł Kaczmarski is a doctoral candidate at the University of Wrocław (Faculty of Historical and Pedagogical Sciences). He is a member of the editorial team of *Praktyka Teoretyczna/Theoretical Practice*, a journal of philosophy, sociology, and culture. Recently, he has been working on the subject of literary autonomy in post-1989 Poland, and the role of literary criticism in a market society.

Marta Koronkiewicz, PhD, is an assistant professor at the University of Wrocław (Faculty of Letters). She is a member of the editorial team of *Praktyka Teoretyczna/Theoretical Practice*, a journal of philosophy, sociology, and culture. Her main areas of interest are modern and contemporary Polish literature—in particular, poetry—and the history of Polish leftist literary criticism.

Lena Magnone, PhD habil, Humboldt fellow at the Institute of Slavic Studies, Carl von Ossietzky University of Oldenburg, previously worked as an assistant professor at the Institute of Polish Literature, University of Warsaw (2007–20) and visiting scholar (Fulbright fellow) at the Center for European and Mediterranean Studies, New York University (2019–20). Author of, among others, two monographs: *Maria Konopnicka. Lustra i symptomy* [Maria Konopnicka. Mirrors and Symptoms] (2011) and *Emisariusze Freuda. Transfer kulturowy psychoanalizy do polskich sfer inteligenckich przed drugą wojną światową* [Freud's emissaries. The cultural transfer of psychoanalysis to the Polish intelligentsia before World War II] (2016; English translation is due to be published in 2022), she is working on a book project about Central European modernist female writers.

Michał Paweł Markowski, is the Stefan and Lucy Hejna Family Chair in Polish Language and Literature and head of the Department of Polish, Russian, and Lithuanian Studies at the University of Illinois at Chicago. He is also a tenured visiting professor at the Center for the Advanced Studies in the Humanities (Jagiellonian University, Kraków, Poland), which he created in 2007. He taught at Harvard (2002), Northwestern (2003), and Brown (2009). Since 1997 he has published more than thirty volumes of individual books, editions, translations on literature and philosophy, and over four hundred essays, articles, and columns in professional journals, cultural monthlies, weeklies, and newspapers. As a translator, he brought into Polish works by Proust, Barthes, Blanchot, Derrida, Foucault, Lyotard, Deleuze, Kristeva, Rorty, and Perec.

Grzegorz Marzec is Associate Professor and Deputy Director of the Institute of Literary Research of the Polish Academy of Sciences. He is the author of four books and numerous scholarly articles, winner of national grants and awards, and a former visiting scholar at Indiana University. His main research interests lie at the intersection of literary theory and criticism, studies in Romanticism, and memory studies. The main effect of these interests is the 2016 book *Ekonomia pamięci* [*The Economy of Memory*].

Ela Przybyło is Assistant Professor in English and Women's, Gender, and Sexuality Studies at Illinois State University. She is the author of *Asexual Erotics: Intimate Readings of Compulsory Sexuality* (2019), an editor of *On the Politics of Ugliness* (2018), and author of many peer-reviewed articles and chapters including in a variety of journals such as *Feminist Formations, GLQ: A Journal of Lesbian and Gay Studies, Sexualities, Radical Teacher, English Studies in Canada*, and *Digital Icons: Studies in Russian, Eurasian and Central European New Media*. Ela is a founding and managing editor of the peer-reviewed, open access journal *Feral Feminisms*.

Emiliano Ranocchi studied Russian and German philology at Urbino University (Italy) and received his PhD in Polish literature at Rome University "La Sapienza." Now, he works as fellow researcher at Udine University where he teaches Polish language and literature. As a dix-huitièmiste and a specialist in Central European literatures, he focuses mainly on this period and area. Since several years, he is working on the Polish francophone writer Jan Potocki. During inquiries in Russia, Poland, and Ukraine he discovered various, until now unknown, manuscripts of Potocki: letters, memoires, and essays. In particular, he investigated the geological corpus of Potocki. He has also reestablished the meeting between Jan Potocki, Goethe, and Herder in Karlsbad in summer 1785. For quite a long time he has been also dealing with modernism, particularly with the literary output of a forgotten interwar Polish writer, Jerzy Sosnkowski. He is deputy editor-in-chief of the quarterly review Autoportret (www.autoportret.pl).

K. A. Wisniewski is the director of Book History and Digital Initiatives at the American Antiquarian Society in Worcester, Massachusetts. His research interests include the History of the Book, literary history, experimental writing, and comedy and popular culture. His critical work has appeared in *Printing History, Genre*, the *Maryland Historical Magazine, Hyperrhiz, Alphaville: Journal of Film and Screen Media*, and the anthologies *Exquisite Corpse: Art-Based Writing Practices in the Academy* and *Kidding Around: The Child in Film and Media*. Wisniewski is also a poet and translator. He is the author of *Making Faces* (2016) and the editor of *The Comedy of Dave Chappelle: Critical Essays* (2009) and the critical edition of *A Pretty Story* by Francis Hopkinson (2023). Wisniewski is the founding editor of the journal *Textshop Experiments*.

Zofia Ziemann is a translation scholar, editor, and translator/interpreter working between Polish and English. She is Assistant Professor at the at the Faculty of Polish, Jagiellonian University, Kraków, where she heads the MA program Literary and Cultural Translation Studies. A graduate of English Studies (MA, University of Gdańsk), Cultural Studies (BA, University of Gdańsk), and Translation Studies (MA, Jagiellonian University), she holds a PhD in Literary Studies from Jagiellonian University. Her research interests are translation history, translator studies, and the reception of translated literature, with particular focus on literary retranslation. Her most recent publication is *Retracing the History of Literary Translation in Poland: People, Politics, Poetics*, a volume co-edited with Magda Heydel.

INDEX

Note: Figures are indicated by page number followed by "f". Endnotes are indicated by the page number followed by "n" and the endnote number e.g., 20 n.1 refers to endnote 1 on page 20.

CPSIA information can be obtained
at www.ICGtesting.com
Printed in the USA
LVHW050607271222
735993LV00002B/41

9 781501 387104